"Few leaders know what it is to step onto a national stage to shape and sustain public opinion and action for a better democracy. Preston Manning has done that, not once but twice, through his leadership in creating political parties, which gave him voice as leader of the Official Opposition to the government of Canada. This book contains Preston Manning's true-north wisdom and is essential reading for reflective leadership."

—Lorna Dueck
CEO, Crossroads Global Media Group

"Preston Manning once again challenges people to wrestle with some big questions—this time, the linkage between faith, leadership, and politics—while making those questions and answers personal to each reader."

—Dr. Colin Harbinson
International Director, StoneWorks Global Arts Initiative

"The worlds of religion and politics are going through a uniquely turbulent time ... or maybe not. Manning's compelling insights from the Bible and his own experience will change your perspective."

—Kevin Jenkins
President and CEO, World Vision International

"Preston's use of storytelling keeps this potentially complex issue interesting and practical. A must-read for those who love politics or faith and want to understand how the two can work together seamlessly."

—The Honourable Chuck Strahl, PC
Former Cabinet Minister and Member of the Parliament of Canada

"Manning's new book connects Jesus to contemporary issues twenty centuries later. It also indicates why a native of Nazareth has a nominal following today of over a billion persons after a public career of only 36 months."

—The Honourable David Kilgour, PC
Former Cabinet Minister and Member of the Parliament of Canada

"This book is replete with wise biblical insight into the most acute challenges of contemporary leadership. It offers a veritable feast to those many believers seeking to follow Christ in the public marketplace and searching for substantial practical help. Preston Manning skillfully narrates a delightfully human and insightful dialogue between his own substantial experience and the rich biblical stories of leaders like David, Moses, Daniel, Esther, and, of course, Jesus himself. He pulls off a marvellous blend of theological insight and practical application that would put most preachers to shame.

I have disagreed sharply with Preston Manning when he told me he was not a theologian. I answered that if anyone could do theology in the world of public leadership, it was him. This book provides all the evidence I need to win that argument!"

—Dr. Paul Williams
CEO, British and Foreign Bible Society

Faith, LEADERSHIP and Public Life

Leadership Lessons from Moses to Jesus

Preston Manning

Faith, Leadership and Public Life: Leadership Lessons from Moses to Jesus

Printed in Canada
ISBN 978-1-927355-91-6 soft cover
ISBN 978-1-927355-92-3 EPUB

Published by: Castle Quay Books
Tel: (416) 573-3249
E-mail: info@castlequaybooks.com | www.castlequaybooks.com

Edited by Marina Hofman Willard
Cover and book interior by Burst Impressions
Printed at Essence Printing, Belleville, Ontario

Library and Archives Canada Cataloguing in Publication

Manning, Preston, 1942-, author
Faith, leadership and public life : leadership lessons from Moses to Jesus / Preston Manning.

Includes bibliographical references
ISBN 978-1-927355-91-6 (softcover)

1. Christian leadership. 2. Leadership--Religious aspects--Christianity. I. Title.

BV652.1.M36 2017 253'.2 C2017-904501-6

CONTENTS

PREFACE

THE PURPOSE OF THIS BOOK IS TO EXAMINE LESSONS IN leadership from the interface of faith and public life, especially the political dimension of public life.[1] But why write or read a book about navigating the interface of faith and public life, especially the interface between the Christian faith and politics? Does not most of the Western world subscribe to the separation of church and state, frown upon expressions of faith in the public sphere, and—if expressions of faith must be tolerated—confine them to the private and personal sphere?

As both a former member of the Canadian Parliament and a practicing Christian, I, too, believe in the merits of keeping the *institutions* of the state separate from the *institutions* of religion. But I also believe that in the long run the attempt to keep the *subjects* and *expressions* of faith and public life in separate watertight compartments is undesirable and untenable because real people in open societies with religious traditions and convictions simply do not do so.

The challenge for us, therefore, is twofold. For the secular decision maker, it is desirable to respect and understand the nature and implications of the religious traditions and convictions of citizens who hold them since, whether one agrees with them or not, they are legitimate and important components of the body politic. For people of faith, the challenge is to learn to live and conduct ourselves responsibly at the interface of faith

[1] Much of the material in this book was originally prepared for lectures on the relationship of faith to politics. I have since been convinced that many of the principles and lessons derived therefrom have an even broader application—useful to any person seeking to be faithful to their most deeply held beliefs while operating in any public arena. Hence the reference in the title, and frequently throughout the following pages, to faith, leadership, and "public life."

and public life so that we are seen by others as non-coercive and credible contributors to public discourse and so that we are a credit, not a discredit, to our own faith and faith communities. It is hoped that some of the experiences and insights related in the following pages will be helpful in meeting these challenges.

But why focus on lessons about navigating the interface of faith and public life from the Judeo-Christian perspective—in particular, from the public life of Jesus, the Israelite leaders he most often referenced, such as Moses and David, and Jewish exiles such as Daniel and Esther, who lived in political systems hostile to their faith?

First, because at least in much of the Western world, this is the most prevalent religious tradition and the one that has impacted most heavily our politics and governance. As a Canadian, it is the tradition and interface with which I am personally most familiar and experienced from both a religious and a political standpoint.

Second, because a better understanding of the lessons from the interface of the Judeo-Christian faith and politics should be of considerable assistance to those wrestling to understand and handle the forceful intrusion of Islam into the global political arena. If we don't thoroughly grasp the lessons to be learned from the faith-political interactions within our own religious and political traditions and culture, it's unlikely that we will be adequately equipped to handle public and political interactions with other faith traditions.

Third, and most important, the lives and experiences of prominent biblical characters who lived and operated at the interface of faith and public life during their lifetimes are highly fascinating and highly instructive.

Consider Jesus. What other figure in history has at least a nominal following of over one billion persons 2,000 years after a public career of only 36 months? And who were the main historical figures he quoted or referenced in his public addresses and teachings? Moses, David, and the prophets—all of whom operated in their times at the interface of faith and public life. Their stories and experiences are recorded in what Christians call the Old Testament, portions of which may today be offensive to the sense and sensibilities of the modern mind. But again let us be reminded that to the best of our knowledge, these are the principal texts that Jesus of Nazareth read and studied—texts that shaped and inspired his life of self-sacrificial love and service. For that reason alone, they and the lessons they contain should commend themselves to our serious consideration.

Finally, allow me to provide a brief defence of the perspective I employ in seeking to derive leadership lessons of contemporary significance from the ancient biblical record of the life and experiences of Jesus and the Israelite leaders and prophets he referenced.

Our modern tendency is to interpret and judge the beliefs and actions of historical figures from the perspective of the beliefs, knowledge, and analytic methodologies of our own age. Thus the modern reader might ask, What can contemporary people, most of whom now believe that the universe is the product of natural forces and that God is a product of the human imagination, possibly learn from Moses, who believed that "In the beginning God created the heavens and the earth"[2] and that God is a real, omniscient being who communicates directly and indirectly with humanity?

Or what might the modern reader who may be persuaded that Jesus was a good man and an influential teacher possibly learn from the perspective of the Gospel writers that he was much more than that—that he was deity incarnate, resurrected from the dead by the power of God, and is eternally present and active in the world?

My own response to these questions is to say, let us—at least for a moment—*not* judge and interpret the lives and experience of Jesus and the Israelite leaders he referenced solely by the beliefs, knowledge, and analytic methodologies of our own age. To do so exclusively would render most of sacred and secular history largely irrelevant to our own times and circumstances. Rather—at least for a moment—let us examine and interpret these ancient lives and experiences as best we can from the perspective of their own beliefs, knowledge, and age. And let us see whether by so doing we might, as I believe we will, derive lessons still highly relevant to our own times and circumstances.

To guard ourselves against the hubris of modernity and postmodernity, would we not be wise to heed the counsel of Jesus himself on judging the motives and actions of others? "Do not judge," he told his earliest followers, "or you too will be judged. For in the same way you judge others,

[2] Genesis 1:1.

you will be judged, and with the measure you use, it will be measured to you."[3]

In future years, if and when posterity looks back on our lives and experiences to see what lessons if any they might learn therefrom, do we not desire that they would first of all seek to interpret our lives and actions through the perspective that actually guided us rather than through some future perspective, different from ours and largely unknown to us at this time? It is this desire to respect and learn, first and foremost from the perspective of the life and times of Jesus and the Israelite leaders he referenced, that has guided me in this study and that I encourage the reader to share.

And so, whether you are a person of faith seeking to learn more about how to conduct yourself at the interface of faith and public life or someone of a secular mindset simply seeking to better understand what can be learned about the interface of faith and public life from the Judeo-Christian perspective, please join me in examining *Faith, Leadership and Public Life: Leadership Lessons from Moses to Jesus.*

Preston Manning
Calgary, Alberta, Canada
September 2017

[3] Matthew 7:1–2.

PART 1:

LEADERSHIP LESSONS from the Public Life of Jesus

INTRODUCTION

FOR 30 YEARS, FROM HIS BIRTH TO EARLY ADULTHOOD, Jesus of Nazareth lived and worked in obscurity. Then for three short years he taught and worked in public, and his public life is well documented in the Gospels of Matthew, Mark, Luke, and John.

Jesus never sought or held public office, yet he and his followers have been politically influential and controversial for twenty centuries. While his ultimate mission was a spiritual one, he nevertheless chose to use a political term—the "kingdom" of God—to define it.

Those of us who believe that Jesus was in fact the one he claimed to be—the Son of God sent by God to reconcile human beings to himself and each other—will tend to attribute the uniqueness and impact of his public life to the presence and power of the supernatural. But even those who do not acknowledge his deity should be drawn to examine the nature and lessons of his public ministry by virtue of its unique and enormous impact from that day to this.

In this regard, I once provided a small group of my political friends who were visiting Israel with a "sealed memorandum" to be opened, read, and discussed only after they had completed their first visit to the Galilean region where Jesus spent much of his life. The memorandum read as follows:

A SPECIAL ASSIGNMENT

Imagine that you have just been parachuted into the Galilee region of Israel to carry out the following special assignment:

- Go into the towns and villages around the lake and recruit a team of twelve people.
- Persuade them to leave whatever they are doing and join you in a venture to change themselves, their community, and the world.
- By formal teaching and example, transform their pursuit of self-interest into the self-sacrificial service of others.
- Equip them to share with others what you will impart to them, so that 2,000 years afterwards more than one billion people will profess to be guided in some way by your teachings and example.
- Fiscal constraints require you to raise your own financial support for this assignment.
- Your initial base of operations will be a carpenter's shop in a small town called Nazareth.
- You have three years to complete this assignment before you must leave the region and entrust the follow-up to your recruits.

Jesus of Nazareth undertook and successfully completed such an assignment, which is why, if for no other reason, I believe that his life and teachings deserve serious examination, especially by those of us who know from our own experience how difficult it is to create and sustain a public movement of any kind, even on a limited scale and for only a brief moment in time.

So, whether we are believers or not, if we are engaged in public life of any sort there is much to learn and profit from examining the public life of Jesus. And if we are operating at the interface of faith and politics this is doubly so.

1.1 INCARNATIONAL COMMUNICATION

To incarnate—to embody in flesh;
to put into a body, especially a human form.

PROVIDENTIAL POSITIONING

PROVIDENTIAL POSITIONING REFERS TO MOVEMENTS BY God's spirit whereby human beings (unbelievers as well as believers) are placed or moved into particular positions and situations to accomplish some aspect of God's work in the world. The biblical record draws attention to such movements at work in the lives of Moses, David, Joseph, Daniel, Esther, Ezra, and Nehemiah as well as in the lives of an Egyptian pharaoh and the kings of the Medes and Persians. It was in reference to such providential positioning that the Jewish exile Mordecai posed the haunting question to Esther when she rose to the position of queen in Medo-Persia, "Who knows but that you have come to your royal position for such a time as this?"[4]

In the entire record of God's dealings with humanity, however, there is no more dramatic and consequential instance of providential positioning than the positioning of Jesus of Nazareth in a particular human family and community within an obscure province of the Roman Empire at a particular time in human history.

The physician Luke begins his Gospel by describing the work of Jesus' *advance man*, John the Baptist. He does so by positioning the time of their public ministry politically:

[4] Esther 4:14.

> In the fifteenth year of the reign of Tiberius Caesar—when Pontius Pilate was governor of Judea, Herod tetrarch of Galilee, his brother Philip tetrarch of Iturea and Traconitis, and Lysanias tetrarch of Abilene—during the high priesthood of Annas and Caiaphas, the word of God came to John son of Zechariah.[5]

Jesus himself, speaking in the synagogue of his hometown of Nazareth, describes his positioning as fulfilling the ancient prophecy of Isaiah:

> He went to Nazareth, where he had been brought up, and on the Sabbath day he went into the synagogue, as was his custom. He stood up to read, and the scroll of the prophet Isaiah was handed to him. Unrolling it, he found the place where it is written:
>
> "The Spirit of the Lord is on me,
> because he has anointed me
> to preach good news to the poor.
> He has sent me to proclaim freedom for the prisoners
> and recovery of sight for the blind,
> to set the oppressed free,
> to proclaim the year of the Lord's favor."
>
> Then he rolled up the scroll, gave it back to the attendant and sat down. The eyes of everyone in the synagogue were fastened on him. He began by saying to them, "Today this scripture is fulfilled in your hearing."[6]

On several other occasions, Jesus implies that his decisions to refrain from certain activities also involved providential timing and positioning. "My hour has not yet come," he tells his mother when she asks him to intervene miraculously at the wedding in Cana.[7] "My time is not yet here," he tells his brothers when they want him to publicly display himself at a feast.[8]

The apostle John, who seemed to be especially aware that the events and circumstances of Jesus' life were providentially ordered, tells us that Jesus was acutely conscious of God's timing and positioning just prior to his arrest, crucifixion, resurrection, and ascension: "It was just before the Passover Festival. Jesus knew that the hour had come for him to leave this world and go to the Father … that he had come from God and was returning to God."[9]

---

[5] Luke 3:1–2.

[6] Luke 4:16–21.

[7] John 2:4.

[8] John 7:6.

[9] John 13:1–3.

With respect to all the events and acts of Jesus' life one might ask, Why *then*? Why *there*? Why *in that way*? We can speculate, but only God knows the definitive answers to these types of questions. What is clearly taught in Scripture is that there was providential purpose in Jesus' being placed at a particular place and time in the history of the world to say and do the things he said and did, just as I believe there is providential purpose in the placement of you and me in the particular places and times in which we find ourselves. The challenge for us is to discern that purpose and to live and act in the light of it, just as Jesus did.

INCARNATION

How do you make the existence and nature of a being as lofty, mysterious, and spiritual as God real and understandable to human beings? God's answer to that question, according to the New Testament writers, is through "incarnation"—by embodying deity in flesh, by incorporating deity into a body, in particular a human man, Jesus of Nazareth.

The apostle John describes it this way: "In the beginning was the Word … the Word was God … The Word became flesh and made his dwelling among us … the one and only … who came from the Father, full of grace and truth."[10] Similarly, the apostle Paul: "When the set time had fully come, God sent his Son, born of a woman … to redeem."[11]

It is at this point that I am in danger of losing the interest and attention of some of my political friends and others of you who simply cannot bring yourselves to believe in the deity of Jesus. He was a good man, you say. He may have been a great teacher. He didn't deserve the cruel fate that he suffered. But he was not divine, you say, and those who believe so are deceived.

Rather than part company over the deity of Jesus, let me try to persuade you to linger a little longer in his company. Because if you are a person with any interest at all in learning how to be effective in public life, particularly in communicating substantive and complex ideas and propositions to ordinary people, there is much to be learned from Jesus of Nazareth and the concept, if not the reality, of incarnation.

To incarnate means to embody in flesh, to put into a body, especially a human form. In Jesus' case, this included not only his physical birth, which

[10] John 1:1–14.

[11] Galatians 4:4–5.

Christians consider miraculous, but also his *un*-miraculous upbringing in a humble family; his apprenticeship, likely beginning at age 12, in a trade; his many years (up to 18) toiling in a carpenter's shop interacting with farmers, fishermen, merchants, and the like; until at age 30 he began to speak and teach in public as an itinerant rabbi, a public ministry that would last only three short years.

The time ratios here are important and worth noting. Up to six years in the community, the carpenter's shop, the marketplace—interacting with the types of people who will one day constitute the bulk of his public audiences, hearing about their troubles and hopes, listening to their stories and conversation, absorbing their vocabulary and reference points—for every one year of teaching and communicating in the public arena. Six to one is the ratio of private preparation to public communication.

INCARNATIONAL COMMUNICATIONS

When Jesus finally stepped into the public arena, he was an "incarnational communicator" and surely one of the most effective public communicators this world has ever seen—someone from whom any public communicator can learn a great deal. He embodied, became the personification of, the truths he sought to communicate. He was fully immersed in the community of human beings he had come to influence. And his choice of words, phrases, and illustrations put flesh upon, made intrinsically human and tangible, spiritual truths and realities so that his audiences could better grasp and accept—virtually see, feel, touch, and embrace—what he was talking about.

Note first of all the lofty and seemingly otherworldly ideas and truths that it was the purpose of his public ministry to communicate: ideas and truths about the nature and will of God, a spiritual kingdom, the foundations of happiness (blessedness), spiritual illumination, the laws of God, spiritual communication (prayer), retaliation and reconciliation, spiritual temptation, heaven and hell, the spiritual consequences of human actions, judgment and justice, spiritual direction, the power and meaning of faith, spiritual deprivation and nourishment, the agents and consequences of evil, the spiritual roots of pain and suffering, spiritual comfort, the reality and meaning of death, spiritual life and death, spiritual and temporal authority, the meaning of truth, spiritual work, self-sacrificial love, spiritual unity, eternal life, the person and work of the spirit of God—the list goes on and on, concepts and truths of a high level of abstraction, seemingly intangible and for the most part beyond the ability of ordinary folk to feel, grasp, and embrace.

But note how Jesus put "flesh" on these concepts and truths to make the seemingly intangible real and tangible. He did so by expressing these truths in words, phrases, and analogies drawn from where? Not primarily from the experience and vocabulary of the religious academy of his day but directly from the circumstances and vocabularies of those he communicated with and among whom he worked and conversed for 18 years. Words, phrases, and analogies that include salt of the earth, the light of a lamp, a cloak given away, rust and moths, birds of the air, lilies of the field, sawdust in the eye, narrow and broad gates, wolves and sheep, the fruit of the tree, houses built on sand or rock, the holes of foxes, the nests of birds, brides and bridegrooms, weddings and other feasts, patches on garments, new and old wineskins, sheep without shepherds, workers for the harvest fields, children in the marketplace, a sheep in a pit, an ox in a ditch, a house swept clean, yeast in the dough, fish in the net, good and bad servants, sowers of seeds, reapers of harvests, the size of a mustard seed, wheat in a field, weeds in a field, stony or thorny ground, landlords and tenants, workers in a vineyard, winepresses and millstones, the fruit of the vine, vines and branches, taxes to Caesar, clean and unclean cups, oil for lamps, fruitful and barren fig trees, sheep separated from goats, a child in the midst, and wine and bread. Often woven into stories and parables, such words and phrases were designed to both enlighten and provoke questions—stories and parables again drawn largely from his own knowledge and experience of the lives and circumstances of his hearers.[12]

Also note the nature of the venues where he met and encountered people: yes, sometimes in a synagogue or formal place of learning, but more often on a hill beside a lake, in a small boat pushed off from the shore, in a disciple's house, at a party with tax collectors and prostitutes, in the marketplace, at a wedding feast, at religious feasts, in a garden, on

[12] "Jesus spoke all these things to the crowd in parables; he did not say anything to them without using a parable" (Matthew 13:34; see also Mark 4:34). When his disciples asked, "Why do you speak to the people in parables?" he replied that it was both to enlighten and to obscure (Matthew 13:10–13).

the road, at a well, and in dozens of other places where he was accessible to sick people, poor people, inquirers, skeptics, critics, lawyers, scribes, priests, soldiers, tax collectors, women, and children.

This is incarnational communication, with three distinctive characteristics: (1) The communicator literally embodies and personifies the truths to be communicated. (2) The communicator has so immersed himself or herself in the community that he or she is an integral part of it, not distant from it. (3) The communication is expressed as much as possible within the conceptual frameworks and in the vocabulary not of the communicator but of the community to be influenced. It is today what communications consultants would call *receiver-oriented communication.*

SOURCE-ORIENTED VERSUS RECEIVER-ORIENTED COMMUNICATION

There is an old and simple model, originating with electronic engineers, of *how communication works* that I have found most helpful in framing my own communication efforts on both political and religious subjects. It conceptualizes communication as originating with a *source* who wishes to generate a *response* from a *receiver* through the transmission of information (*messages*) via a *medium*. The communication occurs in a *context* that significantly influences it and is complicated by the existence of *noise*—competing information and messages.

The communication is further complicated by the fact that messages from the source and responses from the receiver both pass through the respective *communication grids* of each—defining aspects of their respective cultures, conceptual frameworks, thought patterns, and vocabularies that shape the formation and reception of the messages and feedback. When the source's grid is significantly different than the receiver's grid, we encounter all the challenges of cross-cultural communication, such as when oil companies communicate with Indigenous peoples, scientists communicate with politicians, or believers communicate with non-believers on spiritual topics.

Source-oriented communicators express their ideas in the way those ideas came to them (the source), in the words and phrases of the source's vocabulary and conceptual framework, and in venues and through media with which the source is most familiar and comfortable. Such communicators often live and operate at considerable psychological, social, and physical distance from the rank and file of the public. They put much of the onus of understanding what is being communicated on the audience rather than assuming that burden themselves.

Scientists and academics, preachers and professors, and persons in positions of authority such as corporate executives and high-level civil servants tend to be source-oriented communicators. Moses and the scribes and Pharisees[13] of Jesus' day were for the most part source-oriented communicators—indeed this is generally the communication style of lawgivers. While this communication style certainly has its place and is highly effective in peer-to-peer communications, it is generally far less effective in communicating with the general public.

If you are a *receiver-oriented communicator* you will also have definite communications objectives and messages that you as the source want to convey in order to generate a desired audience response. But you do not start planning your communications from the source-oriented perspective of "what do I want to say?"; rather you start with "who are these people I am communicating with?" What are they like—their hopes, their fears, their attitudes, their backgrounds? What do they know or not know about me and my subject? What is their vocabulary? What are their venue and media preferences? What competing information and messages are they receiving? What will be the physical circumstances and psychological climate when and where I will be communicating with them? Then, having asked and answered these questions about the intended receivers of your communication—much easier to do accurately if you have lived and worked among them—you now proceed to framing your communication

[13] "The Pharisees were a religious party or school among the Jews at the time of Christ, so called from the Aramaic form of the Hebrew *perushim*, the separated ones. This name may have been given them by their enemies, as they usually called themselves *Haberim*, associates. They were formalists, very patriotic but bigoted in their patriotism as in their religion. Their political influence was great, though they were only about 6000 to 7000 in number. Jesus denounced the Pharisees for their hypocrisy, which was shown by their care for the minutest formalities imposed by the traditions of the elders, but not for the mind and heart which should correspond. They were ambitious, arrogant, and proudly self-righteous, all of which qualities were contrary to the teachings of Jesus. This explains in part their intense hostility to him" (Alexander Cruden, *Cruden's Complete Concordance to the Bible* [Toronto: G.R. Welch Company Limited, 1980], 494).

and messages with the needs and character of your audience (the receivers) uppermost in your mind.[14]

Genuine democratic discourse requires that politicians and political communicators be more receiver-oriented than source-oriented.[15] And I would argue that as Christians desirous of effectively communicating to others the spiritual truths of the gospel of Jesus Christ we also need to be much more receiver-oriented—personally embodying the gospel's central characteristic of self-sacrificial love, fully immersing ourselves among those we seek to serve, and framing our messages in the terms and words that they would use if they understood our message and were communicating it to someone else.

The psalmist (and political leader) David was a receiver-oriented communicator, as were many of the Old Testament prophets. But Jesus of Nazareth was the master of this style of communication. By embodying the truths he sought to communicate, by practising the self-sacrificial love that he preached, he gained an authority in spiritual matters that exceeded that of the scribes and Pharisees. As he spoke and taught in terms and words that the common people used and could understand, people were willing to listen to him, flocked to hear him, and were amazed at what they saw and heard.[16] The Sermon on the Mount was effective because the sermonizer was not some distant moralizer but a communicator incarnate and embedded in the lives and culture of those whom he addressed in words and phrases drawn from

[14] Note that this form of communication is not simply *finding out what people want to hear* and then communicating that to them—a communication style to which unprincipled politicians are particularly prone. The receiver-oriented communicator has definite communication objectives and distinctive messages to offer, some of which the audience may definitely not want to hear but should. The difference between the source-oriented communicator and the receiver-oriented communicator is that the latter has the audience rather than himself or herself much more in mind at every stage of the preparation and delivery of the communication.

[15] In my own experience with public communication, first as a management consultant and then as a candidate for public office and a politician, I first began to use a receiver-oriented communication planning framework in meeting the challenges of cross-cultural communication on behalf of energy companies with Indigenous people. I then began to use this same communication planning framework in preparing my speeches to public audiences as a candidate for public office and as a political leader, including most of my addresses in the Canadian House of Commons.

[16] "The common people heard him gladly" (Mark 12:37 [KJV]).

their own experiences.[17] As even the temple guards sent to arrest him acknowledged, "No one ever spoke the way this man does."[18]

IMPLICATIONS FOR US

As previously mentioned, if we believe in the providential placement of ourselves as human beings in particular places and times in order to participate in achieving God's purposes in the world, the first challenge for us is to discern those purposes and to live and act in the light of them, just as Jesus did.

But if those purposes require us to communicate in the public sphere, the second challenge is to become incarnational communicators, with Jesus again serving as the great example.[19] So if you are someone in a position to communicate spiritual or political truths and messages to individuals or public audiences,

- To what extent do you yourself embody and personify the truths and messages you seek to communicate?
- To what extent have you immersed yourself in the lives and community of those you seek to influence?
- To what extent have you framed your communication within the conceptual frameworks and vocabulary of those with whom you are communicating?
- How much time and effort have you devoted in preparation to become an effective incarnational communicator?

---

[17] "The people were amazed at his teaching, because he taught them as one who had authority, and not as the teachers of the law" (Mark 1:22). Much of this perceived "authority" came from the content and style of his communication rather than from his position in society.

[18] John 7:46.

[19] Some may argue that the existence of modern communication technology—in particular radio, television, the Internet, and social media—has so radically changed public communication that the example of Jesus, whose primary method of communication was in direct personal contact with his audiences, is no longer relevant. This is not the place to address this concern fully, but I would suggest that one of the major effects (and problems) with modern communication technology is that while it greatly broadens the ability of the source to reach multitudes of receivers, it tends to depersonalize the relationship and increases rather than decreases the *distance* between source and receiver. Consequently, modern communicators using modern technology will be more believable and effective if they embody the truths they are attempting to communicate, have fully immersed themselves in their receivers' world, and employ to the maximum extent possible the conceptual frameworks and vocabulary of their audiences—the distinguishing characteristics of Jesus' incarnational communication.

Imagine if we required anyone wanting to enter the public arena to spend six years of incarnational preparation—learning the troubles, hopes, habits, stories, and vocabulary of his or her constituents—for every year of intended public service.

Imagine if we required anyone wanting to enter the Christian ministry to spend six years immersing themselves not just in theological textbooks and Scripture study, important as these are, but in direct and daily interaction with the troubles, hopes, habits, stories, and vocabulary of their future parishioners for every one year of intended public ministry.

Might not the results be more like those achieved by Jesus of Nazareth—minds and hearts of ordinary, busy, and distracted human beings moved and changed for the better by a unique and authentic style of communication?

1.2 THE FIRST TEMPTATION: FEED THEM AND THEY WILL FOLLOW

Then Jesus was led by the Spirit into the wilderness to be tempted by the devil ... The tempter came to him and said, "If you are the Son of God, tell these stones to become bread."[20]

THE TEMPTATION

THE TEMPTATION OF JESUS IN THE WILDERNESS BY EVIL personified is referred to directly by three of the Gospel writers and alluded to indirectly by the fourth (John). The event occurred at the very outset of his public ministry. Whether one interprets the Gospel writers' description of it literally, as most Christians do who believe in the literal existence of a spiritual being (Satan) dedicated to the destruction of human beings and the work of God, or one only believes that the event described by the Gospel writers was some internal struggle that occurred in Jesus' mind and imagination, the story is immensely instructive to anyone preparing for spiritual or political leadership, especially at the beginning of a public life.

The temptation may of course be interpreted as a straightforward attempt by Satan to get Jesus to sin—literally, *to miss the mark*. It is therefore instructive to anyone facing temptation to do something contrary to the revealed will and purposes of God. A subtler interpretation is that the temptation was a devious and clever attempt by the forces of evil to influence in a very destructive way the entire direction and character of Jesus' leadership and public influence—to *get him on the wrong track*—at the very beginning of his public ministry. It is this interpretation that

[20] Matthew 4:1–3.

is particularly relevant and instructive to anyone contemplating and preparing for spiritual or public leadership today.

FYODOR DOSTOYEVSKY'S PERSPECTIVE AND INTERPRETATION

The interpretation of the temptation of Jesus in the wilderness that I (and many others with political interests) have found most illuminating and helpful is that of the famous Russian author Fyodor Dostoyevsky, as described in his last and greatest novel, *The Brothers Karamazov*.[21]

Fyodor Dostoyevsky was born in 1821, nine years after Napoleon's ignominious departure from Russia. He died in 1881, thirty-six years before the Communist Revolution, the character and evils of which he predicted with great insight. His father was a military doctor and serf owner, extremely cruel and constantly drunk, who was murdered by his serfs when Fyodor was eighteen years of age. Fyodor then joined the army and served in it for four years, where he acquired many bad habits—in particular excessive drinking, womanizing, and gambling—vices that plagued him for the rest of his life and kept him in constant trouble and poverty.

Dostoyevsky lived at a time of intellectual and political turmoil in Russia. He joined a socialist group agitating for reform and at age twenty-nine was arrested and charged with sedition. He was sentenced to death by a firing squad, but at the very last moment the tsar commuted the sentence to exile and hard labour in Siberia. He spent the next nine years there, mainly in the company of murderers, robbers, and other criminals. As he grew older he was subject to violent epileptic attacks, while his gambling and drinking habits kept him constantly on the brink of personal disaster. Some of his best writing was done in a fevered frenzy to pay gambling debts.

For all of his character flaws, however, Fyodor Dostoyevsky was a literary genius with an extraordinary interest in and insight into the nature of good and evil, especially evil.

This interest and insight is particularly evident in his four most important novels, the last and greatest of these being *The Brothers*

[21] Fyodor Dostoyevsky, *The Brothers Karamazov*, trans. Constance Garnett, foreword by Manuel Komroff (New York: Signet, 1957, 1986). In the following section I have relied heavily on the excellent introduction to this novel by the Russian scholar and translator Manuel Komroff.

Karamazov, completed just one year before he died.[22] It is the story of a dysfunctional family headed by an alcoholic and lecherous father (likely modelled after Dostoyevsky's own father) who has four sons, all of whom become involved in a murder. The four brothers are Dimitri, who symbolizes the flesh; Ivan, who represents the intellect; Alyosha, the youngest, who represents the spiritual; and Smerdyakov, the illegitimate son who represents the insulted, the injured, and the disinherited.

In a famous chapter entitled "The Grand Inquisitor" the intellectual Ivan challenges the spirituality and Christian commitment of his younger brother Alyosha by telling him he is working on a poem set in Spain in which Jesus returns to earth during the Spanish Inquisition. In the poem, Ivan imagines that Jesus is immediately arrested and imprisoned by the church authorities on charges of heresy—of adding to what he had said of old, which in the opinion of the church he has no right to do. One dark night, the Grand Inquisitor himself visits the Christ to interrogate and lecture him, arguing that Jesus' greatest mistake was to ignore the advice of that "wise and dread Spirit, the spirit of self-destruction and non-existence" (Satan) when he met with Jesus in the wilderness.[23] If only Jesus had heeded that advice ("the temptation") and based the direction and tenor of his leadership upon it, the work of the church would have been so much more successful, and humanity would have been so much happier and more fulfilled.

THE FIRST TEMPTATION: FEED THEM AND THEY WILL FOLLOW

And so the tempter comes to Jesus and says, "If you are the Son of God, tell these stones to become bread."[24]

---

[22] These, in the opinion of the Russian scholar and translator Manuel Komroff, are *Crime and Punishment*, dealing with the morality, benefits, and problems of the 6th commandment, thou shalt not kill; *The Idiot*, in which the Christlike hero ends up as a wise but loveable fool despite his practice of virtue, self-sacrifice, and saintliness; *The Possessed*, dealing with the evils inherent in the character of both the ruthless revolutionary and the conservative opponents of revolutionary ideas; and *The Brothers Karamazov*, dealing with the spiritual warfare between God and the devil, between good and evil, on the battlefield of the human heart.

[23] Dostoyevsky, *The Brothers Karamazov*, 244–245.

[24] Matthew 4:3; see also Luke 4:3.

From Dostoyevsky's perspective, what Satan is really saying here is that if you, Jesus, really want human beings to give you their allegiance and follow you, you should only appeal to their most immediate and urgent physical needs. Feed them! Give them bread—real, tangible, edible bread that they can see with their eyes, hold in their hands, and put in their mouths. Do that and they will follow you by the thousands. But don't go offering them some kind of "heavenly bread," which it is apparently your intention to do. Don't go talking to them about deliverance from spiritual hunger and offering them spiritual freedom and nourishment—they won't have the faintest idea what you are talking about and will reject rather than accept your leadership.

In the picturesque language of the Grand Inquisitor, Satan's meaning was

> "Thou wouldst go into the world ... with some promise of freedom which men in their simplicity and their natural unruliness cannot even understand ... But seest Thou these stones in this parched and barren wilderness? Turn them into bread, and mankind will run after Thee like a flock of sheep, grateful and obedient."[25]

The Grand Inquisitor says, "Thou didst promise them the bread of Heaven, but, I repeat again, can it compare with earthly bread in the eyes of the weak, ever sinful and ignoble race of man?"[26]

JESUS' RESPONSE TO THE FIRST TEMPTATION

So what was Jesus' response to the first temptation? He did not deny that humanity has tangible and immediate needs that the would-be leader must recognize and address. He himself was deeply moved by human want and acted with compassion when confronted with the needs of the poor, hungry, oppressed, and sick. He knew all about the need for bread, teaching his disciples to pray, "Give us today our daily bread."[27] In fact, he was several times so moved by the immediate physical hunger of those who came to hear him that he resorted to the miraculous in order to feed them.[28]

---

[25] Dostoyevsky, *The Brothers Karamazov*, 245.

[26] Dostoyevsky, *The Brothers Karamazov*, 246.

[27] Matthew 6:11.

[28] See Matthew 14:13–21 and John 6:1–13 to read about the feeding of five thousand and Matthew 15:29–38 and Mark 8:1–10 to read about the feeding of four thousand.

But to the tempter in the wilderness, who sought to influence the direction and principal thrust of his public ministry at its very outset, he responded by saying, "It is written: 'Man shall not live on bread alone, but on every word that comes from the mouth of God.'"[29] In other words, he rejected the first advice of the tempter, who would have had him focus his public work solely on meeting the most immediate physical needs of humanity, by declaring that human beings have deeper spiritual needs that cannot be satisfied by bread alone or the products of business and industry alone or the services of governments alone—important as these may be in their place.

There are needs that the would-be spiritual, business, or public leader must recognize as being beyond his or her ability to satisfy, needs that cannot be satisfied by the products of industry or politics or governments, even if those outputs were supernaturally blessed. These needs ultimately can only be satisfied in a different way and from another source—the full range of grace and truth ("every word") emanating from God himself. It is necessary that human beings' need for bread—for the products of industry and the services of governments—be met, but that is not sufficient in itself to give us the abundant life that Jesus came to offer.

The Grand Inquisitor vehemently insists that Jesus made a huge mistake by failing to take this initial advice offered by the wise and dread spirit. "Thou didst reject the one infallible banner which was offered Thee to make all men bow down to Thee alone—the banner of earthly bread; and Thou hast rejected it for the sake of freedom and the bread of Heaven."[30]

Later during Jesus' public ministry he encountered this temptation again, this time not in the wilderness but in the public arena, and he responded in the same way.[31] He was teaching on the far shore of the Sea of Galilee, and a great crowd gathered. He observed that they were hungry (he was not indifferent to hunger) and asked his disciples, "Where shall we buy bread for these people to eat?"[32] They protested that it would take eight months' wages just to buy enough bread for each one to have a

[29] Matthew 4:4.

[30] Dostoyevsky, *The Brothers Karamazov*, 247.

[31] John 6:1–16, 22–70.

[32] John 6:5.

bite. But Jesus took what they had—five small barley loaves and two small fishes that a boy had brought for lunch—and miraculously multiplied these to feed the multitude.

When the crowd realized what had happened, they reacted precisely as Satan predicted they would if Jesus had turned stones into bread—they formed the intention to make him king by force.[33] What was Jesus' reaction? The disciple John, who recorded this incident, says Jesus rejected their advances, withdrew into the hills, and hid himself from them.

When they continued to seek him out he rebuked them, as he did Satan in the wilderness, saying, "Very truly I tell you, you are looking for me, not because you saw signs [the work of God] I performed but because you ate the loaves and had your fill. Do not work for food that spoils, but for food that endures to eternal life, which the Son of Man [Jesus] will give you."[34] Jesus went on to preach a sermon on "bread from heaven" and did so in language and imagery so repugnant and offensive to his audience that even his closest followers said to each other, "This is a hard teaching. Who can accept it?" And, John added, "From this time many of his disciples turned back and no longer followed him."[35]

IMPLICATIONS FOR US

So what are the contemporary equivalents of this first temptation for would-be spiritual or political leaders today and how would we—how should we—respond to them?

On the religious front, is not one of the modern equivalents the temptation for the spiritual leader to offer people some version of the *prosperity* gospel? "Follow Jesus, and he'll give you economic prosperity and security here and now"—a very compelling and persuasive argument, particularly when offered to people in desperate economic circumstances as in much of the developing world.

On the political front, a contemporary equivalent is for the political leader or candidate for public office to offer voters only that which addresses their most tangible and immediate needs. "Vote for me and I'll pave your road, reduce your taxes, increase your benefits." This appeal

[33] John 6:15.

[34] John 6:26–27.

[35] John 6:60–66.

can be refined and focused by doing extensive public-opinion polling, identifying the voters' most immediate and palpable desires or grievances, and then promising to meet those regardless of the appropriateness of doing so or even the capacity of the candidate, leader, or government to do so.

Thus the tempter whispers to the political leader, "Base your appeal exclusively on an offer to meet their most tangible and immediate needs, and they'll vote for you by the thousands. But stray off that message—for example, into challenging them with the responsibilities of citizenship and liberty or the sacrifices required to maintain freedoms or achieve equality or the demands of rendering service to others—and they'll simply reject both you and your platform."

As a former leader of a political party I have been very much involved in the development of election platforms, based in part on polling and in-depth assessments of "what the voters want." In a democratic society where the needs and demands of the public are to be respected and responded to by those aspiring to public office, there is a place for doing so.

People do need bread—Jesus did not deny it—and they need jobs, incomes, housing, roads, schools, hospitals, and many of the services of the welfare state. But I think the temptation for us, those involved in democratic politics, is to come to believe that that is *all* they need, that if we could only satisfy the material and service needs of our electors we will have done all that can and should be done to achieve what the Grand Inquisitor referred to as the universal peace and happiness of man.

Perhaps the most important lesson from the first temptation is for leaders to recognize the *limits* to what political leadership, legislatures, and governments have to offer humanity. We can offer our people goods and services (and these are important), but we cannot in reality provide them with that which will satisfy their deeper human needs—deliverance from evil in their own lives, forgiveness for the wrongs of the past, the healing of broken relationships, or hope for the future that is independent of their material and temporal circumstances. These must ultimately come in a different way from another source.

It is Jesus' response to the first temptation that cautions leaders against appealing solely to the immediate and the physical. It reminds us that human beings have basic needs that go beyond the material and the temporal. Jesus alerts us to the limits of what the market and the state can offer and deliver.

How do we—how should we—respond to the contemporary equivalents of the first temptation? The Grand Inquisitor says, Accept as offered the advice of the wise and dread spirit. Jesus says, Reject it—man does not live by bread alone, but by every word that comes from the mouth of God.

1.3 THE SECOND TEMPTATION: GIVE THEM A SHOW AND THEY WILL FOLLOW

Then the devil took him to the holy city and had him stand on the highest point of the temple. "If you are the Son of God," he said, "throw yourself down. For it is written: 'He will command his angels concerning you, and they will lift you up in their hands, so that you will not strike your foot against a stone.'"[36]

THE SECOND TEMPTATION

HAVING FAILED TO INFLUENCE THE DIRECTION OF JESUS' ministry and leadership via the first temptation in the wilderness, the wise and dread spirit now tries a different tack. From Dostoyevsky's perspective, what Satan is really saying here is, If you, Jesus, really want people to notice and follow you, then give them a show! Do something spectacular to attract their attention and something mysterious, defying explanation, to pique their curiosity and something seemingly miraculous to win them over. Come here to the highest point of the temple in Jerusalem where everybody can see you. Call out, "Look at me! Look at me!" until every eye and every camera is fixed upon you. Then hurl yourself down, and just before you hit the pavement stones, have your Father's angels swoop down and catch you. (In support of this argument, Satan even quotes Scripture, Psalm 91.) Do that, Jesus, and you will make the evening news on every television network and the headlines in every newspaper. The scene will go viral on YouTube. People will be attracted to you by the millions. But whatever you do, Jesus, don't go about trying to win the masses by asking them to choose to follow you by the uncoerced and unsupported exercise of their free will. They can't do it. They won't do it. Instead, they'll go running after whoever gives them the show that you refuse to give them.

---

[36] Matthew 4:5–6.

JESUS' RESPONSE TO THE SECOND TEMPTATION

What was Jesus' response to this second temptation? Note that he did not deny that there was a role for the miraculous in his public ministry. But most often he performed miracles *in response* to faith, not as a means of generating it.[37] In fact, he rebuked those who followed him only to see or experience a miracle and who were constantly looking for "signs" that would compel them to believe.[38]

Therefore, Jesus rejects Satan's invitation to leap from the pinnacle of the temple and to demonstrate his deity through a spectacular deliverance. Jesus does so by again quoting Scripture: "It is also written, 'Do not put the Lord your God to the test.'"[39] Caesar and the political leaders of the Roman Empire might win the temporary allegiance of the masses by offering them bread and circuses, but Jesus rejects both of these as illegitimate and unacceptable means to acquire a following.

Again the Grand Inquisitor strongly rebukes him: "Thou didst crave for free love [i.e., love freely given] and not the base raptures of the slave before the might that has overawed him forever."[40] "Is the nature of men such, that they can reject miracles and at the great moments of their life, the moments of their deepest, most agonizing spiritual difficulties, cling only to the free verdict of the heart?"[41] Of course not!

> "There are three powers, three powers alone, able to conquer and to hold captive forever the conscience of these impotent rebels for their happiness—those forces are miracle, mystery and authority. Thou hast rejected all three and hast [regrettably, in the opinion of the Grand Inquisitor] set the example for doing so."[42]

IMPLICATIONS FOR US

What are the contemporary equivalents of this second temptation for leaders today, and how would we—how should we—respond to it?

In our day, is much of so-called televangelism—the Hollywood-style entertainment excesses of many of the television preachers—anything other

[37] Two examples of this can be read in Matthew 9:20–22 and 27–29.

[38] John 6:26–27. Matthew 12:39 states, "A wicked and adulterous generation asks for a [miraculous] sign!"

[39] Matthew 4:7.

[40] Dostoyevsky, *The Brothers Karamazov*, 249.

[41] Dostoyevsky, *The Brothers Karamazov*, 248.

[42] Dostoyevsky, *The Brothers Karamazov*, 248.

than succumbing to this second temptation? Are we not also succumbing to this temptation when we attempt to fill our churches by substituting religious entertainment for worship and substantive communication of the gospel with its demands for service and self-sacrificial love?

Similarly, with respect to public and political life, is not this the temptation to put image ahead of substance, to substitute appearances for reality, and to employ all of the techniques and stratagems of *image politics* to win support for our cause or candidacy?

This is a theme that Malcolm Muggeridge, a famous British correspondent and one-time editor of *Punch*, elaborated on under the heading of "The Fourth Temptation."[43] Muggeridge imagines that a wealthy Roman tycoon passing through Galilee happens to hear Jesus speaking and teaching and concludes that there would be a public appetite for his message. He proposes to "puff" Jesus using all the techniques of modern communications and employing the highly respected public relations firm of Lucifer Inc. to put on the Jesus Show and make him a superstar. But Jesus turns him down, for the same reasons that he resisted this second temptation in the wilderness.

Again, like with most powerful temptations, there is an element of truth to it. Effective and influential leadership requires powerful communications, and there was no public communicator more powerful than Jesus Christ. The work of God in the world is both miraculous and mysterious, and Jesus understood and used both miracle and mystery in conducting that work.

Yet, what was his response to this temptation to use the spectacular, the marvellous, and the mysterious to capture and entertain the masses of his day and sweep them into his kingdom camp on an emotional flood of temporary euphoria?

He resisted it! He used miracles to reward faith but not to create it. He said it was a wicked and adulterous generation that sought after a sign. He also quoted the scriptural prohibitions against tempting God by asking him to bless and honour spiritual circuses.

How then do we—how should we—respond to this temptation? The Grand Inquisitor says, Accept as offered the advice of the wise and

[43] Malcolm Muggeridge, *Christ and the Media* (London: Hodder and Stoughton, 1979), 39–41.

dread spirit to win men's allegiance by employing the spectacular, the marvellous, the mysterious. Jesus says, Reject it—do not put the Lord your God to the test.

1.4 THE THIRD TEMPTATION: COMPEL THEM TO FOLLOW BY SEIZING POLITICAL POWER

Again, the devil took him to a very high mountain and showed him all the kingdoms of the world and their splendor. "All this I will give you," he said, "if you will bow down and worship me."[44]

THE THIRD TEMPTATION

TWICE REBUFFED BY JESUS, THE WISE AND DREAD SPIRIT still persists and comes yet a third time with his most powerful and persuasive temptation.

On one level this temptation can be interpreted as the temptation to accept power and influence whenever it is offered, no matter by whom, no matter on what terms. In this case, Jesus is offered such power at the very outset of his public life from the hand of the wise and dread spirit on the condition that he bow down and give his allegiance to the one offering it.

To Dostoyevsky this temptation is much more diabolical than that. It is the temptation to exercise spiritual leadership—to bring about obedience to God's laws and standards, to bring about the kingdom of heaven on earth—not by grace, not by inviting men and women to freely choose to follow and serve Christ, but by seizing the authority and powers of the state and using them to *compel* obedience to the spiritual agenda.

What an awe-inspiring and irresistible temptation! The wise and dread spirit of this world, whom Jesus himself three times referred to in his later ministry as the prince of this world, takes Jesus up to the top of

[44] Matthew 4:8–9. Luke also quotes Satan as saying "I will give you all their authority and splendor; it has been given to me, and I can give it to anyone I want to. If you worship me, it will all be yours" (Luke 4:6–7).

a high mountain—the symbol in the Scriptures of political authority.[45] Then in a flash, in a moment of time, he shows him the kingdoms of this world—*all* of them:

From the absolute power and authority of the Egyptian pharaohs and the ancient Chinese emperors to the cumulative power and authority of the British Empire at its peak. From the power and authority of Prussia and the kaiser to the Third Reich; from the Kremlin and the Soviet Empire to the United States Senate and Congress to the Asian superpowers of the 21st century …

From the power and authority of the Greek city states to the vast empires of the valley of the Euphrates; from the court of Alexander the Great to the ancient kingdoms of the Mayas and Incas and Aztecs and the Khmer people of Angkor Wat; from the great colonial empires of Spain, Portugal, France, and England to the great democracies of today …

From the power and authority of the theocratic kingdom of David and Solomon to the popes of the Holy Roman Empire; from the power and authority of the princes of the Reformation to that of the princes and caliphs of Islam. From the military camps of Attila the Hun to those of the Vikings and the Gauls, to the Roman Senate and the household of Caesar himself …

And then, having shown Jesus *all* these kingdoms and governments of the world—from the dawn of time to the ends of the ages—Satan says, All this power and authority I will give you so that you can compel people everywhere to follow and obey your teachings. The one condition is that you bow down and worship the spirit of this world, the spirit that says the key to achieving the peace and universal happiness of humanity is the holding and exercise of political power and authority.

JESUS' RESPONSE TO THE THIRD TEMPTATION

So what was Jesus' response to this temptation? It was, again, clearly and emphatically to reject it, saying, "Away from me, Satan! For it is written: 'Worship the Lord your God, and serve him only.'"[46]

Note that in this case, he names the source of his temptation—Satan, evil personified—and that, whereas Satan offers power and authority,

---

[45] John 12:31; 14:30; 16:11.

[46] Matthew 4:10.

Jesus commands service. And as we will see, it is this rejection by Jesus of worldly power that most infuriates the Grand Inquisitor.

IMPLICATIONS FOR US: SHOULD WE SEEK POLITICAL POWER IN ORDER TO COMPEL ALLEGIANCE TO CHRIST?

Does this temptation have a familiar ring? Of course it does. This temptation has been presented to, and has often been embraced by, Christian leadership in every century from Jesus' time right down to our own.

Have you not heard the following argument advanced by well-meaning Christian leaders and their supporters in the public arena?

The atheists, agnostics, materialists, and secularists have got hold of the levers of political power and have used those levers to impose a non-Christian and even anti-Christian agenda on our nation. They have promoted and legalized abortion. They have curtailed prayer in the schools. They have made secular humanism the governing philosophy of the education system. They are redefining marriage to obliterate its traditional and spiritual meaning and promoting state-sanctioned euthanasia. They pursue social and taxation policies that weaken the traditional family. They have replaced the God of the Scriptures with the gods of the state and marketplace and the goddess of sexual promiscuity.

And so, what should good Christian people who oppose these trends and want to reverse them do? They should—by public and political action—get *their* hands on the political levers and then use those same levers to impose a *Christian* agenda: to ban or at least regulate abortion; to restore prayer and the promotion of Christian values in the schools; to adopt social and taxation policies that support and strengthen the traditional family; to constrain rather than feed economic and sexual appetites; to restore traditional spiritual beliefs and practices based on the Christian Scriptures to their rightful place in government, the marketplace, and society.

What a laudable and appealing proposition from the standpoint of the Christian community! Seize the levers of political power and authority in your society, and use those to promote and establish the kingdom of heaven on earth. What a noble temptation!

It is of course a very old temptation—one as old as Christendom itself, one to which many Christians and Christian leaders have succumbed—and we should learn from their experience.

During the first three centuries after Jesus' earthly sojourn ended, the Christian community was a minority in the Roman Empire—at first a tiny minority—bitterly persecuted by both the political and the religious establishments. But with the passage of time it grew in numbers and influence.

Then, in the words of the Grand Inquisitor as he recounted this history to the Christ,

> Just eight centuries ago, we took from *him*, the wise and mighty spirit in the wilderness, what Thou didst reject with scorn, the last gift *he* offered Thee, showing Thee all the kingdoms of the earth. We took from *him* Rome and the sword of Caesar, and proclaimed ourselves sole rulers of the earth … But Thou mightest have taken even then the sword of Caesar. Why didst Thou reject that last gift? Had Thou accepted that last offer of the mighty spirit, Thou wouldst have accomplished all that man seeks on earth—that is, someone to worship, someone to keep his conscience, and some means of uniting all in one unanimous and harmonious ant heap, because the craving for universal unity is the third and last anguish of men … Hadst Thou taken the world and Caesar's purple, Thou wouldst have founded the universal state and have given universal peace. For who can rule men if not he who holds their conscience and their bread in his hands.[47]

Yet Jesus, to the bitter disappointment of the Grand Inquisitor, rejected it all!

The Roman Empire declined and eventually disappeared, to be followed centuries later by the Holy Roman Empire, a marriage of professedly Christian institutions and a Christian agenda to the political instruments of the evolving state, a marriage that begot the Crusades and eventually produced the Spanish Inquisition—an institution characterized by a fusion of the powers of the state with those of the professing Christian church so absolute that the powers of the state were used to burn at the stake those whom the church deemed to be heretics and a danger to the purity and the practice of the faith.

Western statesmen today profess to be alarmed at the fusion of religion and government preached and practised by Islamic fundamentalists, and they should be. But in communicating our concerns, let us do so with the

[47] Dostoyevsky, *The Brothers Karamazov*, 250–251.

frank acknowledgement that for over 800 years Christendom attempted very much the same thing, with results even more disastrous for religion than for politics.

In my own political experience, the biggest single public fear of electing strongly professing Christians to public office is the public's fear that we will use the persuasive and legislative powers of elected office to impose our Christian values and beliefs on those who do not share them. And the biggest single criticism from the Christian community of me as a professedly Christian legislator in office was that I did not use the persuasive and legislative powers of my office to do precisely that.

The irony in all this is that if the general public actually knew what Jesus of Nazareth himself taught on this subject, if they knew of his own personal and categorical rejection of that option when it was presented to him at the outset of his own ministry, they would see him and genuine Christianity as the great guardians *against* the very thing that they fear. The further irony—a tragic irony—is that when well-meaning Christians advocate the use of the coercive power of the state to bring in the kingdom of heaven they are actually taking not Jesus' side but the side of Satan when he advocated precisely that position in the wilderness temptation.

But what true believer, zealous for the cause of right and desirous of seeing the kingdom of heaven on earth, can resist the temptation to grasp the power and the authority of the state if it appears within reach?

Well, we know one who did resist—Jesus himself, the author and finisher of our faith. He called the one who offered him that power by his name: "Away from me, *Satan*!"[48] He then quoted the Scripture that says, if a believer is going to bow down to authority or receive authority, there is only one authority to whom that believer should ultimately surrender himself or herself and only one purpose for that surrender. "Worship the Lord your God, and *serve* him only."[49]

Does this mean that Christian believers should not be involved in secular governments or the politics of the world or seek to advance the values and truths that proceed from the word of God in the secular, humanistic, and materialistic political and cultural arenas of our times? Not at all! But

[48] Matthew 4:10, emphasis added.

[49] Matthew 4:10, emphasis added.

let us recognize that the Jesus way of advancing those values and truths—of advancing the kingdom of God, of securing public support for a spiritual agenda—is fundamentally different from the way urged upon him by Satan in the wilderness. More on this *Jesus way* in subsequent chapters.

1.5 TRAINING: ETHICS

INTRODUCTION

PRIOR TO MY ENTRY INTO FEDERAL POLITICS IN CANADA I spent 20 years as a management consultant, mainly focused on long-range strategic, communication, and community relations planning for clients in the energy industry. In that context I tried to keep up on the various techniques and strategies published every year in a variety of journals and books on the subject of effective management, especially the management of people. Some of these were quite helpful and would eventually be of use to me in managing the executive and organization of a political party, including a parliamentary caucus. But of all the management texts I have read and studied, perhaps the most insightful and helpful from my perspective has been a book by a 19th century Scottish clergyman and theologian, A. B. Bruce, entitled *The Training of the Twelve.*[50]

The language of his book will strike the modern reader as quaint and out of another era, which it is. And Bruce occasionally digressed into giving his side of various theological disputes that were apparently important at the time but no longer resonate with us. But the depth and breadth of Bruce's descriptions and insights into exactly how Jesus of Nazareth, in three short years, took a motley crew of twelve young men and moulded them into the founding members and leaders of an organization, the Christian church, which has lasted over twenty centuries and greatly

[50] Alexander Balmain Bruce, *The Training of the Twelve, or Passages Out of the Gospels Exhibiting the Twelve Disciples of Jesus Under Discipline for the Apostleship* (Edinburgh: T & T. Clark, 1871). Note that Bruce focused on the twelve male disciples; however Jesus also had many female disciples who were included in his inner circle and whom he trained.

affected the lives of hundreds of millions of people, are profound and instructive.

The disciples were not the smartest, the wealthiest, or the best educated of the many people Jesus encountered. They were not the best connected or the most religious. Far from it. Most were from a rural region, Galilee, of which one of its own is recorded as wondering "Can anything good come from there?"[51] Bruce described them as follows:

> In a worldly point of view they were a very insignificant company indeed,—a band of poor illiterate Galilean provincials, utterly devoid of social consequence, not likely to be chosen by one having supreme regard to prudential considerations. Why did Jesus choose such men? Was He guided by feelings of antagonism to those possessing social advantages, or of partiality for men of His own class? No; His choice was made in true wisdom. If He chose Galileans mainly, it was not from provincial prejudice against those of the south; if, as some think, He chose two or even four of His own kindred, it was not from nepotism; if He chose rude, unlearned, humble men, it was not because He was animated by any petty jealousy of knowledge, culture, or good birth. If any rabbi, rich man, or ruler had been willing to yield himself unreservedly to the service of the kingdom, no objection would have been taken to him on account of his acquirements, possessions, or titles ... The truth is, that Jesus was obliged to be content with fishermen, and publicans, and quondam zealots, for apostles. *They were the best that could be had.*[52]

Nevertheless, now looking back over twenty centuries, it is truly astounding to see what this humble band became under his tutelage and what was accomplished through them. What might those of us responsible for forming, motivating, and managing small groups of people today—especially for religious or political purposes or for operating at the interface of faith and public life—learn from Jesus' methods and example in this regard?

LESSONS IN LEADERSHIP

As Bruce observed, the record of the work of Jesus contained in the Gospels has two distinct dimensions—a public dimension in which he

[51] John 1:46.

[52] Bruce, *The Training of the Twelve*, 37, emphasis added. "They were the best that could be had" is Bruce's summation of the twelve at the time of their recruitment. Jesus himself, however, viewed them from a different perspective, describing them to his Father toward the end of his ministry as "those whom you gave me" (John 17:6).

spoke, taught, and acted in public and dealt with public audiences and a more private and intimate dimension in which Jesus devoted himself specifically to the training and cultivation of the disciples. Be reminded, Bruce said,

> There were *two* religious movements going on in the days of the Lord Jesus. One consisted in rousing the mass out of the stupor of indifference; the other consisted in the careful, exact training of men already in earnest, in the principles and truths of the divine kingdom. Of the one movement the disciples ... were the agents; of the other movement they were the subjects. And the latter movement, though less noticeable, and much more limited in extent, was by far more important than the former; for it was destined to bring forth fruit that would remain—to tell not merely on the present time, but on the whole history of the world.[53]

It is this second dimension of Jesus' work that Bruce examined and explained in great detail. Three aspects of the training of the disciples that I find particularly relevant to those of us with interests in public service, whether we are believers or not, pertain to the inculcation of high ethical standards, the management of ambition, and the reform of existing practices and institutions. In this chapter let us begin with Jesus' approach to the inculcation of ethics and its contemporary relevance.

THE INCULCATION OF ETHICS

The cultivation of high ethical standards among those who seek public service is absolutely essential today if public trust in public leaders is to be restored, especially trust in political leaders, parties, candidates, democratic processes (such as elections), and democratic institutions. This is particularly true for candidates for public office with a faith commitment, as they are often held to an even higher standard than others are and will be mercilessly castigated as hypocrites if and when they fall short.

In a national public-opinion survey conducted by the Manning Centre for Building Democracy (January 2015) we asked respondents to indicate on a scale of 1 to 10 (with 1 being totally unimportant and 10 being very important) the importance they attached to the following:

---

[53] Bruce, *The Training of the Twelve*, 106.

- Whether candidates for public office are "knowledgeable."
- Whether candidates possess certain "skills," such as the ability to communicate, make decisions, etc.
- Whether candidates possess certain "character traits," such as honesty, compassion, transparency, and integrity.

Predictably, character trumped knowledge and skills by a large margin. In fact, many respondents implied that they didn't care how knowledgeable or skilful a political candidate or leader was; if they couldn't be trusted because of character deficiencies, they shouldn't be supported for public office.[54]

This survey also indicated that the those surveyed held a very low opinion of the ethical standards of Canada's current political class, with 90 percent seeing elected officials as being more concerned with advancing their own interests (e.g., making money) than serving their constituents, and 55 percent considering elected officials to be unprincipled in general.

Another survey conducted around the same time by Ryerson University indicated that the unethical behaviours of politicians that respondents found most objectionable were the breaking of election promises (75 percent), the use of tax dollars to buy votes (55 percent), and the adoption of policies favouring particular interest groups, lobbyists, or family members solely to advance those interests and win their support (55 percent).[55]

RELIANCE ON ETHICAL CODES

So how do we go about raising the ethical tone and standards of a nation or a society? More particularly, how do we go about raising the ethical tone of those in public service?

From ancient times down to the present, the most frequently utilized approach is to develop and enforce a code of ethics, with positive incentives for adherence, penalties for violations, and a system for monitoring and enforcing compliance.

---

[54] "2015 Manning Barometer," national public opinion survey carried out January 20 to 23, 2015.

[55] "Public Perceptions of the Ethics of Political Leadership," Jim Pattison Ethical Leadership Program at Ryerson University.

For the people of Israel, from the days of their liberation from Egypt right down to Jesus' day, it was the code of ethics embodied in the law of Moses and all the processes and institutions developed for its communication, expansion, and enforcement that constituted the traditional approach to securing ethical behaviour. Not dissimilarly, in our day we have seen the same approach taken, as evidenced by the plethora of ethical codes and compliance regimes adopted by many companies, professional organizations, and governments. In the case of the latter, codes of conduct for civil servants and elected officials may be enshrined in legislation and reinforced by the appointment of compliance officers and ethics commissioners.[56] This was the situation that prevailed when my colleagues and I were first elected to the Canadian Parliament in 1993.

INSUFFICIENCIES OF THE CODE OF ETHICS APPROACH

Unfortunately, the sad reality is that this approach by itself has generally proved to be insufficient in achieving the goal of securing consistently ethical behaviour on the part of those committed or subjected to it. For example, this insufficiency was demonstrated by the four-hundred-year experience of ancient Israel with the law of Moses, as recorded in the Old Testament, and the conclusion of the latter prophets that unless the law could be written on the tablets of the heart—that is, internalized—reliance on a code of ethics alone was insufficient to guarantee ethical behaviour.

My own experience as a Canadian parliamentarian from 1993 to 2002 has led me to conclude that reliance on an external code of ethics is an insufficient approach today as well. When the Chrétien government was elected in 1993 it introduced a code of ethics for parliamentarians and civil servants, accompanied by the appointment of an ethics commissioner and a tightening of laws and regulations governing lobbying and conflicts of interests. The government insisted that all of this would lead to a higher degree of ethical behaviour on the part of the administration and parliamentarians. But the sad reality was that the parliaments of which I was a part exhibited the following:

---

[56] *Federal Accountability Act: An Act Providing for Conflict of Interest Rules, Restrictions on Election Financing and Measures Respecting Administrative Transparency, Oversight and Accountability* (S.C. 2006, c. 9).

- A chronic inability to recognize moral and ethical issues when they arose, especially with respect to old practices sanctioned by time, routine, and habit.
- A persistent defaulting to "moral relativism" as an excuse for inaction when confronted with moral and ethical issues.
- An overreliance on ethical pragmatism and utilitarianism rather than code-based or "deontological" ethics when an ethical decision could not be avoided.

INSUFFICIENCIES ILLUSTRATED FROM MY PARLIAMENTARY EXPERIENCE

The word *parliament* is derived from the French *parler,* meaning to speak. Communication is the essence of political and parliamentary discourse, and the principal ethical test of a communication is "Is it true?" This test can be applied to a speech, a news release, a ministerial statement, a party platform, a policy declaration, and so on, but when we do so in today's world, what do we find? That of all our public communications it is political discourse that is so riddled with near truths, half-truths, outright lies, and political spin that the public has justifiably ceased to believe much of what politicians say.

Did the proclamation of a code of ethics for the 35th parliament of Canada change any of this? Did it increase the sensitivity of members as to whether what they were saying in debate or in committee or from a political platform met even the most elementary test of truthfulness? Not at all. Politicians, in general, simply do not see a moral or ethical aspect to our long-established habits of communication in the public arena, just as some business people see no moral issues in their long-established business practices and some media people see no moral issue in how they filter and present information and some bureaucrats see no moral issues in how they treat or mistreat people. Codes of ethics, no matter how well worded or communicated, seem insufficient to increase awareness of ethical issues or standards in areas where indifference, callousness, or habitual practices have blinded the practitioners to them.

To illustrate, let me cite just one bizarre incident that demonstrated for me how ineffective, in the final analysis, the Standing Orders of the House of Commons are in guaranteeing any degree of truthfulness in parliamentary debate. On this particular occasion a government member asserted that a certain opposition member was a "racist," an assertion that I and others knew to be a lie.[57] In the heated exchange that followed, the opposition member in question said so and labelled the first member a "liar." The Speaker immediately ruled both members out of order and threatened them with expulsion from the chamber if they did not retract and apologize. In doing so, he was much more censorious of the second member than the first, giving the impression that the use of unparliamentary language—the word *liar*—was a much greater offence than the lie that provoked it. I later sought clarification from the Speaker, who ruefully confirmed that, as he interpreted the Standing Orders governing members' conduct, the House is offended by the use of the word *liar* but not necessarily offended by the lie itself. Obviously there is a great need for upgrading the ethics of the House in regard to truth telling, but something much more than a code of ethics or amendments to the Standing Orders is required to achieve that objective.

At about the same time as this incident, several other issues involving serious violations of ethical standards were swirling about the head of the government. These included the alleged cover-up of the murder of a Somali civilian by Canadian Special Forces on a peacekeeping mission; the deaths of scores of Canadians from tainted blood and the allegations that an earlier Liberal administration had ignored early warnings of this danger because it did not want the matter to become an election issue; and the denial by the government that its leadership had ever promised to "kill, scrap, or abolish" Canada's goods and services tax during the previous election campaign, when there was overwhelming evidence to the contrary.[58]

During the daily Question Period I asked the prime minister, "Do any of these activities violate the prime minister's ethical standards, or by his standards are all these activities ethically acceptable?" Later in the day at a meeting of a special joint committee of the House and Senate on a code of ethics for members of Parliament I asked the prime minister's ethics counsellor the same question.

In both cases, each professed to see no ethical issues with respect to the activities in question, only "differences of opinion on matters of

---

[57] See Preston Manning, *Think Big: My Adventures in Life and Democracy* (Toronto: McClelland & Stewart, 2002), 117.

[58] See Manning, *Think Big*, 118–120.

policy between the government and the opposition." In essence, this was a fall back to *moral relativism*, which eviscerates many ethical discussions in the political arena and elsewhere by adhering to the notion that you are entitled to your ethical standards and I am entitled to mine, but neither of us is entitled to judge or challenge the standards of the other, because there are no absolute moral standards, only differences of opinion as to what constitutes ethical conduct.[59]

On one further occasion during my last year in Parliament, I again became acutely aware of the insufficiency of the instinctive approach of politicians to ethics while dealing with an important piece of legislation. As a member of the Standing Committee on Health, I was involved in reviewing a draft bill for the regulation of assisted human reproduction, related stem cell research, and human cloning. These activities are fraught with ethical considerations, and we sought the advice of several expert ethicists to assist us in dealing with them. It soon became apparent, however, that a majority of my colleagues on the committee favoured a utilitarian approach to the ethical issues in question—an approach that pragmatic politicians instinctively favour. Simply identify the costs and benefits of the activity in question, and if the benefits outweigh the costs, then the activity is ethically justifiable. If the ratio of benefits to costs is not favourable enough, keep expanding the definition and scope of benefits until you get the justification you want.

This approach does not even rely on a code of ethics and is in conflict with so-called deontological ethics, which insist that we have an inherent obligation or duty to act in accordance with certain specific rules of conduct derived from reason or accepted beliefs, regardless of whether to do so maximizes some defined good or minimizes some defined harm.[60] This is why attempts to ensure that the bill included a clause recognizing an inherent obligation on the part of Canadians to respect human life—

[59] In this regard I am reminded of a study of political integrity by the historian D. C. Somervell that focused on the lives of two 19th century British statesmen. These were William Gladstone, the moralist, who if he didn't see right and wrong in an issue was uninterested, and Benjamin Disraeli, the pragmatist, who rarely saw right or wrong in any issue, only differences of opinion. And what was Somervell's conclusion? That while it is an error to discover moral issues when none are in fact at stake, *it is a greater error to be blind to them when moral issues really arise* (see D. C. Somervell, *Gladstone and Disraeli* [Garden City: Garden City Publishing Company, 1928], 66).

[60] *Deontological* is derived from the Greek word for duty or "that which is binding."

regardless of pragmatic arguments for taking, preserving, or manipulating it based on the costs and benefits of doing so—were completely disregarded.

A DIFFERENT ROAD TO ETHICAL BEHAVIOUR

So what were the distinguishing features of Jesus' approach to ethics and which features characterized his training of the disciples in this regard? And how does his approach differ from the conventional approach to ethics today?

First of all, he presents and demonstrates love—self-sacrificial love—as the supreme ethic, which if practised will ensure that all the other ethical demands of the law (the code) will be met. "Love the Lord your God" and "Love your neighbor as yourself. All the law and the Prophets hang on these two commandments."[61]

According to Bruce,

> [Jesus] described the *ethics* of the kingdom, as a pure stream of life, having charity [i.e., love] for its fountainhead; a morality of the heart, not merely of outward conduct; a morality also broad and catholic, overleaping all arbitrary barriers erected by legal pedantry and natural selfishness.[62]

Of course, in the end he not only taught this ethic, he demonstrated it in an unforgettable way by his own self-sacrifice on the cross.

Note that this ethic is not a utilitarian ethic—it does not rest on a calculation of costs and benefits to either the individual or the society embracing it—but is presented as inherently worthy of adoption because of its source. As described later by the apostle Paul, love keeps no record of wrongs or of its own accomplishments (that is, it keeps no record of its costs or benefits). "Love is patient, love is kind. It does not envy, it does not boast, it is not proud. It does not dishonor others, it is not self-seeking, it is not easily angered, it keeps no record of wrongs. Love does not delight in evil but rejoices with the truth. It always protects, always trusts, always hopes, always perseveres."[63]

Second, Jesus teaches his early followers that the inner transformation required to adopt and practise this ethic involves committing yourself to

[61] Matthew 22:37–40.

[62] Bruce, *The Training of the Twelve*, 43.

[63] 1 Corinthians 13:4–7.

and following a being morally superior to yourself who already embodies and practises this supreme ethic. As a result, he draws the disciples to himself, saying, "Love each other as I have loved you," and points them and other seekers to a loving God as the ultimate source of this morality.[64] When one such seeker asks, "Good teacher … what must I do to inherit eternal life?" Jesus replies, "Why do you call me good? … No one is good—except God alone."[65] God himself is the being who is morally superior to us all. Draw near to him, and you will draw near to the ultimate source of morality.

Note that Jesus does not disparage those who honestly strive to adhere to a code of ethics, in particular the law of Moses. In fact, Jesus says,

> "Do not think that I have come to abolish the Law or the Prophets; I have not come to abolish them but to fulfill them. For truly I tell you, until heaven and earth disappear, not the smallest letter, not the least stroke of a pen, will by any means disappear from the Law until everything is accomplished. Therefore … whoever practices and teaches these commands will be called great in the kingdom of heaven."[66]

But he teaches that the code of ethics contained in the law of Moses is to be fulfilled not by adding regulation on regulation or constantly tightening its compliance and enforcement regime but by committing ourselves to a *person* who embodies and practises it fully, in this case Jesus himself. Therefore, the code of ethics becomes a means to an end—a guardian or schoolmaster, as the apostle Paul was later to write—to drive us toward a relationship with that morally superior being who embodies and fulfills it.[67]

Third, Jesus demonstrates to the disciples that in the hands and company of himself, the embodiment of self-sacrificial love, his followers will begin to see moral and ethical issues in situations that the mere adherents to the law are blind to. For example, in his Sermon on the Mount he actually tightens the ethical demands of the law rather than relaxing them, saying,

---

[64] John 15:12.

[65] Mark 10:17–18.

[66] Matthew 5:17–19.

[67] See Galatians 3:24.

> "You have heard that it was said to the people long ago, 'You shall not murder, and anyone who murders will be subject to judgment.' But I tell you that anyone who is angry with a brother or sister will be subject to judgment ... You have heard that it was said, 'You shall not commit adultery.' But I tell you that anyone who looks at a woman lustfully has already committed adultery with her in his heart."[68]

He rebukes the Pharisees in particular for professing to see a moral obligation to practise tithing even with respect to their use of spices but being blind to their moral obligations in weightier matters demanding justice, mercy, and faithfulness.[69] At the same time, he cautions his followers against the opposite extreme—the danger to which moralists of every kind are particularly susceptible—of seeing moral and ethical issues in every particular situation involving others, even when such issues do not exist, while ignoring their own moral condition.[70]

Fourth, Jesus forms his followers into a "moral community," one where the ethic of love is to be its distinguishing moral characteristic and whose members support one another and hold each other accountable for their behaviour. It is this moral community that is to sustain and extend the ethical teachings of Jesus, and his last recorded prayer is a prayer for its unity and endurance.[71]

It should be noted that the size of the original community of disciples was small; that the relationships among them grew more personal and intimate as they lived and worked together; and that the moral tone of their community was definitely set by the high ethical standards of their leader. Where these three characteristics do not exist—as in large, impersonal

---

[68] Matthew 5:21–22, 27–28.

[69] "Woe to you, teachers of the law and Pharisees, you hypocrites! You give a tenth of your spices—mint, dill and cumin. But you have neglected the more important matters of the law—justice, mercy and faithfulness. You should have practiced the latter, without neglecting the former. You blind guides! You strain out a gnat but swallow a camel" (Matthew 23:23–24).

[70] "Now there were some present at that time who told Jesus about the Galileans whose blood Pilate had mixed with their sacrifices. Jesus answered, 'Do you think that these Galileans were worse sinners than all the other Galileans because they suffered this way? I tell you, no! But unless you repent, you too will all perish. Or those eighteen who died when the tower in Siloam fell on them—do you think they were more guilty than all the others living in Jerusalem? I tell you, no! But unless you repent, you too will all perish'" (Luke 13:1–5).

[71] See John 17.

organizations with distant or ethically challenged leadership—the inculcation and maintenance of high ethical standards are compromised.

IMPLICATIONS FOR US

I must first of all readily admit that I have personally wrestled long and hard—often with limited success—with precisely how to internalize high standards of ethical behaviour among members of business and political organizations of which I have been a part and that I still have much to learn myself in this area.

But it would seem to me that the ethics of the political organizations and communities of which I have been a part, including the Parliament of Canada, would be strengthened by acknowledging the following:

- Codes of ethics and associated compliance and enforcement regimes are insufficient in themselves to achieve a high standard of ethical behaviour.
- The ethics of an organization will never rise higher than those of its leadership, and high ethical standards should therefore be an essential prerequisite in choosing and cultivating political leadership.
- Putting the interests of others—our fellow countrymen, our constituents, our colleagues, our families—ahead of our own selfish interests should constitute our highest ethical commitment. (Is not this the essence of self-sacrificial love as Jesus taught it?)
- The ethical life is not static; we should be growing in ethical sensitivity—increasingly seeing ethical and moral dimensions in issues and situations where we might not have seen them before, while avoiding the extreme of seeing moral issues where in fact none exist.
- We are in need of the fellowship of others who share our moral commitments and will hold us accountable to keep those commitments. We therefore should seek to be part of a moral community and contribute to its sustenance and activity.

If you are ever responsible for establishing the moral tone and standards of a group—a church, company, charity, political organization, or government—surely these lessons drawn from the teachings and example of Jesus constitute an excellent starting point.

Make self-sacrificial love the supreme ethic to be pursued and practised, encouraging and rewarding those who put the interests of others ahead of their own while constraining those who consistently put their own self-interest ahead of everything else. Commit yourself to following and learning from someone who personally practises that ethic, and seek to become that person yourself, recognizing that the ethical standards of an organization will never rise higher than those of its leadership. And form or join a moral community or fellowship—preferably a small and intimate one—where that highest of ethical standards will be practised and where you will be supported and held accountable by others for doing so.

1.6 TRAINING: MANAGING AMBITION

THE AMBITIONS OF THE DISCIPLES

IN ALMOST ALL POLITICAL SYSTEMS, FROM THE authoritarian one-party regime of Communist China to the multi-party democratic systems of the West, personal political ambition plays a major part in initiating and sustaining the involvement of those desiring positions and offices of influence. Personal ambition is also frequently present as a driving force among persons desiring positions of influence in religious and charitable organizations.

It should not surprise us therefore to find personal ambition thrusting itself to the fore among Jesus' band of initial followers. And since Jesus was offering the "kingdom of heaven"—"kingdom" being a political concept and "heaven" being a spiritual one—it should not surprise us that their ambitions were a combination of the spiritual and the political.

On one occasion, for example, we are told that James and John, two of Jesus' closest and most faithful associates, accompanied by their mother, came to him requesting that they be given key cabinet posts in the future government of the kingdom.[72] Needless to say, this open display of ambition by James and John stirred up indignation on the part of the other ten disciples.

On yet another occasion, while they were travelling along the road to Capernaum, the disciples fell to arguing among themselves as to who would be "the greatest" in the future kingdom.[73] Apparently, they sensed that this was an unseemly argument among the followers of one who was

---

[72] See Matthew 20:20–28; Mark 10:35–45.

[73] Mark 9:33–34; Luke 9:46.

teaching them to put the interests of others ahead of their own, because they conducted it out of Jesus' hearing and were embarrassed when he later asked them what they had been quarrelling about.

Even on the sad and dramatic occasion of the Last Supper, when Jesus addressed his disciples for the last time and predicted his own self-sacrificial death, it is recorded that, again, "a dispute also arose among them as to which of them was considered to be the greatest."[74] Ambition—how to advance themselves, how to be the greatest—always seemed to be not far from their minds no matter what the occasion or circumstance.

THE MANAGEMENT OF PERSONAL AMBITION

So how did Jesus deal with personal ambition on the part of his followers? In particular, how did Jesus deal with ambition combined with spiritual motivation—a potentially dangerous mixture and one often found among believers operating at the interface of faith and public life?

Significantly, he did not directly disparage the ambition of the disciples. He did not renounce it as misguided or evil. Rather Jesus sought to redirect their ambition away from the service of self and toward the self-sacrificial service of others. He did so in four ways.

First, he contrasted the *route to the top* in his kingdom with the politics of power and authority in the kingdoms of this world. This was his reply to James and John when they came to him requesting cabinet posts in his government, and it was his response to the surfacing of political ambitions at the Last Supper. "The kings of the Gentiles lord it over them ... But you are not to be like that. Instead, the greatest among you should be like the youngest, and the one who rules like one who serves."[75]

Second, he repeated on each occasion when their unseemly and misdirected ambition surfaced the same maxim, in words that are as piercing and relevant to politically ambitious believers today as when he first spoke them: "Whosoever would be chief among you, let him be your servant."[76] In other words, "You want promotion and advancement in

[74] Luke 22:24.

[75] Luke 22:24–29. See also Matthew 20:20–28; Mark 10:35–45.

[76] Matthew 20:27 (KJV).

my kingdom? You want to be chief—a leader, a cabinet minister, a first minister? Fine! Then go out and serve better and more self-sacrificially than anybody else."[77]

Third, he offered himself and his work as the model of the self-sacrificial service of others that leads to advancement in his kingdom. He told the disciples, "I am among you [not as the Gentile rulers who lord it over others, but] as one who serves."[78] And on the occasion of the Last Supper it was Jesus who assumed the role of the servant, washing his disciples' feet.

> "Do you understand what I have done for you?" he asked them. "You call me 'Teacher' and 'Lord,' and rightly so, for that is what I am. Now that I, your Lord and Teacher, have washed your feet, you also should wash one another's feet. I have set you an example that you should do as I have done for you."[79]

THE CHILD IN THE MIDST

Fourth, Jesus offered *humility* as the quality most required to temper spiritually motivated political ambition. But how do you teach humility to the passionately ambitious? Well, watch how Jesus did it.

On each occasion where it is recorded that the disciples quarrelled among themselves as to who would be the greatest, it is also recorded that Jesus did a most unusual thing. He interrupted their quarrelling by bringing a small child into their midst and declaring that until they became like the child in humility, trustfulness, and guilelessness they were not yet fit for service or advancement in his kingdom.[80] "Truly I tell you," he said, "unless you change and become like little children, you will never

---

[77] No one modelled this "downward route to the top" for us better than Jesus. As the apostle Paul wrote to the Philippians, "In your relationships with one another, have the same mindset as Christ Jesus: Who, being in very nature God, did not consider equality with God something to be used to his own advantage; rather, he made himself nothing by taking the very nature of a servant, being made in human likeness. And being found in appearance as a man, he humbled himself by becoming obedient to death—even death on a cross! Therefore God exalted him to the highest place and gave him the name that is above every name, that at the name of Jesus every knee should bow, in heaven and on earth and under the earth, and every tongue acknowledge that Jesus Christ is Lord, to the glory of God the Father" (Philippians 2:5–11).

[78] Luke 22:27.

[79] John 13:12–15.

[80] See Matthew 18:1–5; Mark 9:33–37; Luke 9:46–48.

enter the kingdom of heaven. Therefore, whoever takes the lowly position of this child is the greatest in the kingdom of heaven."[81]

IMPLICATIONS FOR US

It requires a certain amount of ambition to enter and participate in the public arenas of our day. If one is a Christian believer, that ambition may well be mixed with spiritual motivation, such as a desire to bring ethical "salt and light" to the political and public arenas and a genuine desire to serve.

If we are to be guided by Jesus, however, we can be sure that he will constantly redirect our ambition away from the service of ourselves and our party toward the self-sacrificial service of others, as he guided the ambitious among the disciples so long ago.

When I was leader of a Canadian political party and leader of the Official Opposition in our House of Commons, I had a small plaque on my office desk, given to me by one of my daughters, that simply read, "Whosoever would be chief among you, let him be the servant of all."

Some very ambitious people came to see me during those years, some of whom became cabinet ministers in the government of Canada, one even becoming prime minister. All ended up rendering genuine and substantial public service to the people of Canada, and it is not my intent to disparage that service in any way. But I wonder to this day if their service might have been more effective if I had more strongly encouraged and rewarded those who were willing to pursue the downward route to the top as Jesus did and if I had more faithfully modelled that route myself.

Even today there is merit in employing, at least in our imaginations, the concept of *the child in the midst* as a means of moderating and tempering environments where partisan ambition to be the first and the greatest is the dominant characteristic.

Imagine the House of Commons during the daily Question Period—a cauldron of mistrust, ambition, and self-aggrandizement if there ever was one. The members of Parliament, egged on by the media, are hurling loaded questions, clever retorts, and assorted insults across the floor as usual, all striving to make the evening news and secure the greatest possible attention and recognition for themselves and their parties.

---

[81] Matthew 18:3–4.

But what if we were also to imagine that the space between the government and opposition benches was occupied not by the mace and the tables of the house officers but by scores of young children representing more truly than any member of Parliament the future hopes of our country?

How would politicians act in the face of *the child in the midst*? Would it be the presence and actions of the children that would be incongruous and out of place in the Commons, or would it be the words and actions of the members that would now appear inappropriate and misdirected?

If only we would listen, Jesus of Nazareth has much to teach us—by word, by example, and through the tempering influence of *the child in the midst*—on the management of ambition.

1.7 TRAINING: MANAGING CHANGE

THE LEADERSHIP OF CHANGE

THE LEADERSHIP OF CHANGE CAN BE ONE OF THE MOST difficult and thankless tasks a leader undertakes—in particular when it involves the reform of entrenched practices or institutions that need to be changed because they have become outdated, deformed, counterproductive, or obsolete but to which those engaged in them are still deeply committed because of tradition, habit, familiarity, and resistance to innovation.

In the case of Jesus, he first focused his ministry of change not on the general public but on his small band of initial followers. As A. B. Bruce pointed out, it was an onerous undertaking:

> At the time of their call they were exceedingly ignorant, narrow-minded, superstitious, full of … prejudices, misconceptions, and animosities. They had much to unlearn of what was bad, as well as much to learn of what was good, and they were slow both to learn and unlearn. Old beliefs already in possession of their minds made the communication of new religious ideas a difficult task.[82]

The three well-established religious conventions of his day that Jesus particularly addressed were the practices and institutions of fasting, ceremonial washing, and Sabbath observance. Jesus specifically addressed the reform of *religious* practices and institutions—those most resistant to change because they are rooted in deeply held beliefs that their adherents believe to be immutable and divinely sanctioned. But the principles and techniques Jesus utilized to induce change under such circumstances are relevant to the reform of *any* deeply entrenched practice or institution.

---

[82] Bruce, *The Training of the Twelve*, 14.

THE CRITIQUE OF CURRENT PRACTICES

In Jesus' day, the most rigorous teachers and practitioners of fasting, ceremonial washing, and Sabbath observance were the Pharisees. As the primary teachers of the law of Moses, their instruction and example with respect to these practices were highly influential with the general public, including the members of Jesus' initial band of followers.[83] So to change the conduct of the latter in relation to these practices, Jesus first had to critique the teaching and practices of the former. His focus was on criticizing not the essence of these practices but the extremes to which the Pharisees carried them.

For example, with respect to ceremonial washing,

> The aim of the rabbinical prescriptions respecting washings was not physical cleanliness, but something thought to be far higher and more sacred. Their object was to secure, not physical, but ceremonial purity; that is, to cleanse the person from such impurity as might be contracted by contact with a Gentile, or with a Jew in a ceremonially unclean state, or with an unclean animal, or with a dead body or any part thereof … Not content with purifications prescribed in the law for uncleanness actually contracted, they made provision for merely possible cases. If a man did not remain at home all day, but went out to market, he must wash his hands on his return, because it was possible that he might have touched some person or thing ceremonially unclean. Great care, it appears, had also to be taken that the water used in the process of ablution was itself perfectly pure; and it was necessary even to apply the water in a particular manner to the hands, in order to secure the desired results.[84]

With respect to Sabbath observance, adherence to the fourth commandment,[85] Bruce again described in considerable detail the

[83] "There are two major characteristics of the Pharisees, their meticulous observance of obligations under the Law for purity, tithing, and Sabbath observances; and their emphasis on oral law as equally binding to the Law. The New Testament witnesses to their great concern over tithing and purity … and the many disputes Jesus had with the Jews over the Sabbath day reflect their concern for that law as well … The other major characteristic of the Pharisees is the value they placed on oral traditions. 'Oral law' refers to traditional rules and observances that were designed to adapt the written Law to the changes of time … In the process of multiplying rulings it was easy for the Pharisees to become hypocritical because in attempting to be faithful to the letter of the Law they lost the spirit of the Law" (Allen Ross, "2. The Pharisees," *The Religious World of Jesus* [Bible.org, 2016]).

[84] Bruce, *The Training of the Twelve*, 80–81.

[85] "Remember the Sabbath day by keeping it holy. Six days you shall labor and do all your work, but the seventh day is a sabbath to the Lord your God. On it you shall not do any work, neither you, nor your son or daughter, nor your male or female servant, nor your animals, nor any foreigner residing in your towns" (Exodus 20:8–10).

extremes to which the Pharisaic interpretation and practice of this institution had been taken.

> Their habit, in all things, was to degrade God's law by framing innumerable petty rules for its better observance, which, instead of securing that end, only made the law appear base and contemptible. In no case was this miserable micrology carried to greater lengths than in connection with the fourth commandment. With a most perverse ingenuity, the most insignificant actions were brought within the scope of the prohibition against labour. Even in the case put by our Lord, that of an animal fallen into a pit, it was deemed lawful to lift it out—so at least those learned in rabbinical lore tell us—only when to leave it there till Sabbath was past would involve risk to life. When delay was not dangerous, the rule was to give the beast food sufficient for the day; and if there was water in the bottom of the pit, to place straw and bolsters below it, that it might not be drowned.[86]

JESUS' CRITIQUE OF RELIGIOUS EXTREMISM

In critiquing the Pharisaic approach to teaching and enforcing adherence to the commandments of the Mosaic law, Jesus illustrated the merits of always taking a hard look at what I call "the dark side of the moon." In other words, whatever doctrine or philosophy of life we may adhere to—be it religious, political, or cultural—in our mind's eye we should push it to its extreme and take a hard look at what that really looks like and the results it may produce. If that image of the extreme is ugly and deformed and the results of its pursuit are evil and deplorable, as the image and products of extremism most frequently are, then that realization ought to strongly incentivize us to back away, to resist movement in that direction, to avoid association with that extreme, and to warn others to do likewise.

For example, the Rule of Law as given to Moses by God when genuinely followed by ancient Israelites was a noble and beneficial concept originally given as an instrument for establishing and maintaining right relationships between God and his people and among the people themselves. But pushed to the fanatical extreme to which the Pharisees pressed it—whereby the Rule of Law was transformed into an arid, crippling, and hypocritical legalism—it became a barrier, not a means, to right relations with God and a burden instead of a boon to the people—the very opposite of the results that it was originally intended to produce.

[86] Bruce, *The Training of the Twelve*, 89.

With respect to Sabbath observance, Jesus dealt with the extreme interpretations and practices of the Pharisees in three distinct ways.

First, he demonstrated his personal disapproval of and opposition to the Pharisaic teachings and practices of Sabbath observance by personally violating certain of their teachings on this subject and defending his followers for doing likewise. For example, on five separate occasions as recorded in the Gospels, Jesus deliberately and publicly performed acts of healing on the Sabbath despite the accusations and protestations of the Pharisees that this constituted Sabbath breaking.[87] On another occasion, he stoutly defended the actions of his disciples, who had plucked some ears of grain on the Sabbath day to satisfy their hunger, again over the objections of the Pharisees that this constituted "work" and was therefore to be condemned.[88]

Second, Jesus drew a distinction between the spirit and the letter of the law, maintaining that acts of mercy (healing) and acts of necessity (satisfying hunger) were completely within the *spirit* of the law, which the Pharisees were violating and quenching by their extreme interpretations and extensions of the *letter* of the law.

Third, he taught that the proper practice of Sabbath observance required an understanding of the original design and purpose of such practices and the need for adjustments to conserve that design and purpose under changing circumstances.

ORIGINAL DESIGN AND THE NECESSITY OF CHANGE IN ORDER TO CONSERVE

Concerning the original purpose of the Sabbath, Jesus taught his early followers that "the Sabbath was made for man, not man for the Sabbath" and that "it is lawful to do good on the Sabbath."[89]

As Bruce observed,

---

[87] Examples are the healing of a man afflicted with an abnormal swelling of his body (Luke 14:1–6); the healing of a man with a shriveled hand (Matthew 12:9–14; Mark 3:1–6; Luke 6:6–11); the healing of a woman crippled for 18 years (Luke 13:10–17); the healing of a man at the pool of Bethesda who had been ill 38 years (John 5:1–18); and the healing of a blind man (John 9:13–17).

[88] Matthew 12:1–4; Mark 2:23–28; Luke 6:1–5.

[89] Mark 2:27 and Matthew 12:12.

> The key to all Christ's teaching on the Sabbath, therefore, lies in His conception of the *original design* of that divine institution ... His doctrine was this: The Sabbath was meant to be a *boon* to man, not a *burden*; it was not a day taken from man by God in an exacting spirit, but a day given by God in mercy to man—God's holiday to His subject; all legislation enforcing its observance having for its end to insure that all should really get the benefit of the boon—that no man should rob himself, and still less his fellow-creatures, of the gracious boon.[90]

Jesus also claimed the right for himself, and ultimately for his followers, to alter the practice of the Sabbath to ensure that it continued to serve its original purpose.[91] Such alterations eventually included opposing any man-made regulations that diverted the Sabbath from that purpose, expanding its observance to Gentile believers, giving it a new name, and even changing the day of its observance.

In dealing with Sabbath observance in this way, Jesus practised and illustrated one of the most important principles of managing orderly and constructive change—conserving the original rationale and purpose of a practice or institution while simultaneously changing it in certain ways to accommodate new demands and circumstances. At first blush, we may think that the idea of conserving something by changing it is illogical and contradictory. But Jesus, particularly in relation to Sabbath observance, teaches us that conservation and change can be, and in some instances must be, complementary.

In criticizing the Pharisaic approach to the law (including laws governing the Sabbath), Jesus made it clear that it was not his intention to destroy the Law; rather it was his intention, by reinterpreting and changing its application, to fulfill the Law.[92] Achieving and maintaining this balance between conservation and change are more easily done if the defenders of the old and the advocates of the new recognize and appreciate their respective roles in conserving and adapting the institution to changing conditions, i.e., see their roles as complementary rather than adversarial.

As Bruce plaintively asks, "When will young men and old men, liberals and conservatives, broad Christians and narrow, learn to bear with one

[90] Bruce, *The Training of the Twelve*, 91–92.

[91] Matthew 12:8; Mark 2:28.

[92] Matthew 5:17.

another; yea, to recognize each in the other the necessary complement of [their] own one-sidedness?"[93]

IMPLICATIONS FOR US

1. Unlearning and learning

When we come to Jesus we should be open to unlearning and learning under his tutelage. The disciples all had their faults, but to their immense credit they were teachable, open to the unlearning and learning that Jesus had to offer. Which raises the question, are we? Most of us are much more highly and broadly educated than the disciples. This should be a blessing, but it may also render us less open to the teaching and influence of Jesus because *we think we know*. Unlearning often needs to precede learning on both the religious and political fronts.

In my own case, for example, I grew up with a fairly narrow conception of what the Christian faith was about, namely that it was primarily the means to my own personal spiritual well-being and salvation. If I had been one of the disciples and held this one-dimensional conception of faith, my unlearning and learning under the tutelage of Jesus would likely have included,

- Unlearning the narrowness and singularity of this vertical perspective of faith without in any way abandoning the importance and necessity of a personal relationship to God through Jesus.
- Learning to expand my conception and experience of the faith to include its horizontal and social dimensions, i.e., adding the crossbar of the cross to my vertical upright.

On the other hand, if you grew up with a conception of the faith that focused exclusively on its social and horizontal dimension but with little or no appreciation of the necessity of attending to your own personal relationship to God through Christ, your learning and unlearning experience under his tutelage might be the reverse but equally necessary.

2. Visiting the dark side of the moon

As previously mentioned, Jesus' approach to guarding his initial followers against the extreme teachings and practices of the Pharisees illustrates

[93] Bruce, *The Training of the Twelve*, 78.

the merit of taking a hard look at the dark side of the moon—the image and results of pushing any philosophy of life to its extreme—and utilizing that visualization as a warning and a caution to avoid the negative and destructive aspects of that extreme.

Jesus' use of this approach provides us with an excellent example of how to guard religious believers today against the extremes to which we in our age are susceptible. But this approach is also highly applicable to guarding political ideologues and activists against the dangers of political extremism.

Political pragmatists, for example, proud of not being committed to any ideology or fixed set of principles and striving only to do the *right thing under the circumstances*, are well advised to take a hard look at what that pragmatic position looks like and leads to when pushed to its extreme. In the extreme, it can lead to a completely cynical and unprincipled *politics of expediency*—weathervane politics and government that merely twist and turn in response to every wind that blows. And is not that extreme pragmatic position something to resist, back away from, and avoid association with? And shouldn't you warn others to do likewise?

Or perhaps you are of the more liberal or socialistic political persuasion and place great faith in the power and instrumentalities of the state and its capacity to protect and advance human well-being. Certainly there is merit in recognizing this positive potential of the state and the utilization of its agencies for the betterment of humanity. But liberals and social democrats are also well advised to take a hard look at what that statist position looks like and leads to when pushed to its extreme. It is the expansion and deification of the state, carried to its extreme, that has led to some of the most dictatorial, brutal, and oppressive governments the world has ever known, such as the Communist regimes of Stalin, Mao Tse Tung, Pol Pot, and Kim Jong-un. Is not that extreme statist position something to resist, back away from, and avoid associating with? And shouldn't you warn others to do likewise?

Or perhaps we are of a conservative political persuasion. We place great faith in the power and potential of markets and freedom of enterprise to advance the well-being of human beings. Or perhaps we are *conservative revolutionaries* who resist various aspects of modernity and advocate changes designed to restore preferred aspects of a golden past.[94] These are legitimate and worthwhile positions when held and practised in moderation but dangerous when pushed to the extreme—capable of legitimizing greed, exploitation, unconstrained consumerism, environmental degradation, and even fascism—extremes that the responsible conservative will want to resist, back away from, and avoid associating with, while warning others to do likewise.

3. Balancing conservation and change

As previously mentioned, in dealing with Sabbath observance as he did, Jesus practised and illustrated yet another important principle of managing orderly and constructive change—the principle of conserving the original rationale and purpose of a practice or institution by simultaneously changing it in certain ways to accommodate new developments and circumstances.

So suppose we want to change a practice or an institution that in our judgment needs to be reformed. Using Jesus' approach to the simultaneous preservation and reform of Sabbath observance as a model, we should identify the original purpose or rationale and whether it is still valid; identify what is still good and needs to be conserved; and also identify the changes that are required to reform or replace the original practice and institution. And then, most difficult of all, seek to implement the new while preserving the best of the old.

In the Canadian political world in which I participated, this was the approach that some of us took, however imperfectly and crudely, in the 1980s and 1990s when we attempted to "reform" Canadian conservatism at the national level.[95] On a deeper and more philosophical level it is also the position taken by the great British parliamentarian and thinker Edmund

---

[94] For an insightful commentary on the extreme version of the conservative revolutionary position, see Fritz Stern, *The Politics of Cultural Despair: A Study in the Rise of the Germanic Ideology* (Berkeley: University of California Press, 1961). In this work, Stern investigates the 19th century ideological roots of 20th century fascism in Germany. He describes the "conservative revolutionaries" of that day as those who "sought to destroy the despised present in order to recapture an idealized past in an imaginary future" (xvi). A contemporary example of this mentality exists today at the interface of faith and politics in the form of Islamic fundamentalism, whose adherents despise modernity and seek to recapture the idealized glories of the ancient Islamic world in an imagined Islamic caliphate of the future.

[95] For my personal description of and perspective on this effort, see Manning, *Think Big*.

Burke in his commentary on how to achieve necessary and effective political change in Britain while avoiding the extremes exemplified by the French Revolution.

According to Burke,

> A state without the means of some change is without the means of its conservation. Without such means it might even risk the loss of that part of the constitution that it wished the most religiously to preserve. The two principles of conservation and correction operated strongly [in concert] at the two critical periods of the Restoration and Revolution, when England found itself without a king.[96]

Burke concludes with this observation: "When the legislature altered the direction, but kept the principle, they showed that they held it [the principle] inviolable."

Just as Jesus taught that the principles of conservation and change needed to be pursued simultaneously in order to preserve the original rationale of the Sabbath, so Burke maintained that the principles of conservation and correction (reform) needed to be applied simultaneously in order to preserve "inviolate" the original design and rationale of the British Constitution and monarchy.

In seeking to conserve the essence of a useful and valuable practice or institution by changing its application or expression, there will always be those who will maintain that any alteration at all to that practice or institution is an abandonment or betrayal of it and to be fiercely resisted. Thus, Jesus was repeatedly accused by the status quo defenders of the Sabbath of wanting to destroy the very institution he sought to preserve in a more appropriate and sustainable form.

In my own experience I sometimes combatted this accusation with the following illustration drawn from my community development days in north central Alberta. It is an illustration that may be useful to conservative reformers of today, whether in the religious or public arenas.

Along an old back road, east of Lesser Slave Lake, there once stood a huge post set in rocks with a signboard affixed to it by heavy bolts. The sign displayed one word, the name of the town of "Sawridge," and an arrow pointing west. That sign did not change or move in over 50 years,

[96] Edmund Burke, *Reflections on the Revolution in France* (London: J.M. Dent & Sons Ltd., 1790), 18–19.

no matter how hard the winds blew or how much snow fell. It always said the same thing, and it always pointed in the same direction.

A reliable guide, some might say. And yet, if you followed the directions on that sign you would never get to the town of Sawridge. Why? Because although the message and the direction of that signpost never changed, *everything else around it had changed.*

The town of Sawridge changed its name. It changed its location, moving to higher ground after a flood in the 1930s. In addition, the roads leading to it had been rerouted half a dozen times since the signpost had been planted. It was the very fact that the signpost had not changed while everything else around it had that made it an unreliable guide to anyone travelling that old road.

And so there is much to learn from Jesus of Nazareth with respect to the management of change. The importance of being open to unlearning and learning under his tutelage; the value of visiting, at least in our mind's eye, the dark side of the moon, no matter what our religious or political philosophy of life may be; and perhaps the most important of all, learning to strike that balance between conservation and change that facilitates constructive rather than destructive change.

To paraphrase A. B. Bruce, how long will it be until young people and old, broad Christians and narrow, liberals and conservatives, the keepers of the old wine and the champions of the new, learn to bear with one another and to recognize, each in the other, the necessary complements to their own one-sidedness?

1.8 THE GREAT GUIDELINE: WISE AS SERPENTS AND GRACIOUS AS DOVES

DURING THE FIRST YEAR OF JESUS' THREE-YEAR PUBLIC life it would appear that the main role of his small band of followers was simply to follow, listen, and observe the master at work. But there came a day when this initial apprenticeship was over, and he began to send them out to do public work—to speak and act publicly on their own in his name.

Jesus' instructions on that day were well remembered by one who was there—Matthew, the former tax collector. He later recorded, in Matthew 10, Jesus' instructions to them. Paramount among those is what I call *the great guideline* for believers called to exercise their faith in public. Jesus said to them, "Behold, I send you forth as sheep in the midst of wolves: be ye therefore wise as serpents, and harmless as doves."[97]

WISE AS SERPENTS, GRACIOUS AS DOVES

The analogies Jesus employs here are striking, particularly to those familiar with the Judeo-Christian Scriptures. In those Scriptures, the serpent is the symbol of the devil—evil personified, the antithesis of God, the "wise and dread spirit, the spirit of self-destruction and non-existence" as Dostoyevsky called him.[98] So in essence Jesus is saying to his followers, "In your public lives, be as shrewd as the devil."

Likewise, in the New Testament the dove is the symbol of the spirit of God. So in essence Jesus is saying to his followers, "In your public lives, be as gracious as the spirit of God."

---

[97] Matthew 10:16 (KJV).

[98] Dostoyevsky, *The Brothers Karamazov*, 244–245.

FOOLISHNESS IN THE NAME OF GOD

Note further what Jesus did *not* say in sending out his followers to do public work. He did *not* say, "Be vicious as snakes and stupid as pigeons," although, sadly, it must be acknowledged that sometimes we believers act as if this is the perverse guideline governing our public conduct.

As believers we must acknowledge that we are quite capable of acting foolishly, even viciously, in the name of God, especially at the interface of faith and public life, and need to be constantly cautioned against doing so.

The Old Testament prophet Samuel was obliged to say to Saul, Israel's first king, "You have done a foolish thing" when as a political leader he disobeyed the instruction of Samuel and expropriated functions that were the domain of the priests.[99] David, a man after God's own heart, nevertheless had to confess, "I have done a very foolish thing" after he conducted an ill-advised census of Israel's army.[100] In addition, the book of Proverbs contains dozens of admonitions, attributed to wise King Solomon, to avoid "foolishness."

In our time, one of the great but often ignored services to the Christian community by the American evangelist Billy Graham is his confession of acting foolishly on his very first excursion into the political world and the lessons he learned from it.

This incident, recorded in the introduction to his autobiography, occurred just after he and his evangelistic team had received national media attention as a result of very large evangelistic crusades in Los Angeles and Boston and throughout New England. As a newborn celebrity it was arranged for him and his team to visit the White House to meet President Truman, an intersection of faith and public life. Graham ruefully describes what happened in the following words:

> I was just a tanned, lanky thirty-one-year-old, crowned by a heavy thatch of wavy blond hair, wearing what *Time* magazine would later describe as a "pistachio-green" suit ... with rust-colored socks and a hand-painted tie. My three colleagues [Jerry Beavan, Grady Wilson, and Cliff Barrows] were similarly attired. But was there something missing, we asked ourselves.
>
> We had seen a picture of the President on vacation in Florida, wearing white buck shoes. That was it! Grady already had a pair. I sent him to the nearest Florsheim store to buy white bucks for Cliff and me. So how could we go wrong? ...

---

[99] 1 Samuel 13:13.

[100] 2 Samuel 24:10.

Promptly at noon, we were ushered into the Oval Office. From the look on President Truman's face, the chief executive of our nation must have thought he was receiving a traveling vaudeville team … I told him about Los Angeles, … Boston, … and my extensive New England tour in the early months of 1950 … I had publicly called on the President of the United States to proclaim a day of national repentance and prayer for peace.

Mr. Truman nodded as though he remembered the incident …

Our allotted time was quickly running out, and what I really wanted to talk to him about was faith. I did not know how to begin.

"Mr. President," I blurted out, "tell me about your religious background and leanings."

"Well," he replied in his Missouri accent, "I try to live by the Sermon on the Mount and the Golden Rule."

"It takes more than that, Mr. President. It's faith in Christ and His death on the Cross that you need."

The President stood up. Apparently, our twenty minutes were up. We stood up too.

"Mr. President, could we have prayer?"

"It can't do any harm," he said—or something similar.

I put my arm around the shoulders of the President of the United States of America and prayed …

When we stepped outside the White House, reporters and photographers from the press corps pounced on us.

"What did the President say?"

I told them everything I could remember.

"What did you say?"

Again I told them everything I could remember.

"Did you pray with the President?"

"Yes, we prayed with the President."

"What did he think about that?" someone called out.

Before I could respond, an enterprising photographer asked us to kneel on the lawn and re-enact the prayer. The press corps roared its approval. I declined to repeat the words we had prayed in the Oval Office, but I said that we had been planning to thank God for our visit anyway, and now was as good a time as any.

The four of us bent one knee of our pastel summer suits, and I led the prayer of thanksgiving as sincerely as I could, impervious to the popping flashbulbs and scribbling pencils.

It began to dawn on me a few days later how we had abused the privilege of seeing the President. National coverage of our visit was definitely not to our advantage. The President was offended … Mr. Truman never asked me to come back.

A White House staff memorandum in late 1951 stated it bluntly: "At Key West the President said very decisively that he did not wish to endorse Billy Graham's Washington revival meeting and particularly he said he did not want

> to receive him at the White House. You remember what a show of himself Billy Graham made the last time he was here. The President does not want it repeated."
>
> I did visit Mr. Truman many years later at his home in Independence, Missouri. I recalled the incident and apologized profusely for our ignorance and naiveté.
>
> "Don't worry about it," he replied graciously. "I realized you hadn't been properly briefed."
>
> After our gaffe, I vowed to myself it would never happen again if I ever was given access to a person of rank or influence.[101]

Other instances of unwisdom by the Christian community can be more serious. In Canada, the actions of a vocal portion of the Christian community in relation to the decriminalization of abortion and the Mulroney government's attempt to establish a regulatory regime might be cited as yet another example of well-intentioned believers nevertheless failing to act wisely at the interface of faith and politics.

In 1968 to 1969 abortion in Canada was made legal by the administration of Pierre Elliott Trudeau, provided a committee of doctors affirmed that it was necessary for the mental or physical well-being of the mother.[102] But in 1988, the Supreme Court of Canada struck down this Criminal Code amendment, and it fell to the new Progressive Conservative administration of Brian Mulroney to propose a new law governing abortion.[103]

The Mulroney government's first attempt was a compromise that provided easy access to abortion in the early stages of pregnancy and criminalized late-term ones, but it was defeated in a free vote in the House of Commons.[104] In 1989, the government introduced a much stricter bill, which, if enacted, would ban all abortions unless a doctor ruled the woman's life or health was threatened.[105] This bill passed narrowly in the House but was defeated by a tie vote in the Senate, where the rules interpret a tie vote on a bill as a defeat.

---

[101] Billy Graham, *Just As I Am: The Autobiography of Billy Graham* (New York: Harper Collins Publishers, 1997, 2007), xxi–xxiii.

[102] *Criminal Law Amendment Act, 1968–69* (S.C. 1968–69, c. 38).

[103] *R. v. Morgentaler*, 1 S.C.R. [1988] 30.

[104] Stephen Bindman, "Abortion Motions Rejected. Govt. Given Little Help on New Law," *The Ottawa Citizen*, July 29, 1988, A1.

[105] Bill C-43: An Act Respecting Abortion, 2d sess., 34th parl., 1989.

Under normal circumstances, the rare defeat in the unelected Senate of a bill already passed by the democratically elected House of Commons would bring about a negative public reaction and increase support for the bill in both houses. But in this case, the issue was proving so divisive and unmanageable for the Mulroney government that it decided not to reintroduce the legislation. Since then, no federal government has introduced any legislation on this subject, and Canada remains one of only a few nations in the world with no legal restrictions on abortion.

Throughout this whole debate much of the pro-life Christian community took an all-or-nothing approach—rejecting compromises and often attacking as perceived "weakness" the compromise positions of the pro-life members within the cabinet and parliamentary caucuses even more vigorously than those positions were attacked by their pro-choice opponents. The end result therefore was not a regulatory regime that would at least have provided a "place to stand" in order to advocate for more pro-life regulation over time but *nothing*, no legal restrictions in Canada on abortion whatsoever.

THE WISDOM OF THE SERPENT DEMONSTRATED

Jesus not only *instructed* his disciples to be wise as serpents in their public conduct; he *demonstrated* this wisdom in his own public conduct and addresses.

This wisdom was most often displayed on the numerous occasions when Jesus' opponents would ask him questions in public for the sole purpose of getting him into trouble. This is often the situation when one is asked questions in public by the media or one's adversaries. On these occasions the questions are rarely asked out of an honest desire for information but are usually intended to publicly embarrass or discredit the answerer no matter how she or he responds.

On one such occasion, for example, Jesus was asked, by his opponents, after a flattering preamble, "Is it right [lawful] to pay the imperial tax to Caesar or not?"[106] It was both a political question (about paying taxes) and a moral or religious question (is it right?), and it was purposely designed to get Jesus into difficulty with either the public or the authorities or both.

[106] Matthew 22:17; see Matthew 22:15–22.

If Jesus answered "yes" he would be in trouble with the crowd, including his own followers, since the Jews hated the Romans and particularly loathed those Jews who co-operated with them in the collection of taxes. But if he answered "no" he could be charged with treason for advocating disobedience to Roman law and authority. So what was he to do? How was he to respond?

Note first of all that Jesus, knowing the motives of the questioners, did not answer immediately. This was not because he didn't know what to say, as it became clear that he knew perfectly well what he was going to say. Rather, I suspect that he was teaching his onlooking disciples one of the most basic lessons in responding to public questions from opponents: If you don't know what to say, shut up until you do. Better to remain silent and appear contemplative or uncooperative than to make a hurried, ill-considered, and foolish reply. "Twitterers," take note.

Next, perhaps again to show his disciples how to bide their time, he asked several questions of his own. (Responding to nasty, loaded questions by asking some of your own is not a bad tactic in itself.) He asked to be shown the coin used for paying the tax. Someone in the crowd, perhaps one of his interrogators, fished around in his purse and produced a coin, likely a Roman denarius. Jesus looked at it and, pointing to the coin, asked two more questions: "Whose image is this? And whose inscription?" Someone answered, "Caesar's."

Then came the zinger, Jesus' reply to the original question, a reply displaying the wisdom of the serpent and the shrewdness of the devil: "So give to Caesar what is Caesar's, and to God what is God's." Fewer than fifteen words, spoken in less than ten seconds. A wise reply, a brilliant reply—the perfect sound bite. A reply that would have made the evening television news had the cameras been rolling, and a graphic demonstration to his followers of what it means to be "wise as serpents" in one's public acts and utterances.

Would God that as followers of Christ today we could, in our time and circumstances, respond with such wisdom to questions designed to embarrass or discredit the Christian faith at the interface of faith and politics.

VICIOUSNESS IN THE NAME OF GOD

As believers we must also acknowledge that not only are we quite capable of acting foolishly in the name of God, especially at the interface of faith and public life, but we are also quite capable of acting viciously. Again, there is a need to be constantly cautioned against doing so.

In the case of Jesus' early disciples, for example, while on their way to Jerusalem for the last time before Jesus' arrest, they and their master passed through a Samaritan village where he was not welcome.[107] This hostility toward Jesus obviously irked the disciples, and two of the most spiritual of them, James and John, suggested that they burn the place down. They did propose holding a prayer meeting first: "Lord, do you want us to call fire down from heaven to destroy them?" But their intent was quite clear, to destroy the enemies of Christ.

How Jesus' heart must have sunk when he witnessed this display of viciousness! He had this gang of disciples under his tutelage for three years. He ceaselessly taught them by word and example that the distinguishing characteristic of their lives and service was to be self-sacrificial love. He was on his way to Jerusalem to demonstrate how far he himself was prepared to practise that teaching by sacrificing himself for the sins of humanity on the cross. Yet here they wanted God to destroy a whole village of Samaritans—men, women, and children—not simply because of their hostility toward Jesus but out of the disciples' own deeply ingrained prejudices toward Samaritans.

When Jesus picked these men he knew very well that they were perfectly capable of such prejudice and viciousness. That is why on the very first day that he commissioned them for public work and told them to be wise as serpents and harmless as doves, he also specifically told them, "Do *not go* among the Gentiles, or enter any town of the Samaritans."[108] He knew then, as became evident later, that they were not yet ready to communicate with, let alone minister to, the Samaritans, against whom they held long-standing racial, religious, and cultural prejudices. There would come a day, of course, when he would send them out again, this time saying, "you will be my witnesses in Jerusalem, and in all Judea *and Samaria,* and to the ends of the earth."[109] But that day would not come until a change of hearts had occurred—a change not in the hearts of the Samaritans but in the hearts of his followers, as a result of the work of the spirit of God.

---

[107] Luke 9:51–55.

[108] Matthew 10:5, emphasis added.

[109] Acts 1:8, emphasis added.

On this occasion, however, when viciousness in the name of God so readily reared its ugly head among his followers, Jesus strongly rebuked them. "You know not what manner of spirit ye are of. For the Son of Man is not come to destroy men's lives but to save them."[110] Then they went on to another village.

THE GRACIOUSNESS OF THE DOVE DEMONSTRATED

Jesus not only *instructed* his disciples to be gracious in their public conduct, rebuking them when they failed to be so; he also *demonstrated* this graciousness in his own public conduct and addresses.

One such occasion is recorded in John's Gospel and involved "a woman caught in adultery" by the Pharisees and teachers of the law.[111] They dragged the poor woman (significantly, the woman but not the man involved) into the presence of Jesus and again publicly posed a difficult question.

This time the question was about sexual morality. In that day, to raise such a question in public was nothing short of scandalous, and even today this is the most difficult type of question for the believer to handle in the public arena. Once again, the sole intent of the questioners was to trap Jesus and get him into trouble.

"Teacher," asked the legalists in the presence of a crowd of onlookers, "this woman was caught in the act of adultery. In the law Moses commanded us to stone such women. Now what do you say?"

If Jesus said, "Spare her," he would be publicly advocating a violation of the law of Moses and guilty of heresy; if he said, "Stone her," he would violate all his own teaching on love, mercy, and forgiveness. So what was he to say and do?

Once again, he didn't respond right away. He didn't rush to judgment as so many of us are inclined to do when confronted with a question on morality. Instead, John (who was present) recorded that Jesus bent down and wrote on the ground with his finger. This prompted his interrogators to question him again, until suddenly he straightened up and delivered the perfect answer—wise as a serpent, but above all, gracious as a dove. "Let any one of you who is without sin be the first to throw a stone at her."

---

[110] Luke 9:55–56 (KJV).

[111] John 8:1–11.

An answer as gracious as it is shrewd—fewer than twenty words, the perfect sound bite, eminently quotable, again sure to make the evening television news if the cameras had been rolling. What could his interrogators say or do in reply? None of them was spotlessly clean when it came to sexual morality. Jesus knew it, and perhaps some of their friends and neighbours in the crowd knew it. They were left speechless and gradually slipped away, leaving Jesus and his disciples alone with the woman, who was about to experience the full extent of his graciousness.

Jesus asked her, "Woman, where are they [your accusers]? Has no one condemned you?" "No one, sir," she replied. "Then neither do I condemn you," Jesus declared. "Go now, and leave your life of sin." In this reply Jesus made it clear that he did not condone adultery. But confronted with the sin of adultery—literally, *missing the mark* with respect to God's intention for sexual relations between married people—he was not condemnatory. "Neither do I condemn you." How many of us would have said likewise in that situation? Instead of condemning, Jesus demonstrated to the woman involved the graciousness of the spirit of God, that loves and forgives notwithstanding our conduct.

Would God that as followers of Christ today we could, in our time and circumstances, respond with such wisdom and graciousness to loaded questions on sexual morality designed to embarrass or discredit the Christian faith at the interface of faith and politics.

IMPLICATIONS FOR US

1. The need for instruction

Jesus did not entrust his followers with public work in his name, nor did he send them out into the public arena, without giving them specific instruction on how to speak and act in that capacity in public. Is it not imperative, therefore, that we follow his example in this regard? That Christian seminaries, schools, churches, and para-church organizations provide specific instruction and training for those who will represent the Christian faith in the public arena so that they will do so with the wisdom and graciousness that Jesus himself modelled? Is this not especially important for Christian members and candidates of political parties, operating in a secular political arena hostile to faith and increasingly dominated by social media?[112]

2. The prayer for wisdom

There is such a thing as *the prayer for wisdom,* and surely it is a prayer that those of us operating at the interface of faith and public life should pray more often and more fervently.

Perhaps the most famous of such prayers by a man about to step into the public arena as a political figure is that prayed by Solomon, the son of David and Israel's third king: "Give me wisdom and knowledge, that I may lead this people, for who is able to govern this great people of yours?" To which God then replied,

> "Since this is your heart's desire and you have not asked for wealth, possessions or honor, nor for the death of your enemies, and since you have not asked for a long life but for wisdom and knowledge to govern my people over whom I have made you king, therefore wisdom and knowledge will be given you. And I will also give you wealth, possessions and honor, such as no king who was before you ever had and none after you will have."[113]

The importance of praying for wisdom was also later emphasized by one of the disciples who first heard Jesus' instruction to be "wise as serpents." Accordingly, the disciple James, who later became one of the principal leaders of the Christian community in Jerusalem, wrote to his fellow believers, "If any of you lacks wisdom you should ask God, who gives generously to all without finding fault, and it will be given to you."[114] James also seemed to be particularly aware that it was not enough to simply pray for wisdom or even to receive it; one had to *act* on it to

---

[112] It is to address this need that the Manning Centre for Building Democracy (manningcentre.ca) has developed a lecture and seminar program entitled "Navigating the Faith-Political Interface."

[113] 2 Chronicles 1:10–12. Sadly, it should be noted that while Solomon prayed for wisdom and received it, he did not always act upon it. Eventually, he was led away from wholehearted worship of God by the influence of his many foreign wives. In addition, his heavy taxation of his people in order to finance the building of his magnificent palaces eventually led to rebellion by the northern tribes, civil war, and the breakup of the kingdom under his son Rehoboam.

[114] James 1:5.

be effective in God's service. "Do not merely listen to the word [wisdom received], and so deceive yourselves. *Do* what it says."[115]

3. Avoiding foolishness in the name of God

Fortunately for us, the grace of God is such that God can redeem the situations in which we Christians have spoken and acted foolishly in his name and convert them into sources of future wisdom through lessons learned.

Billy Graham acted foolishly as a representative of the Christian faith in his first encounter with American president Harry Truman. But he learned from that experience and went on to become an increasingly respected and trusted spiritual friend to a number of other presidents, from Dwight Eisenhower to George W. Bush. Should we not also learn from our mistakes, especially when we have acted foolishly in his name?

Similarly, the one redeeming feature of acknowledging the unwisdom of Canadian Christians who as a minority group took an *all-or-nothing* position on the abortion issue in a majoritarian political arena is that a wiser course of action may be taken by the faith community in the future. The opportunity for a second chance will likely come when advances in genetics, medical practice, and science-based jurisprudence force a reframing of "beginning of life" issues beyond the old pro-life, pro-choice paradigm and oblige future legislators to establish new policies and regulatory regimes based on that reframed understanding. Let Christians be prepared to conduct themselves wisely and graciously in that future debate.

4. Avoiding and mitigating viciousness in the name of God

Do not we as believers in our time and circumstances need to be strongly cautioned against acting viciously in the name of God and urged to take corrective action when such viciousness rears its ugly head?

It is sad but true (and I speak from experience) that some of the most vicious letters received by elected officials, especially over moral issues such as abortion, same-sex marriage, and euthanasia, come from people professing to represent a Christian perspective. Similarly, what are we to think of those overly zealous pro-life advocates who threaten the lives

---

[115] James 1:22, emphasis added.

of abortionists and would readily burn down abortion clinics just as the early followers of Jesus were prepared to burn down the Samaritan village that refused to receive him?

What should those of us of the Christian community say and do when we see and hear such threats and acts of viciousness made or committed in the name of Christ? Should we remain silent and therefore appear to condone them? Or should we not be in the forefront of correcting and mitigating them after the example of Jesus himself?

What would Jesus say to those believers today who are prepared to act viciously in his name? Would he encourage them in those attitudes and actions, or would he respond in the same vein as he did to his earliest followers long ago: "You know not what spirit you are of—certainly it is not my spirit … I sent you forth not to be vicious as snakes but gracious as doves, gracious as the spirit of God himself. Now conduct yourselves accordingly if you profess to be speaking and acting in my name."

5. Drawing closer to him who exemplified wisdom and graciousness in his public work

Jesus' initial followers undoubtedly learned as much about what it meant to be wise and gracious in the public arena by simply drawing closer and closer to their master as they ever did from studying his explicit instruction on this subject. This should remind us, yet again, of the need to draw ever closer to Jesus in every aspect of our lives so that how we conduct ourselves in the public arena is not some contrived strategy but a natural outworking of our relationship to him.[116]

Let us also cultivate, in our time and circumstances, Christian leaders and spokespersons who not only teach and advocate the wisdom and graciousness of Jesus in the public arena but actually model that wisdom and graciousness in their own public work and conduct.

---

[116] What does it mean to "draw ever closer to Jesus"? If one is not a believer, a good starting point is to read the record of his life and teachings in the Gospels and then decide whether to follow him or not. If one is already a believer, it means cultivating a closer and deeper relationship through prayer, study, and fellowship with other believers.

1.9 WISDOM AND GRACE IN ACTION: THE WILBERFORCE ANTI-SLAVERY CAMPAIGN

WE HAVE EXAMINED THE KEY INSTRUCTION GIVEN BY Jesus of Nazareth to his earliest followers before he sent them out to do public work in his name: "Be wise as serpents and harmless as doves." But can this guideline actually be followed faithfully and effectively by Christian believers in the rough and adversarial public arena of politics? In this chapter we examine a most encouraging and instructive example.

In the long and colourful history of politics within the tradition of British democracy, there is probably not a better example of a campaign conducted with the wisdom of the serpent and the graciousness of the dove than that conducted by William Wilberforce and his associates to eliminate slavery throughout the British Empire.[117]

It was an organized political and spiritual effort to eradicate a great evil, the institution of slavery, and to achieve a great moral good, the freedom of hundreds of thousands of human beings previously held in brutal bondage. There is great benefit, therefore, in examining it in detail to identify features and principles that will be helpful to Christians today who are involved in combatting great evils and advancing moral causes in the rough and adversarial arena of contemporary politics.

---

[117] While there is a large body of documentation and literature on this subject, for the purposes of this chapter I have relied mainly on, and quoted extensively from, three sources, to whose authors I am deeply indebted: Kevin Belmonte, *William Wilberforce: A Hero for Humanity* (Grand Rapids: Zondervan, 2007); Adam Hochschild, *Bury the Chains: Prophets and Rebels in the Fight to Free an Empire's Slaves* (New York: Houghton Mifflin, 2005); Eric Metaxas, *Amazing Grace: William Wilberforce and the Heroic Campaign to End Slavery* (New York: Harper Collins, 2007).

THE CAMPAIGN

"The Campaign," as we refer to it, was a long one. It began in earnest on May 22, 1787, when 12 humble but determined abolitionists met at a print shop at Number 2 George York Street in London, and it did not fully achieve its objective until 51 years later on August 31, 1838, when nearly 800,000 black slaves throughout the British Empire became legally free.

While the issue it addressed had enormous economic and social implications, at its core was an ethical question—was slavery morally defensible or not? Political campaigns involving moral issues are among the most difficult to successfully manage and conduct, which makes the Wilberforce campaign particularly instructive in that regard.

Of special significance to Christians interested in successfully navigating the interface of faith and public life is the fact that this campaign was directed primarily by people who were personally motivated, guided, and sustained throughout by their Christian faith. Many (though not all) were evangelical Christians, products of the first evangelical awakening in Britain, led by John Wesley and George Whitfield.

Key contributors to the campaign included Granville Sharpe, a legal beagle; Thomas Clarkson, an indefatigable organizer; Hannah More, an intellectual and spiritual leader of the Clapham Circle; Olaudah Equiano, a freed slave whose two-volume autobiography bore eloquent witness to the evils of the slave trade; John Newton, a former slave ship master, clergyman, and the composer of the hymn "Amazing Grace"; James Stephens, a lawyer and strategist; and of course, the parliamentarian William Wilberforce and his small band of political colleagues.[118]

This campaign was first and foremost what in our times would be called an issue or advocacy campaign as distinct from an election campaign.[119]

---

[118] See Olaudah Equiano, *The Interesting Narrative of the Life of Olaudah Equiano, or Gustavus Vassa, The African, Written by Himself* (London: Author, 1789), available at http://www.gutenberg.org/files/15399/15399-h/15399-h.htm. For an excellent movie depiction of the Wilberforce campaign, see *Amazing Grace*, 2006, starring Ioan Gruffudd, Albert Finney, et al.; directed by Michael Apted (20th Century Fox).

[119] My own experience with modern issue campaigns, which to some extent informs my perspective on the Wilberforce anti-slavery campaign, comes primarily from my involvement in Canadian federal politics. The three most prominent issue campaigns in which I was personally involved are (1) a successful campaign to defeat the Charlottetown Constitutional Accord (a proposal to amend the Constitution of Canada in ways that my colleagues and I deemed unfavourable to western Canada and national unity), conducted within the context

As such, the campaign to abolish slavery is highly instructive to those wishing to engage in advocacy campaigns today.

Its main objectives were twofold: first, to raise the issue of slavery in the public consciousness and in the political arena so high and insistently that it could not be ignored by the politicians and lawmakers of the day; and second, to raise public support for a particular solution to the issue—i.e., laws to curtail the slave trade and eventually abolish slavery itself—again, so high and insistently that elected officials would be forced by the weight of public opinion to act.

As in many issue campaigns, this campaign had its forerunners—people who became exercised about the issue earlier than most and whose efforts to address it, while generally unsuccessful, awakened the consciences of others and paved the way for the success of the latter campaign. Successful issue campaigns recognize their forerunners and seek to integrate their advance work into the latter campaign rather than regarding the forerunners as failures or unwelcome competitors. In this case, the forerunners included the English Quakers, whose opposition to slavery was theologically based, and crusaders like Granville Sharp, who very early on sought to have slavery curtailed through the courts.[120]

The key functions that need to be performed in the conduct of an issue campaign—strategizing, planning, identifying supporters, motivating, coalition building, counteracting opponents, communicating, persuading, fundraising, and mobilizing volunteers—are almost identical to those

of a national referendum on the issue initiated by the government of Canada in 1992; (2) a successful campaign, from 1987 to 1998, to force the government of Canada to balance its budget; (3) a long-running but unsuccessful campaign from 1987 to 2014 to reform the Senate of Canada. The ethical or moral dimension of each of these campaigns centred around "fairness"—inter-generational fairness in the case of the budget campaign, and regional fairness in the case of the Charlottetown and Senate campaigns.

[120] The Religious Society of Friends movement, known as the Quakers for their reputation to "tremble" in the way of the Lord, began in the mid-17th century in northern England. Despite strong opposition and persecution, the movement expanded across the British Isles and to the Americas and Africa. The Quakers had a significant role in the abolition of slavery, equal rights for women, and peace.

Granville Sharp, a committed Anglican Christian who held a minor post in the ordinance office in the Tower of London, was an eccentric genius of diverse talents and enormous energy that he increasingly devoted to the cause of abolishing slavery. See Hochschild, *Bury the Chains*, 41–48.

that must be successfully performed in election campaigns. As a result, the skills acquired by those who participated in this campaign placed them in good stead in later campaigns to elect pro-abolition members to the British House of Commons, particularly after the *Reform Act* of 1832 broadened the franchise and greatly increased the representativeness and power of that chamber.

What then were the noteworthy features and guiding principles of the campaign to abolish slavery from which people today, especially Christians operating at the interface of faith and public life, can learn and benefit? To what extent did this campaign demonstrate adherence to the great guideline given by Jesus to his followers in carrying out public work? That is, to what extent were the objectives, tactics, and communications of these faith-motivated campaigners "wise," as shrewd as those of the devil, and as "gracious" as the spirit of God himself?

GUIDELINES APPLICABLE TO THE WISE AND GRACIOUS CONDUCT OF MODERN ISSUE CAMPAIGNS

1. Choose the initial campaign objective and strategy wisely

In issue campaigns of any kind, great care and attention need to be given to defining the initial campaign objective and the initial strategy for achieving it. If these definitions and choices are unwise or misguided, the entire campaign effort may be doomed to failure before it even begins. Launching such campaigns is like launching a canoe. Accidents most frequently occur at the very beginning of the venture—getting into the canoe successfully and pushing off from the shore.

In the case of this campaign, after considerable internal debate, it was wisely decided to proceed incrementally rather than *to go for broke*—to seek first the abolition of the *slave trade*, the activity that fed the institution of slavery, rather than to immediately seek the abolition of the institution itself. The objective was, as Thomas Clarkson put it, to lay "the axe at the very root" of the tree rather than to immediately try to chop down the tree itself.[121]

Even in our day, let alone in 18th century Britain, if the aim of a campaign is to move public and parliamentary opinion from *A* to *C*, it is usually advisable to first secure support for *B*—a more modest objective

[121] Hochschild, *Bury the Chains*, 110.

than *C* but a move in the right direction.[122] In the case of the Wilberforce campaign, *A* was the status quo, which tolerated both slavery and the slave trade; *C* was the ultimate objective of abolishing slavery altogether; but *B* was the more immediately attainable objective of curtailing the slave trade.

With respect to Wilberforce himself, because he was a parliamentarian, he might have been forgiven for adopting a one-track strategy, namely that of pursuing abolition solely through changes in the law. But instead, wisely as it turned out, Wilberforce personally adopted a two-track strategy involving both a legal and a social-activist approach.

On Sunday, October 28, 1787, he wrote in his diary, "God Almighty has placed before me *two great objects*, the suppression of the slave trade and the reformation of manners [that is, morals]."[123] With respect to the reformation of manners and morals, Wilberforce specifically targeted public and political indifference to the suffering caused by a host of social evils—poverty, the unavailability of education, child labour, the abuse of animals, and prison conditions. He attacked this indifference, not so much by preaching against it but by launching and supporting numerous volunteer societies and agencies to provide help and service to those suffering the consequences of these evils and to urge changes in related public and private policies.[124]

If Wilberforce and his colleagues had only attacked the slave trade by legislation and had done nothing to address in visible and practical terms the general indifference to human suffering that was a characteristic of the times, their campaign would have commanded far less public support and been far less effective than it was.

We, in addressing the social evils of our times, must be careful not to make the most frequent mistake of religious moralists and political legalists in addressing a moral issue—that is, to immediately focus on declaring moral or legal principles and prescriptions while doing little to offer personal and practical service to those afflicted by the social ills we are seeking to redress.

---

[122] This is particularly true in Canada, where our tendency is to always seek a middle way rather than taking the shortest and most direct route to the objective. Why did the Canadian cross the road? To get to the middle.

[123] Belmonte, *William Wilberforce*, 97.

[124] The "little platoons" as Edward Burke called such instrumentalities are what we call the instruments of civil society.

For example, a Christian response in Canada to the growing demands for amendments to the Criminal Code to facilitate assisted suicide cannot be only a legal response (opposing such amendments and/or proposing legislative alternatives), important as such a response may be. To be effective after the manner of Wilberforce the response must be a legal response *and*—And *what*? Wilberforce would likely propose a vast increase in Christian sympathy, ministry, and service to those facing the end of life through a great expansion of our support and involvement in the provision of palliative and hospice care.

2. Seize the high moral ground by first strongly identifying with the suffering to be alleviated

This strategic guideline is quite similar to that just described. But the principle on which it is based is so important to the proper positioning of campaigns to address moral and ethical issues that it bears restating in a slightly different form.

The initial stages of the campaign to abolish slavery were characterized in the political arena not so much by preaching against the evils of slavery and the slave trade but by publicizing and empathizing with the *suffering* that those institutions created. For example, the campaign

- Publicized the horrors of the Zong case (a slave ship whose captain threw 136 slaves into the sea and whose owners filed an insurance claim for the value of the dead slaves).
- Confronted members of Parliament and attendees at public meetings with the actual chains and shackles used to bind slaves to their stations on the trans-Atlantic voyage.
- Arranged tours for members of Parliament along the docks where the slave ships were moored so that they could smell for themselves the stench of death that clung to them.
- Published the logs of slave ship doctors and the accounts of escaped slaves themselves, telling of the indescribable horrors of life and death on the slave ships.

People suffering from the operation of evil institutions and practices have an understandable right to say to those proposing the reform of those institutions and practices, "We don't care how much you know and talk about this—religiously or legally—until we know how much you care. *Show us*, don't just tell us, how much you care."

The Sermon on the Mount was effective because the sermonizer was not some distant moralizer but deity incarnate embedded and active in alleviating pain and sorrows in the lives of those whom he addressed. Jesus got his moral authority in the eyes of the common people, a moral authority that exceeded that of the teachers of the law, by *actively identifying and empathizing* with the suffering of the poor, the sick, the imprisoned, and the oppressed.

Thus, for example, it is those who can *demonstrate*—by personal empathy and acts of care—that they truly care about those facing end-of-life situations who will be most listened to and respected when it comes to deciding what public policies and laws should apply to those situations.

3. Reframe the issue to position it within a conceptual framework best suited to advancing the campaign

When engaging in any political debate, you may often find yourself debating initially within a hostile conceptual framework defined primarily by your opponents (or often, in our day, by prejudiced and unsympathetic media). Under such circumstances, your chances of winning the debate are slim unless you can *reframe the issue* to the advantage of your cause. This may involve directly challenging the old conceptual framework as inadequate and if possible replacing it with one in which your arguments and cause have a better chance of succeeding.

In the case of the campaign to abolish slavery and the slave trade, the abolitionists had little chance of swaying public opinion or winning the argument for abolition as long as slaves were merely considered to be "property." Within that framework, any debate on the pros and cons of slavery would be mainly focused on the economics, not the morality or inhumanity, of slavery—the financial benefits of sustaining it and the financial costs of limiting or abolishing it. Within that context it could be argued that the death of slaves being transported by the slave ships to America was simply a "property loss" that could be (and was) insurable; that any curtailment of slavery would do great damage to British trade and commerce and the livelihood of those dependent upon it; and that the abolition of slavery would constitute a massive and prohibitively expensive confiscation of property.

Therefore, the abolitionists from the very outset of their campaign sought to shift the public and parliamentary perception of slaves from "property"—which could be bought, sold, used, and abused as economic objects—to "human beings" who deserved to be recognized, appreciated, and treated as such.

This attempt to shift the public perception of slaves was carried out by a variety of tactics, such as identifying slaves by name, publishing their horrific personal stories, and bringing parliamentarians and public-opinion leaders into direct contact with freed slaves such as Olaudah Equiano. Josiah Wedgewood, a pottery manufacturer, aided the cause in this regard by producing a special line of china showing a kneeling African with chains uplifted and beseechingly asking, "Am I not a man and a brother?"[125]

4. Move the debate, if possible, into the decision-making arena most conducive to success

Just as it is often prudent in a political debate to shift the conceptual framework within which it occurs to one more favourable to the cause, so it is also often necessary to try to change the arena—the venue in which the requisite policy decisions and legal actions must occur—in order to have a better chance of securing the desired outcome.

In 18th century Britain, the House of Lords, not the House of Commons, was the dominant parliamentary chamber. The Lords were appointed by the Crown rather than elected by the people and were therefore less susceptible to influence by public opinion and more susceptible to influence by powerful special interests such as the pro-slavery lobby.

As a result, it was very much in the interests of the abolitionists to get the slavery issue debated and decided in the House of Commons, whose members they could influence by swaying the views of their electors. The abolitionists were, therefore, generally supportive of any reform that strengthened the Commons at the expense of the Lords. It was significant that the legislation that ended slavery throughout the empire was not passed until after the passage of the *Reform Act* of 1832, which significantly strengthened the power and representativeness of the Commons by broadening the franchise.

[125] Hochschild, *Bury the Chains*, 128. Note that the phrase "Am I not a man and a brother?" is based on the apostle Paul's letter to Philemon (Philemon 1:16) in which Paul writes to Philemon, a slave owner, on behalf of the slave Onesimus.

In our day, the success of a particular issue campaign may likewise depend in part on how successfully the campaigners are able to shift the debate and the decision-making on the issue to the arena most favourable to it. If the legislators are indifferent or hostile to an issue or a particular policy for addressing it, there may be merit in trying to shift the debate and decision to the courts, or vice versa.[126] In Canada, where there are ten provincial legislatures and governments, there is often merit in determining which provincial jurisdiction provides the most favourable climate for advancing an issue and its solution and beginning the issue campaign there in order to achieve some initial success.

5. Build a principled coalition to advance the cause

In Wilberforce's day there was not nearly the party discipline that exists in many of the Commonwealth parliaments and legislatures (such as those of Canada or Australia) today. In the early days of the anti-slavery campaign, William Pitt, the prime minister and Wilberforce's close friend, personally opposed the slave trade and supported Wilberforce's resolutions. But this in itself did not guarantee majority or government support in Parliament.

Wilberforce therefore had to build a coalition of support both outside and inside the Parliament for his legislative proposals. His coalition consisted of those who may have disagreed on many points but were agreed on the principle that slavery and the slave trade were evils to be resisted and eradicated. As much as they held differing views on how to go about this, they also came to agree that the immediate objective should be to abolish the slave trade, and they were willing to work together to achieve that specific objective.

It is important to note that the coalition to abolish the slave trade was a principled coalition as distinct from a coalition of expediency. Participants in coalitions of expediency generally participate out of short-run self-interest or purely *to oppose for opposing's sake*. Such coalitions have

[126] In Canada this tactic may even be used by governments who command majority support in their legislature. Canadian legislators, for example, are often very reluctant to deal with polarizing moral issues such as abortion, same-sex marriage, and euthanasia. So rather than tackle such issues in the legislature and run the risk of dividing their own caucuses, they may refer the matter to the courts. This may be done directly, but also indirectly by passing a bill addressing the issue but deliberately neglecting to state clearly the intent of the legislature in passing it, so that ultimately the courts will be called upon to *fill in the blanks*.

little capacity for moral suasion with others who do not share those interests or the opposition mentality. On the other hand, coalitions founded on principle, demanding self-sacrifice from their members and adherents, and ultimately committed to pursuing a positive and principled objective (such as the liberation of slaves) have a moral authority that places them in good stead when endeavouring to persuade others of the worthiness of their cause.

Wilberforce once wrote that the "bringing together [of] ... men who are likeminded and who may at some time or other combine ... for the public good" is a principle "of first rate importance." He "always sought to be a bridge builder and would work with anyone in pursuit of common philanthropic goals."[127] Indeed, ironically in the end, his abolition bill, which did not pass during the administration of his friend Prime Minister Pitt, finally passed under the short-lived administration of Lord Grenville, who was never a strong ally of Wilberforce, with the influential support of Charles Fox, who had originally opposed abolition.[128]

If there are two skills absolutely essential to political success today—and especially essential to the conduct of issue campaigns with moral and ethical dimensions—one of them is the skill of communication. But the other is the skill of coalition building, which requires us to recognize our forerunners, identify potential coalition partners, define the principled common ground on which they can be induced to work together, and then use our powers of persuasion to get them to work together for the common cause.

6. Legitimate the discussion, graciously

When Wilberforce was first elected at the tender age of 21[129] there was an unspoken but very strong agreement among members of Parliament *not* to

[127] Belmonte, *William Wilberforce*, 167.

[128] Fox was not only an initial opponent of the abolition effort; he was "internationally known for his immoral and rakish behavior" and for encouraging the Prince of Wales (the future king) in his "outrageously dissolute lifestyle" (Metaxas, *Amazing Grace*, 31). His eventual acceptance into the Wilberforce coalition indicates the extent to which its members had to bury their differences, not only over policy matters but also with respect to each other's lifestyles—all for the sake of the greater cause.

[129] Note the youthfulness of some of the key leaders of the campaign. Wilberforce was 21 when first elected to Parliament. Pitt became prime minister at 24. Thomas Clarkson was a 25-year-old Cambridge student when he first became engaged.

raise the subject of slavery in Parliament at all; to do so was taboo.[130] This was not because the members were slaveholders themselves but because many, particularly in the House of Lords, personally profited from the slave trade and the colonial plantations and enterprises it supplied. In addition, most members of Parliament were uncomfortable with the moral aspects of slavery and the political ramifications of debating it. They therefore preferred that the subject not be raised or discussed at all.

So the first challenge for Wilberforce and his associates became one of legitimating the discussion of the issue of slavery in a democratic chamber where even the mention of the word was unwelcome. To meet this challenge required both the wisdom of the serpent and the graciousness of the dove, and Wilberforce's approach demonstrated both.

As a passionate Christian moralist, Wilberforce was undoubtedly tempted and urged to ride into the House on a white horse, denouncing slavery as an abomination from hell, castigating anyone profiting from it as being in league with the devil, and calling for the immediate and total destruction of the institution of slavery and all its works. But he was warned—perhaps by that still small voice of the spirit of God within but also most likely by Pitt the Shrewd—that if he took such a course the overwhelming reaction of the House would be negative, and it would be years before the subject of slavery could be raised in that chamber again.

Note, therefore, the innocuous wording of the initial resolution whereby Wilberforce proposed to legitimate the discussion of slavery in the British House of Commons: "That this House will, early in the next Session of Parliament, proceed to take into Consideration the Circumstances of the Slave Trade."[131]

The wording of this resolution is about as inoffensive as it was possible to make it, and we can just imagine the angry reaction of the moral zealots in the abolitionist camp when they first saw the draft: *What kind of an insipid, mealy-mouthed resolution is this?* With respect to timing, you defer to the convenience of the House when the urgent and inconvenient truth is that men, women, and children are dying daily in slavery? You ask the House to merely take the issue into "consideration" when it is bold

---

[130] A contemporary equivalent would be trying to raise the issue of abortion in the Canadian Parliament, which considers the issue taboo.

[131] *Journals of the House of Commons* 44 (Great Britain: House of Commons, 1803), 232.

action that is required. You meekly ask the House to merely take into consideration "the circumstances" of the slave trade when what should be demanded is the immediate and complete abolition of slavery itself and everything connected with it!

And yet the wisdom of Wilberforce's approach to legitimating the discussion became apparent in retrospect as the subject of his resolution was grudgingly accepted. This began, however modestly, the long debate that eventually led to the total abolition of the slave trade and slavery itself within British territory.[132]

7. Do the necessary research thoroughly and well

In seeking to advance an issue with moral dimensions in the public arena—an issue where your own position and zeal for the cause is rooted in deeply held, emotion-stirring convictions and experiences—it is tempting to believe that such convictions, emotions, and zeal will be sufficient to carry the day with others. But wisdom and experience suggest that mastering the facts surrounding the issue is equally important, which means doing your research and doing it thoroughly and well.

The abolitionists working with Wilberforce were zealous for the cause, and their zeal was rooted in convictions and experiences that stirred and energized them emotionally, but they didn't rely exclusively on these elements in communicating their cause. They also meticulously and assiduously armed themselves with *the facts*, and this required research—exhaustive, thorough, and comprehensive research.

It involved researching the existing laws and policies affecting slavery and the trade; documenting evidence from slave ship crews, ships' doctors, and slaves themselves as to the death toll and terrible conditions that characterized the voyage from Africa to America; researching and dissecting the interests and arguments of the pro-slavery lobby and their

---

132 Wilberforce became seriously ill just before his resolution was to be presented to Parliament, so it was his friend Pitt, the prime minister, who began the debate. When Wilberforce himself was able to participate, the wisdom and graciousness of his first resolution was further reflected in the tone and wording of his first speech to the House on that subject: "I mean not to accuse anyone, but to take the shame upon myself, indeed, with the whole Parliament of Great Britain, for having suffered this horrid trade to be carried on under their authority. We are all guilty—we ought all to plead guilty, and not to exculpate ourselves by throwing the blame upon others" (*The Parliamentary Register, or History of the Proceedings and Debates of the House of Commons* XXVI [London: J. Debrett], 131).

parliamentary allies; and constantly monitoring public attitudes and shifts in public sentiment over the long course of the campaign.[133]

However, if there was one area where the research and preparation of the campaign to abolish slavery was deficient until late in the day, it was with respect to the tactics involved in securing support for a controversial bill in the British Parliament. Wilberforce was an idealist, an excellent communicator, and a tireless worker, but he was not a tactician. He understood the broad arena—the public square, where public opinion in support of abolition had to be stimulated and shaped—but he was not particularly adept at managing the passage of an initially unpopular bill through the narrower, specialized arena of the House of Commons, nor does it appear that he had anyone in his immediate parliamentary circle who was expert and shrewd in this regard.

Eventually, this deficiency would be remedied by the involvement of James Stephens, one of the empire's leading maritime lawyers, a prominent authority on international law with tactical sense and expertise, and one who had a visceral hatred of slavery born out of living in the West Indies. But for many years the abolitionists were repeatedly outfoxed in the House by their anti-abolition opponents, and Wilberforce's abolition bills were to suffer many defeats before he and his colleagues were able to match and then outwit their opponents at the tactical level.

Knowing their own cause, knowing their opponents, knowing their audiences, and, eventually, coming to know the intricacies of the decision-making arena were essential elements of the campaign to abolish slavery, just as they are essential to any successful advocacy campaign today. Exhaustive, thorough, and comprehensive research is essential to securing such knowledge and being able to act upon it.

8. Make maximum use of existing law

The campaign to abolish slavery and the slave trade did not occur in a legal vacuum. Some laws and legal rulings pertaining to slavery already existed, and the abolitionists learned to take advantage of them.

[133] Abraham Lincoln, in his references to moving the public on an issue, tended to stress the need to appeal to "public sentiment"—the need to take into account what the public is "feeling"—rather than focusing on "public opinion" (i.e., what the public is "thinking") as we are more apt to do today. The Wilberforce campaign to abolish slavery researched "the facts" but it primarily aimed its communication of them at the hearts of the British public, not just their heads.

The right to petition the Crown, for example, was recognized in *Magna Carta* of 1215 and restated in the *English Bill of Rights* of 1689.[134] The abolitionists turned "the right to petition" those in authority into a powerful tool for advancing their cause.

A further use of existing law was made by Granville Sharp, one of the forerunners mentioned earlier, who provided the legal defence of James Somerset, an escaped slave whose owner was trying to recapture him. Sharp argued forcefully that British law allowed no one to be a slave in England itself. The case was heard by Lord Chief Justice Mansfield, who did everything possible to avoid having it decided by trial. When eventually obliged to rule, Mansfield's carefully worded judgment, rendered on June 22, 1772, set Somerset at liberty without automatically freeing other slaves.[135] But almost everyone, including many lower court judges, believed that Mansfield had indeed outlawed slavery in England.[136] It was also a significant moral victory for the abolitionists to get Mansfield to declare, however reluctantly, that slavery was "odious" to the court; the task of the abolitionists was to now make it odious to the public and to the lawmakers in Parliament.

Many Canadian Christians regard the *Canadian Charter of Rights and Freedoms* (*Charter*) as hostile to faith-based arguments and causes because the Supreme Court of Canada has ignored the *Charter*'s reference to the

---

[134] *Magna Carta 1215*, S. 61, states, "If we, our chief justice, our officials, or any of our servants offend in any respect against any man, or transgress any of the articles of the peace or of this security, and the offence is made known to four of the said twenty-five barons, they shall come to us—or in our absence from the kingdom to the chief justice—to declare it and claim immediate redress." The relevant section of *English Bill of Rights [1689]* declared, "That it is the right of the subjects to petition the king, and all commitments and prosecutions for such petitioning are illegal" (1 Will. and Mar. sess. 2, c. 2).

[135] Mansfield's decision in the Somerset case: "The power of a master over his slave has been extremely different, in different countries. The state of slavery is of such a nature, that it is incapable of being introduced on any reasons, moral or political, but only by positive law, which preserves its force long after the reasons, occasion, and time itself from whence it was created, is erased from memory. It is so odious, that nothing can be suffered to support it, but positive law. Whatever inconveniences, therefore, may follow from the decision, I cannot say this case is allowed or approved by the law of England, and therefore the black must be discharged" (*The Founders' Constitution*, article 4, section 2, clause 3 [Chicago: The University of Chicago Press, 2000, originally published 1787], available at http://press-pubs.uchicago.edu/founders/documents/a4_2_3s2.html).

[136] Hochschild, *Bury the Chains*, 50.

supremacy of God, affirmed Canada to be a secular society, and rejected faith-based arguments in striking down laws prohibiting abortion, same-sex unions, and physician-assisted suicide.

But neither the court nor the secularists, who use the *Charter* and the secular bias of the judges to their advantage, can erase the fact that the *Charter* explicitly guarantees freedom of conscience, religion, thought, belief, and expression.[137]

These rights as exercised by people of faith do not need to be written into the Constitution in response to interest group pressure through test cases; they already *are* in it. What faith-oriented Canadians need to learn is to how to take greater advantage of these fundamental rights, just as the Wilberforce abolitionists learned to take full advantage of the provisions of *Magna Carta*, the *English Bill of Rights*, and the eventual willingness of the court, however reluctantly, to declare "odious" practices and institutions previously considered morally and judicially acceptable.

9. Make maximum use of the tools of democracy

The campaign to abolish slavery did not occur in a legal vacuum; nor did it occur in a political vacuum. British politics in the 18th century was in transition. A new breed of politician—more independent and less tied to hereditary privilege and tradition than the parliamentarians of the past—was entering the arena. The informal organization of voting coalitions formed in and sustained by membership in the old political clubs was giving way to what would eventually become the party system. There was a constant and growing demand to expand the franchise (i.e., the right to vote)—more and more people were insisting on a greater say in their public affairs. The abolitionists learned to harness the energies behind these changes to their own cause and also to engage in political innovation themselves.

One of the most influential forerunner groups, the Quakers, were non-hierarchical with respect to church and community organization, and their democratic organizational techniques were infused into the anti-slavery movement from its beginning.[138]

---

[137] *Constitution Act, 1982*, c. 11, p. 1, s. 2.

[138] Hochschild, *Bury the Chains*, 108.

Petitioning Parliament,[139] direct-mail fundraising and pamphleteering, public rallies featuring prominent spokespersons, the use of graphic symbols (e.g., Wedgwood's china depiction of a slave in chains beseeching recognition of his humanity), sermons and music (e.g., John Newton's "Amazing Grace" and the story behind it), promotional efforts, including book tours giving victims a voice (e.g., Olaudah Equiano)—all tools used in issue campaigns by civil society organizations today—were pioneered in many respects by the campaign to abolish slavery.

A particularly innovative tactic employed by the abolitionists was the boycott whereby they strongly encouraged the British public to boycott sugar from the slave-oriented West Indies in favor of sugar from India.[140] The boycott was essentially the work of women, many of whom were thus introduced to political activism for the first time. Their activism was not through election participation, since British women did not get the right to vote until 1928, but through the issue campaign to abolish slavery. The boycott was such a novel idea that the very word would not come into common use in the English language for nearly another century.

The relevance of all this to issue campaigning today should be obvious: use the existing law where possible to advance the cause; effectively use all the tools that have been invented or employed by issue campaigners in democratic societies over the last 200 years; use the issue campaign to introduce political activism to people who have been excluded or alienated from the current political system (e.g., the under-30 crowd today in many Western democracies); and make innovative use of new instrumentalities, the most significant in our time being social media.

10. Communicate wisely and graciously

Issue campaigns for the most part are *communication* campaigns, so it is imperative that the campaign communications be aligned to the maximum extent with the overall campaign objective and strategy. This was generally the case with the campaign to abolish the slave trade.

The key messages of the campaign—slaves are human beings, terrible human suffering is the main product of the slave trade, abolish the trade

[139] By the late 1780s petitions opposing slavery signed by up to 100,000 people were reaching Parliament; by 1792 parliamentarians were confronted with over 500 such petitions signed by 380,000 to 400,000 individuals.

[140] Hochschild, *Bury the Chains*, 193–195.

to relieve this suffering, pass a law to do so—were well aligned with the initial campaign objective and strategy, enabling the campaigners to seize the high moral ground and to reframe the issue to their advantage.

As mentioned, before these messages could be extensively communicated, the communication had to be *legitimated* in forums such as Parliament, where the subject of slavery was still considered taboo. This legitimizing process was facilitated by keeping the tone of the initial communications gracious and flooding the decision-making arena with well-researched, undeniable facts.

THE ROLE OF PRAYER

One communication feature of issue campaigns managed by faith-oriented people is the prevalence of prayer. The Wilberforce campaigners, like the Quakers before them, regularly prayed to the God in whom they earnestly believed. They not only petitioned Parliament; they petitioned God to deliver Britain from the evil of slavery and beseeched him for the wisdom and grace to achieve the goals that they believed he had set before them. The Wilberforce campaigners, like the Quakers, took literally and acted upon the instruction of the apostle Paul to the Christians in the faith-hostile Roman city of Philippi: "Let your gentleness be evident to all. The Lord is near. Do not be anxious about anything, but in every situation, by prayer and petition, with thanksgiving, present your requests to God. And the peace of God, which transcends all understanding, will guard your hearts and your minds in Christ Jesus."[141]

In our day, of course, public prayer at public events and gatherings is virtually unknown or so generalized and sanitized in the name of political correctness that it has no impact whatsoever on the hearers (God included). In 18th century England, however, this was not so, and hearing the abolition of slavery called for in public prayers and in the prayers of respected clergymen before their congregations aided the public communication efforts of the campaign.

CHOOSE THE RIGHT LANGUAGE

As in all communication campaigns, careful attention had to be paid to the *language* employed by the anti-slavery campaigners. Was the right language being used and, if not, how should it be changed?

---

[141] Philippians 4:5–7.

In this case, the initial language of the campaign had been set by the forerunners, especially the Quakers. But the Quakers spoke and wrote differently than most other Englishmen, using the pronouns "thee" and "thou" and employing other quaint habits of speech. They also refused—both in writing and in personal contact—to address lords, judges, and other government officials by their titles, which severely hampered communication with the very people empowered to change the laws.

Changes, therefore, needed to be made early on in the language of the campaign. This was initially facilitated by Granville Sharp and Thomas Clarkson, who were not Quakers but respected them and joined with them early on in the anti-slavery effort.[142]

DISMANTLE THE MYTHS

A major portion of the initial communication thrust of the campaign also had to be focused on dismantling the myths that sustained the status quo and public support of the slave trade. One of the most pernicious of these myths was that the slave trade ships provided a useful nursery for the training of British seamen required by the British Navy and Merchant Marine. This myth was systematically destroyed by assembling and presenting evidence collected from the logbooks of slave ships and the testimony of ships' doctors and crewmen themselves. It showed that the crews of the slave ships, many of them shanghaied by press gangs, suffered many of the same horrors of disease and malnutrition as the slaves, with the death toll among slave ship crews crossing the Atlantic often being as high as 20 percent.[143]

OUT OF WHOSE MOUTH?

Then there is one of the most important communication questions of all to be answered in planning and executing an issue campaign. That is, *Out of whose mouth will our message(s) be most credible?*

To Clarkson and Granville, who shared many of the same spiritual values as the Quakers, if not their quaint habits of speech and dress, the Quakers were credible and influential spokespersons on the slavery issue. But the anti-slavery message coming from Quakers and rooted

---

[142] Hochschild, *Bury the Chains*, 107–109.

[143] Hochschild, *Bury the Chains*, 94–95.

in a spiritual perspective was far less credible in the ears of a titled and irreligious member of the British House of Lords.

In Parliament, because of their backgrounds and oratorical skills, Pitt and Wilberforce were still credible spokespersons to their fellow parliamentarians, even though most of the latter vehemently disagreed at first with the messages being delivered. But with the general public, perhaps the most credible spokespersons of all on the horrors and sufferings caused by the slave trade were ex-slaves like Olaudah Equiano—those who spoke from undeniable first-hand experience and to whom the anti-slavery campaign gave a platform and a voice.

Out of whose mouth will our message(s) be most credible? needs to be insistently asked and wisely answered for any issue campaign, especially today in our media-dominated age and especially for those campaigns where moral and ethical issues are prominent.

For instance, on beginning of life issues such as abortion, who is the more credible spokesperson: a well-meaning and well-informed 55-year-old male or a passionate and articulate woman in her child-bearing years? As the genetic testing of the preborn becomes increasingly sophisticated and targeted, enabling prospective parents to know more and more about the most probable personal characteristics of the fetus, who would be the most credible spokesperson for stronger, more ethical regulation of medical interventions, including abortion: someone with an established reputation for pro-life advocacy or a former pro-choice advocate who has come to see completely unrestricted abortion as a potential instrument for the practice of genetically based discrimination?

Out of whose mouth will our message(s) be most credible? And when wisdom, as it often does, says to the crusading politician or interest group zealot, "Not yours," will we reject that advice? Or will we have the wisdom and grace to accept it as the Quakers did and for the sake of the cause pass the podium, the microphone, and the social media megaphones to the most credible source, whoever that may be?

11. Be clear and honest about your motives

In the case of the Wilberforce campaign, the motives of the original campaigners were so transparently altruistic that there was little point, even from the standpoint of their opponents, in questioning or attacking them on that ground. The campaigners had nothing to gain personally by seeking the abolishment of slavery, and their persistent pursuit of that objective in the face of stiff opposition and censure involved much pain and self-sacrifice.

But in moral crusades of this type there usually comes a time, particularly as the cause becomes more popular politically, when those joining the cause do so from mixed motives. In order to protect the integrity of the campaign there is, therefore, wisdom in recognizing, right from the outset, the importance of at least being clear and honest about one's own motives for participating in it.

Jesus, in preparing his disciples for their public work in his name, once told his disciples a parable to show them that they should always pray and not give up.[144] But then he immediately warned them against praying and doing good works from wrong motives, in particular out of a conviction that they were morally superior to other people—and using their good works to publicize that superiority. Joining and participating in the work of God in order to demonstrate moral superiority to others was to participate from wrong motives, motives that could not be justified or blessed.[145]

This guideline is particularly relevant in our time where increasing numbers of participants in the political arena are afflicted with what might be called the Desperately Seeking A Righteous Cause (DSARC) syndrome. The motives of individuals afflicted with this syndrome, in joining an issue campaign with moral objectives such as justice for the poor or equality for the victims of discrimination, may have little to do with a genuine concern for justice and equality. Instead, the underlying motive is more likely rooted in a desire to demonstrate moral superiority to one's opponents and to increase one's own popularity thereby.[146]

[144] Luke 18:1.

[145] "To some who were confident of their own righteousness and looked down on everyone else, Jesus told this parable: 'Two men went up to the temple to pray, one a Pharisee and the other a tax collector. The Pharisee stood by himself and prayed: "God, I thank you that I am not like other people—robbers, evildoers, adulterers—or even like this tax collector. I fast twice a week and give a tenth of all I get." But the tax collector stood at a distance. He would not even look up to heaven, but beat his breast and said, "God, have mercy on me, a sinner." I tell you that this man, rather than the other, went home justified before God. For all those who exalt themselves will be humbled, and those who humble themselves will be exalted'" (Luke 18:9–14).

[146] For an excellent commentary on the issue of doing right things from wrong motives see T. S. Eliot, "Murder in the Cathedral," in *The Complete Poems and Plays, 1909–1950* (New York: Harcourt Brace & Company, 1950, 1980). It portrays the assassination of

It is of course a dangerous and extremely difficult business to judge the motives of others in joining an issue campaign in support of a righteous cause, and as Christians we are told "Do not judge, or you too will be judged."[147] Discerning the true but hidden motives of others is best left to him who knows the hearts of all, including those of politicians and issue campaigners. But in choosing to join issue campaigns in pursuit of righteous causes, we can, particularly as Christian believers, ask God to examine and purify *our own motives*. Hence the wisdom of making one of the guidelines for the conduct of the issue campaigns in which we are involved to *be clear and honest about your motives*.

12. Avoid foolishness and viciousness

It would, of course, be erroneous to characterize the Wilberforce campaign to abolish the slave trade and slavery as perfectly executed and free from the foolishness and viciousness that Jesus so clearly warned his followers to avoid in any public work.

Sometimes, regrettably, foolishness and viciousness go together, and in the case of the anti-slavery campaign this fateful combination almost brought the campaign to ruin. As bill after bill put forward by Wilberforce and his colleagues was defeated, the more impatient members of the campaign team, such as Clarkson, began to believe that stronger and more radical tactics would be necessary to succeed.

They looked across the English Channel and began to wonder out loud and in public whether the radical approach to change being taken by the French revolutionaries—notwithstanding vicious excesses—offered a better and faster way forward, not only to achieve the emancipation of slaves but also to emancipate the poor and downtrodden of England from the bondage of poverty and exploitation by the ruling classes.

Clarkson and other abolitionists visited Paris and met with the revolutionaries they admired. Some of the abolitionists even began to speak approvingly of the slave revolts in the West Indies—understandable,

---

Archbishop Thomas Becket in Canterbury Cathedral in 1170. Beckett is tempted to seek his own martyrdom in order to enhance his own reputation as a righteous champion of the church, but he resists it with the oft quoted lines "Now is my way clear, now is the meaning plain: Temptation shall not come in this kind again. The last temptation is the greatest treason: To do the right deed for the wrong reason."

[147] Matthew 7:1.

but also characterized by vicious excesses—and wondered again out loud and in public whether only violent actions could break the chains that bound the oppressed both abroad and at home.

Wilberforce, a conservative reformer if there ever was one, was appalled by these developments but could do little to curtail or counteract them. As Britain went to war with France, Pitt warned Wilberforce and his colleagues that he and his government would regard any consorting of the abolitionists with the French as treason. Pitt was now lost to the abolitionist cause as he became totally focused on the war.

Needless to say, the opponents of the anti-slavery campaign were delighted with this turn of events. They now seized on every opportunity to paint the abolitionists as extremists and radical revolutionaries who, if they got their way, would destroy the very foundations of British society. So impatience begot foolishness and desperation begot viciousness, and together they begot suspicion and disillusionment with the abolitionist cause. The anti-slavery campaign sank to its lowest ebb with even its most ardent supporters wondering if it could ever recover.

13. Endure setbacks and persevere despite adversity

The French Revolution brought social reform in Britain, indeed any reform supported by the masses, to a halt. But there were many other setbacks both before and after. When the king became mentally ill, Britain was plunged into a constitutional crisis that virtually paralyzed Parliament. Then, war with France diverted the attention of Pitt and the nation away from anything else but the war effort.

At the same time, there was the regular and discouraging defeat of Wilberforce's parliamentary resolutions and bills. His initial resolution, while warmly received in the Commons, was rejected by the House of Lords. In 1792 his bill was gutted by an amendment to pursue abolition but only *gradually*. In 1796, he came closer to carrying his bill in the Commons than he ever had before but lost the vote on third reading 74 to 70 when a dozen of his supporters were induced to attend a comic opera that night instead of staying in the House for the vote.

Every year from 1797 to 1803, either his bills were defeated or the votes postponed. As mentioned, his friend and ally Thomas Clarkson flirted in despair with the radicalism of the French Revolution; then, suffering from ruined health and financial distress, he retired from the abolitionist cause and didn't rejoin it for 12 years. Wilberforce himself was physically exhausted and discouraged, and he came close to a mental breakdown.

Clarkson once wrote,

> We are taught the consoling lesson, that however small the beginning and slow the progress … we need not be discouraged as to the ultimate result of our labours; for though our cause may appear stationary, it may only become so, in order that it may take a deeper root, and thus be enabled to stand better against the storms which may afterwards beat about it.[148]

In the end, both he and Wilberforce took this advice. Both recovered and persevered. As an issue campaigner, therefore, be prepared for reversals and setbacks. But persevere, for reversals and setbacks are invariably part of any principled campaign to advance a worthy cause, just as dogged perseverance will be essential to its ultimate success.

14. Wisely and graciously manage the middle

In democratic assemblies or decision-making bodies of any kind, when it comes to deciding the appropriate course on a moral issue there will usually be three major groups of members to be dealt with:[149]

- Those who are fervently seized by the issue and strongly in favour of some remedial measure.
- Those who have an opposite view of the issue and are strongly opposed to the remedial measure proposed.
- Those in the *middle* who are ambivalent or undecided about the issue and simply wish it would go away.

---

[148] Thomas Clarkson, *The History of the Rise, Progress, and Accomplishment of the Abolition of the African Slave-Trade by the British Parliament*, 2 vols. (London: L. Taylor, 1808), available at http://oll.libertyfund.org/pages/abolition-of-the-slave-trade.

[149] For an excellent commentary on this subject, see *Lincoln*, the 2012 American epic historical drama film directed by Steven Spielberg, starring Daniel Day-Lewis as President Abraham Lincoln and loosely based on Doris Kearns Goodwin's biography *Team of Rivals: The Political Genius of Abraham Lincoln*. The primary focus of the film is the efforts of Lincoln and his associates to win the support of those in the *middle*, between the pro-slavery and anti-slavery elements of the 1865 House of Representatives, for the 13th amendment to the United States *Constitution* abolishing slavery throughout the union. A major portion of this effort had to be directed toward constraining the most fervent abolitionists in the House from going *over the top* and driving those in the *middle* into the pro-slavery camp.

How these middle members are treated and courted—whether or not they are offended or attracted by the tactics and arguments of the competing sides—becomes crucial to deciding the outcome.

In the case of the campaign to abolish slavery, the graciousness of Wilberforce's language, entreaties, and initial approach stood him and the cause in good stead with these middle members of the British Parliament. Some were eventually won over, and others, by abstaining from crucial votes, were at least constrained from going over to the "dark side."

Clarkson and the more radical members of the abolition campaign were inclined to castigate as moral and political cowards those middle members who were reluctant to openly side with the anti-slavery campaign because they represented port cities and constituencies with factories and businesses benefiting from the slave trade or its products. Wilberforce, on the other hand, as an elected member himself who also had to take constituent interests into account, better understood the political dilemma of these members and tried to provide them with the tools and arguments for resolving it rather than attacking their characters and driving them over to the other side.

15. Master shrewd tactics for dealing with opponents

How an issue campaign, especially one with moral dimensions, deals with those in the *middle* is often crucial to its success or failure. Equally important are the tactics adopted for dealing with the outright opponents of the campaign, particularly those with decision-making power, such as parliamentarians. Just as the graciousness of the dove is required to win over the former, it is usually the shrewdness of the serpent that is required to triumph over the latter.

As mentioned earlier, the resolutions and bills introduced by Wilberforce and his colleagues to curtail the slave trade were defeated time and time again in Parliament, notwithstanding all the effort that had been expended on rallying public support for them. So what was to be done?

Eventually, it was the lawyer James Stephens, likely with some assistance from the veteran parliamentarian Charles Fox, who came up with an answer. Britain was at war with France, and most of the ships sailing in opposition to British interests were sailing under American flags of convenience to protect them from attacks by the British navy and privateers. These included the slave ships sailing from Africa to America, many of which were actually manned by British crews and outfitted from Liverpool. If a bill removing that protection could be framed and introduced as a trade regulation measure to frustrate the French and advance the British war effort, it would be impossible for the anti-slavery members of Parliament to vote against it without appearing to be siding with the French.

Consequently, such a bill was framed and introduced to the House in as dull and boring a fashion as possible by a member not strongly identified with the anti-slavery caucus, so as not to arouse unnecessary suspicion. Before the opponents of slavery realized what was happening, the bill secured sufficient support from the anti-slavery members, the ambivalent middle members, and its conflicted opponents in order for it to pass.

It was not until 1833, after many more years and much more campaigning, that the House passed the final legislation, completely abolishing slavery throughout the British Empire. However, the first major legislative victory in the battle, curtailment of the slave trade, had now been won, in part through the graciousness of the dove but also through the wisdom of the serpent, by campaigners who were now as skilled at navigating the narrow corridors of Parliament as they were at navigating the broad streets of the public square.

Successful issue campaigns need winsome and diplomatic communicators like Wilberforce. They need zealous and indefatigable activists and organizers like Clarkson. But, invariably, they also need tactical shrewdness and serpentine wisdom like that of Stephens and Fox to ultimately succeed.

16. Support the campaign with spiritual resources

The key participants in the campaign to abolish slavery needed physical, financial, and political resources to succeed. But because of the moral dimensions of their cause and the spiritual roots of their motivation, they—above all—needed spiritual resources to guide and sustain them through the long nights occasioned by opposition attacks, numerous setbacks, and debilitating defeats.

The support that sustained Wilberforce and his colleagues during this long campaign came from four sources, all of which are essential to supporting and sustaining those who engage in moral and ethical campaigns today.

In the case of Wilberforce personally, there were his own internal spiritual resources, acquired before he ever became engaged in the abolition campaign and instrumental in causing him to choose to engage in that campaign in the first place. He himself described the acquisition and outworking of these resources as "The Great Change"—brought about by contact with a godly uncle and aunt, the influence of a former tutor Isaac Milner, the reading of books on the spiritual life by Philip Doddridge and Blaise Pascal, personal prayer, attendance at religious services, especially communion, and a constant searching of the Scriptures for comfort and guidance. If a leader is urging others to change, it is helpful if that leader has undergone a major change in his or her own life so as to have a true appreciation of what he or she is now demanding of others.

Second, there was Wilberforce's wife, Barbara Spooner, and eventually his family. The life partner and family of a moral crusader are rarely given their due in political commentary on issue campaigns. But their role is usually crucial to success in providing honest assessments of the crusader's strengths and weaknesses and in providing badly needed support and encouragement during the dark days of the campaign. In most of the early accounts of the anti-slavery campaign, not nearly enough attention was paid or credit given to the role of women such as Barbara Spooner and Hannah More in conducting the campaign and in supporting, encouraging, and sustaining the frontline activists.

Third, there was the counsel of godly pastors—for example, long and insightful letters to Wilberforce from John Newton—that provided spiritual counsel but also demonstrated an understanding of the political pressures and circumstances to which Wilberforce was subject.

Fourth, and perhaps most important to the campaign team as a whole, was the Clapham Circle. It consisted of Wilberforce's cousin Henry Thornton (also an MP), Edward Eliot (Pitt's brother-in-law), Hannah More (the most prominent female among the abolitionists), and several other leading evangelicals serving in Parliament and in business, all of whom decided to live together in the pastoral village of Clapham just outside of London.

They dined together, worshipped together, prayed together, and shared each other's burdens during all the dark years when the cause of abolition seemed hopelessly lost. Like some of the Christian prayer fellowships that exist among the Christian members of our legislatures, including the Parliament of Canada, they met regularly to provide spiritual support to the personal and family lives of those in attendance. But unlike our fellowships of this kind, they were also free and able to fully discuss and debate from a faith perspective, without becoming dangerously divided, the political and public issues of the day and, as a result, to better equip and fortify each other for their public lives.

IMPLICATIONS FOR US

There is a need for advocacy campaigns today—campaigns to raise important issues and remedies so high and insistently in the public consciousness and political arena that they cannot be ignored by politicians and lawmakers and so that they will be forced by the weight of public opinion to act. Some of the most important of those campaigns will involve moral issues engaging faith-oriented citizens at the faith-political interface, for example,

- Campaigns to combat the terrible resurgence of human trafficking in our time, in particular the global sex trade with Internet-based pornography as its communication and marketing arm.
- Campaigns to achieve equality for females and the protection of young girls from sexual exploitation, as well as equality and dignity for Indigenous peoples.
- Campaigns to establish and communicate what "death with dignity" means for faith-oriented people and to create safe and spiritually sensitive hospice and palliative care environments where state-sanctioned euthanasia and physician-assisted suicide are neither promoted nor practised.
- Campaigns to establish ethically based laws and regulatory regimes to deal with beginning of life issues, from assisted human reproduction and abortion to the genetic modification of human beings.
- Campaigns to awaken and mobilize faith-oriented citizens to the challenges of creation care, environmental stewardship, and the voluntary constraint of consumerism as spiritual responsibilities.
- Campaigns to reorganize and strengthen the charitable sector of civil society as a partner and/or alternative to the welfare state in providing care and services to the poor, the oppressed, the disadvantaged, and the elderly.

In the Wilberforce campaign just examined we have a great example of a faith-oriented campaign to eradicate a great social evil and achieve a great social good, conducted by people operating with the wisdom of serpents and the graciousness of doves at the interface of faith and politics. Those of us who want to conduct such campaigns today to eradicate the social evils of our time and advance worthy social causes should study this campaign backward and forward and apply the lessons it teaches.

More specifically, learning from Wilberforce and his associates, let us,

- Choose the initial campaign objective and strategy wisely.
- Seize the high moral ground by first strongly identifying with the suffering to be alleviated.
- Reframe the issue to place it within the conceptual framework best suited to advancing the campaign objective and strategy.
- Move the debate, if possible, into the decision-making arena most conducive to success.
- Build a principled coalition to advance the cause.
- Legitimate the discussion, graciously.
- Do the necessary research thoroughly and well.
- Make maximum use of the existing law.
- Make maximum use of the tools of democracy.
- Communicate wisely and graciously.
- Be clear and honest about our motives.
- Avoid foolishness and viciousness.
- Endure setbacks and persevere in adversity.
- Wisely and graciously manage the middle.
- Master shrewd tactics for dealing with opponents.
- Support the campaign with spiritual resources.

And if in fact spiritual resources are an essential element of any campaign on behalf of great moral causes, it is appropriate for us who may be involved in such campaigns today to ask and answer the following questions:

- What personal spiritual resources and experience can *we* bring to or draw upon in undertaking such campaigns at the interface of faith and politics?
- Have *we* ever personally experienced the Great Change that Wilberforce experienced and that strengthened his capacity to become a change agent among his generation?
- Who and where are the pastors, spiritual directors, and counsellors in our time who can be to *us* what John Newton was to Wilberforce?
- Who and where will be *our* Clapham Circle, providing spiritual and social support to our campaign endeavours, especially when the road gets hard and difficult?

1.10 THE MINISTRY OF RECONCILIATION: THE JESUS WAY

AS PREVIOUSLY MENTIONED, TWO OF THE GREAT RIVERS of religious thought that cut across the Canadian prairies, where much of my own political and religious experience is rooted, are the *evangelical stream* and the *social gospel stream*.

According to social gospel adherents, the primary purpose of the Christian religion is to heal and strengthen relationships between people. Their favourite New Testament passage is the story from Luke's Gospel of the Good Samaritan, the man who loved his neighbour as himself.[150] According to evangelicals, the primary purpose of the Christian faith is to establish right relations between people and God. Their favourite New Testament passage is John 3, which speaks of the necessity of a spiritual new birth before one can enter or work for the kingdom of God.[151]

Perhaps the most significant thing about these perspectives is that reconciliation is the principal concern of both. For evangelicals, it is reconciliation between human beings and God, or personal salvation; for social gospel adherents, it is reconciliation among people, or social justice. But reconciliation and how to achieve it is at the heart of both professions.

Obviously, reconciliation *should* be at the heart of any Christian profession since reconciliation was at the very heart of Jesus' mission and public work.

But how Jesus went about it, how he practised reconciliation, was very different from the methodologies most frequently prescribed by the conventional religious and political wisdom of both his time and ours.

---

[150] See Luke 10:25–37.

[151] See John 3:1–21.

Since democratic politics at its highest level is very much about the reconciliation of conflicting interests by non-coercive means, anyone involved in democratic politics today should find Jesus' approach both relevant and instructive. Of course, his approach should be most relevant and instructive to Christian believers engaged in public life and politics, since we are called to follow in his footsteps.

RECONCILIATION THROUGH THE RULE OF LAW

The conventional religious wisdom of the Jewish society in which Jesus was born and raised was that right relationships between human beings and God and between human beings themselves could be achieved by adherence to the Rule of Law, in particular the law of God as given to Moses, contained in the Hebrew Scriptures and expounded and expanded by the scribes and the Pharisees. This notion had its non-religious and political counterpart in the strong belief by the Romans that societal order and progress could be achieved and maintained by adherence to and the enforcement of Roman law.

The story of reliance on the Rule of Law to reconcile conflicting interests and restore broken relationships in ancient Israel (more about this in part 2) is one of the most instructive that anyone responsible for law or rule-making and administration can examine. In ancient Israel, the law of God, and subsidiary regulations derived from it, was used to govern every aspect of Israel's economic, social, political, and personal life. This exercise was conducted for hundreds of years, with lasting peace and great prosperity promised to those who would obey the laws and the direst of penalties meted out to those who failed to keep them.

The most significant thing about this whole socioreligious exercise is that it did not succeed in attaining its ultimate objective—the reconciliation of human beings to God or to each other. Therefore, the latter prophets emphasized this sobering conclusion: unless laws can be inscribed on the human heart, and not merely written on parchment or tablets of stone, law by itself is insufficient to restore or regulate relationships between people and God or among themselves. In other words, the Israelites came up against the limits to the Rule of Law and to the conclusion that something more than law and law enforcement is required to heal and restore strained and broken relationships and to establish harmonious future relationships.

RECONCILIATION THROUGH SELF-SACRIFICIAL MEDIATION

The latter prophets, therefore, looked forward to another divinely initiated approach to reconciliation—one that Christians believe found its fulfillment in the life and work of Jesus. This approach, reconciliation through non-coercive, self-sacrificial mediation, is thoroughly described in the New Testament. Here, God is portrayed as sending not another lawgiver but a uniquely constituted and positioned mediator to restore the relationship of human beings to himself and to each other through sacrificing his own life and interests on their behalf. If the story of the Old Testament is the settlement of relations between estranged parties through law and judgment, the story of the New Testament is that of an out-of-court settlement.

Significantly, this reconciliation effort is initiated by the party sinned *against* and is motivated by love. It is motivated not primarily by a love of justice, although the demands of justice must be satisfied, but by the love of God for human beings themselves—"God so loved the world that he gave ..."[152] Love in this instance is presented not as an emotion or sentiment but as decisive and continuous action to establish and restore relationships, even turning bad relationships into good. It is the polar opposite of evil, which strains and destroys relationships, even turning good relationships into bad.

The New Testament makes clear that this greatest of divine initiatives—reconciliation through self-sacrificial mediation motivated by love—is non-coercive. Human beings are free to accept or reject it, free to accept or reject the person and work of the mediator and the offer of healed relationships that he presents. So if there is one supreme test for distinguishing the expression of genuine Christianity in practice from spurious Christianity (professing Christians seeking public office, take note), it is that genuine Christianity does not seek to impose itself or its solutions on those who choose not to receive it.

At the heart of this mediation effort is Jesus. He came not as a judicial mediator, aloof and impersonal, distancing himself from the parties to be reconciled so as to avoid a conflict of interest. Instead, he was intimately related to the alienated parties; he embodied and incorporated the interests

[152] John 3:16.

of both in himself, calling God his father and human beings his brothers and sisters. Rather than avoiding the conflict of interest between them, he accepted, internalized, and resolved it.

Initially, his mediation effort focused on communicating extensively with both parties. He represented the people to God in prayer and represented God to the people through teaching. He taught those who would listen how to pray effectively to God themselves. The restoration of communication, in this case through a third party intimately related to both parties, is necessary for the healing and restoration of relationships to begin.

Finally, the mediation effort was consummated through self-sacrifice—the initiator of the reconciliation process (God) and the mediator (Jesus) paying the price of reconciliation rather than requiring the estranged party to do so. The mediator yielded himself to the forces opposed to reconciliation in such a way that their attacks on him—his life, his teachings, his work, and all he represented—actually facilitated the reconciliation process.[153] The alienated parties were then presented with the option of accepting the mediator's sacrifice as payment of the price of reconciling each to the other or rejecting it.

In the final analysis, the efficacy of this approach to reconciliation, whether it *works* or not, depends on whether both parties accept the work and sacrifice of the mediator. According to the New Testament writers, the resurrection of Jesus and his acceptance back into fellowship with the Father was conclusive proof that the initiator of the reconciliation process accepted the work of the mediator. Whether human beings accept or reject it is up to us.

Whether *you*, as a 21st century person, accept this approach to reconciliation and seek to apply its principles to your own relationships with God and your fellow human beings is ultimately your decision to make. But in my case, as a young management consultant with political interests and dealing with conflicting interests all the time, when I first began to see Jesus' approach to reconciliation in this light, I thought it was the most intriguing, otherworldly, and ingenious approach to that challenge that I had ever encountered.

---

[153] I think of this as a sort of spiritual jujitsu whereby the strength and ferocity of the opponent's attacks are levered against him to the advantage of the one attacked.

APPLICATION OF THE JESUS WAY TO RECONCILIATION IN ANCIENT TIMES

It is in the Gospels that Jesus' personal ministry of reconciliation is most thoroughly described, with the Gospel of John having the most to say about its application to the reconciliation of human beings to God—the vertical application.

But it is in the book of Acts, written by the Gentile doctor Luke, and in the letters to the early Christians by Paul of Tarsus, the converted Pharisee, that we begin to see the application of Jesus' approach to the reconciliation of conflicts among human beings themselves—the horizontal application and the application most relevant to those who serve in public and political arenas.

Consider the following two illustrations: the reconciliation of Jews to Gentiles in the early church and the reconciliation of a runaway slave to a slave owner described in Paul's letter to Philemon.

THE RECONCILIATION OF JEWS AND GENTILES

As is well known, a great gulf existed between Jews and Gentiles in Jesus' time, the alienation being so complete and antagonistic that Jesus had to initially warn his first disciples to refrain from even attempting to minister to Gentiles until his disciples' hearts and habits had been changed through their personal relationship with himself, his teachings, and his spirit.[154]

The principal mediators of relations between Jews and Gentiles in the early church were the apostles Peter and Paul, in particular the apostle Paul. Note the distinguishing elements of Paul's ministry of reconciliation in this regard and how closely they mirrored the non-coercive, self-sacrificial approach taught and modelled by Jesus:

- Paul, once "a Pharisee, descended from the Pharisees," was willing to transform and position himself however he needed to in order to minister to those alienated from God and himself as a Jew. "Though I am free and belong to no one, I have made myself a slave to everyone, to win as many as possible. To the Jews I became like a Jew, to win the Jews … To those not having the law [Gentiles] I became like one not having the law … so as to win those not having the law."[155]
- His ultimate motivation in doing so was love—the self-sacrificial love modelled by the Jesus whom he followed. "If I speak in the tongues of men or of angels,

[154] Matthew 10:5.

[155] 1 Corinthians 9:19–21.

but do not have love, I am only a resounding gong or a clanging cymbal ... If I give all I possess to the poor and give over my body to hardship that I may boast, but do not have love, I gain [achieve] nothing."[156]

- He communicated constantly with God through his prayers, but he also increasingly communicated the gospel to Gentile audiences through his preaching and writings. He did so often at great risk to himself physically and to his relationship with others (Jews) in the early church who themselves were alienated from Gentiles and suspicious of Paul's overtures to them.[157]
- His approach to the Gentiles was non-coercive. He did not seek to bring Gentiles "under the law" given to Moses and resisted the efforts of those who would do so. He did not attempt to compel them to accept either the gospel or a new relationship with the Jewish community within the church. He could only offer Jesus' way of reconciliation and pray that they would accept it.
- His ministry of reconciliation involved not the assertion of his rights but his sacrifice of them. As an apostle who had seen Jesus, Paul asked the Corinthians, did he not have the right to make a living (i.e., to receive physical and financial support) from those to whom he ministered? Yes, he did, and he quoted Scripture in support of those rights. And yet, he declared, "I have not used any of these rights ... that in preaching the gospel I may offer it free of charge, and so not make full use of my rights as a preacher of the gospel." In this regard, he likened himself to an athlete who has the right to indulge his body as he pleases but forgoes that right in order to win the race.[158]
- And finally, in carrying out this ministry of reconciliation he ultimately sacrificed not just his rights but his own life, being executed by the Romans just as Jesus was.

RECONCILIATION OF A SLAVE OWNER TO A RUNAWAY SLAVE

In Jesus' time, slavery was a widespread and accepted institution throughout most of the ancient world, and one often reads criticisms that the Christian Scriptures and the early proponents of the gospel of Christ have so little to say about the evil of this institution and the need for its abolition.

I personally find these criticisms odd because when I first began to read the New Testament as the ultimate textbook on the reconciliation of conflicting interests, I discovered that there was an entire New Testament book (though admittedly a short one)—the letter of the apostle Paul to Philemon—that is entirely focused on this very issue.[159] However, it

[156] 1 Corinthians 13:1–3.
[157] See Acts 21 and 22.
[158] See 1 Corinthians 9.
[159] See Philemon.

approaches the abolition of the master-slave relationship in such a very different way from what we might expect (i.e., without reference to laws and political actions to secure abolition) that we can easily fail to recognize it as such.

Philemon, the man to whom Paul's letter is addressed, was an early Christian. Paul described him as a dear friend, a fellow worker who shared his faith, a believer who hosted meetings of fellow Christians in his home and who "refreshed the hearts of the Lord's people."

But Philemon was also a slave owner, and one of his slaves, named Onesimus, had run away from his household. Onesimus had also become a Christian believer and had apparently become a servant to Paul while Paul was imprisoned in Rome. Paul had come to have great affection for Onesimus, whom he described as his son in the faith, just as he had great affection for Philemon. He loved them both.

But now Paul was sending Onesimus back to Philemon, and his intent was to reconcile each to the other and address the relationship between slave and slave owner. He did so without any reference whatsoever to either Jewish or Roman law but in accordance with the principles of Jesus' approach to the reconciliation of conflicting interests. Key aspects of Paul's letter to Philemon are as follows:

- *Love is the motivation*: Paul loved justice, but here his reconciliation effort was motivated by his love of both Philemon and Onesimus as human beings and fellow believers. "I am sending him [Onesimus]—who is my very heart—back to you" and "I appeal to you [to receive him] on the basis of love."
- *A new and better relationship is the objective*: "Perhaps the reason he was separated from you for a little while was that you might have him back forever—no longer as a slave, but better than a slave, as a dear brother." Significantly, Paul went out of his way to describe Onesimus, the runaway slave, not as property, as was the common conception of a slave at that time, but as "a fellow man and as a brother."
- *The approach is non-coercive*: In appealing to Philemon to receive and treat Onesimus as a man and a brother Paul sought Philemon's voluntary acceptance of his mediatorial efforts. Paul was not trying to coerce Philemon's acceptance; he was particularly not trying to coerce Philemon's acceptance by exercising ecclesiastical authority (contemporary Christians, take note). "Although in Christ I could be bold and order you to do what you ought to do, yet I prefer to appeal to you on the basis of love … I did not want to do anything without your consent, so that any favor you do would not seem forced but would be voluntary."

- *The mediator is willing to pay the price of reconciliation*: It is in this respect that Paul's effort to reconcile Philemon and Onesimus—abolishing the master-slave relationship and replacing it with a brotherhood based on love—most closely paralleled Jesus' approach to reconciliation.

Paul, the mediator, wrote to Philemon, "If you consider me a partner, welcome him [Onesimus] as you would welcome me. If he has done you any wrong or owes you anything, charge it to me. I, Paul, am writing this with my own hand. I will pay it back."

One can imagine Jesus, in opening up the way for humanity to be reconciled to God, using similar language in addressing the Father. "If you consider me a partner, welcome them as you would welcome me. If they have done you any wrong, as they have; if they have sinned against you, as they have; if they owe you anything, as they do, *charge it to me; I will pay*." And he did so, on Calvary.

So Paul, practising the ministry of reconciliation after the fashion of Jesus, abolished slavery in the household of Philemon, at least as far as the relationship between Philemon and Onesimus was concerned. Paul's approach was not dependent for its success on law, politics, or the exercise of force, unlike the means whereby slavery would one day be abolished throughout the British Empire and the United States. True, it did not abolish the *institution* of slavery; it did, however, begin to undermine it from within, the slow but certain route to eventual abolition. Neither Paul nor the early church, from their minority positions politically, were yet in any position whatsoever to influence the laws of Rome or to dismantle evil institutions by political and legal means. Nevertheless, the master-slave relationship was broken in this instance, with the potential for multiplication throughout the Christian community, long before the opportunity would present itself to harness the authority of law or political power to the task of institutional abolition.

IMPLICATIONS FOR US

Is the *Jesus way* to reconciliation relevant and applicable to conflict resolution in our time? Can it be practised by Christians operating at the interface of faith and public life today? These questions are addressed in the following chapter.

1.11 RECONCILIATION: THE JESUS WAY APPLIED

APPLICATION OF JESUS' APPROACH TO CONFLICT RESOLUTION IN OUR TIMES

AS A CHRISTIAN LAYMAN, NOT A THEOLOGIAN OR academic expert in the interpretation of the Judeo-Christian Scriptures, and as someone who has sought to relate my Christian faith in the complex and often confusing worlds of business and politics, I must acknowledge that my understanding and application of Jesus' approach to reconciliation in such arenas is incomplete and quite likely flawed. But I have had enough positive experience in witnessing and attempting the application of his approach to some of the conflict situations with which I have been involved to come to believe that it is indeed highly relevant to conflict resolution in our time, and that a better informed and more rigorous application of this approach to contemporary conflict resolution would be well worth the effort, especially by those with Christian convictions already embedded (perhaps providentially) in such conflicts.

Early in my management consulting practice I sought to translate Jesus' approach to reconciliation as described in the New Testament into a form that I could use in addressing some of the conflict situations we were encountering in our work. Those situations included our involvement in attempting to resolve actual or potential conflicts between energy companies and Indigenous bands, particularly in northern Alberta.

Our firm specialized in applying systems analysis to conceptualizing and addressing the problems and challenges faced by our clients, so I worked out (initially just for my own use) a description of Jesus' approach to reconciliation in "systems terms."[160] This involved stripping out all the religious language so that the engineers and executives I was largely dealing with would not even recognize its Christian origins unless they themselves were believers.

In identifying the key components and actors in applying this model to conflict resolution situations faced by our clients, man the sinner became the *alienated* party, God the Father became the *initiator* (of the reconciliation process), John the Baptist became the *advance man*, Jesus became the *mediator*, evil personified became the *opposition*, the scribes and Pharisees became the *agents of the opposition*, the Holy Spirit became the *facilitator*, the church became the *reconciled community* with a capacity to continue the reconciliation process, and so on.

Conceptualized in this way, the process of reconciliation, now described in systems terms, could be represented via a functional flow diagram (the kind that oil patch engineers and executives understand and love), with a series of boxes describing the key functions to be performed and linked with arrows and feedback loops. This functional flow diagram is in effect a "model" of the reconciliation ministry practised by Jesus but expressed in systems terms rather than theological language.

Lastly, I identified thirty operating guidelines for the application of the model so I could consider their relevance and application to at least some of the conflict situations I was encountering in my consulting practice. This is not the place to fully list or elaborate on these, but the principal ones included the following:

- The model is particularly applicable where there have been previous reconciliation attempts (especially via legal or jurisprudential means) that have failed. In fact, the model requires a previous and failed reconciliation attempt in order to be operationalized.
- The objective of the reconciliation process is not to achieve a compromise between the parties but to establish a new relationship between them superior to any relationship that may have previously existed.
- The reconciliation action is ideally initiated by the *offended* party rather than the *offending* party and must be rightly motivated (expressing *love* in systems terms was a challenge).
- The reconciliation process is persuasive but non-coercive, respecting the freedom of the alienated party to accept or reject the reconciliation initiative.

[160] For a more detailed description of this model, see Preston Manning, *With Heart, Mind & Strength: The Best of Crux 1979–1989*, vol. 1 (Langley: Credo, 1990), 237–253.

- The mediator is not independent of the parties to the conflict but is intimately related to both and internalizes the conflict between them.
- Constituting and positioning the mediator is the most time-consuming aspect of the reconciliation process.
- The most dangerous agents of the opposition are those drawn from and loyal to the institutions established and processes employed by the previous reconciliation attempt.
- The mediator is willing to sacrifice his or her own position and interests in order to establish the new and reconciled relationship between the initiator and the alienated party.
- The implementation of the reconciliation process is extremely costly. The costs are not equally distributed among the parties but are borne primarily by the initiator and the mediator.

ILLUSTRATIVE APPLICATIONS

To illustrate the application of this approach to reconciliation in real world situations, allow me to share some of my own limited but relevant experience with the attempted application of Jesus' approach to conflict resolution in the business and political world. In doing so, let me also urge each of you, particularly if you are a professing Christian, to think seriously about more faithfully and systematically applying Jesus' approach to some of the conflict situations in which you may find yourself.

A Business Application

I once observed a Christian executive as he mediated a strained relationship between a financially distressed company and its creditors in such a way that it reminded me of how Jesus might have acted in such a situation. The company was in the homebuilding business but had fallen into financial difficulties when the market collapsed and interest rates skyrocketed. Its largest creditors were a bank and a lumber supply company. The bank proposed to the supplier that they co-operate in putting the homebuilder into receivership, close down its operations, and sell its assets while they were still of sufficient value to at least cover its obligations to the bank and the supplier. If this plan had been followed, the owners of the homebuilding company, its employees, and its other creditors would have been left out in the cold.

One of the executives of the lumber supply company was a Christian gentleman named Gordon. He was uniquely positioned to be a mediator because he had a close relationship with the bank, the supply company, and the homebuilder and was trusted by each. Gordon volunteered that he, rather than some distant and indifferent third party, be appointed as a "friendly receiver" to see what could be done to reconcile the interests of all concerned. This offer was accepted—the homebuilder had little choice—and Gordon moved into a small office at the headquarters of the homebuilding company, acting and appearing to outsiders as if he were just another member of their executive team.

He had all the powers of a receiver, and had the lumber supply company decided to take over the homebuilder, Gordon would have been appointed the president and CEO. Instead, Gordon simply positioned himself as the comptroller—with the blessing of the bank and the principal creditors—whose job was to rectify the homebuilders' financial affairs if he could. He was in constant communication with the homebuilder, the lumber supply company, and the bank. He gradually implemented measures that eventually led to the financial recovery of the homebuilder and the satisfactory retirement of all its obligations. In the process, which took years, Gordon sacrificed his own opportunities to secure a more prominent executive position and the increased compensation and prestige that would have accompanied such a promotion. When the homebuilder was eventually restored to financial health, Gordon, at the homebuilder's request, remained in his comptroller position, serving the company that he had rescued from bankruptcy in that capacity until his retirement fifteen years later.

If you asked the owners and senior employees of that home building company, as I once did, why they thought Gordon had acted the way he had, they simply replied, "We think it had something to do with his Christian faith."

A Political Application

In the 1990s in Canada (for those not familiar with our politics), a concerted effort was made to realign the conservative side of the political spectrum at the national level—an effort in which I was very much involved.[161] Growing disillusionment with the governing Progressive Conservative (PC) Party of Canada, particularly in western Canada and

[161] For a more detailed description of this effort from my perspective see Manning, *Think Big*.

among fiscal conservatives, led to the formation of the Reform Party of Canada (Reform) with myself as leader.

In the 1993 federal election, the PC Party's representation in the House of Commons was reduced from 156 seats to 2. The Reform Party elected 52 members, but vote splitting between the federal PCs and Reform greatly assisted the Liberal Party of Canada (Liberal) to form a majority government. Over the next four years, Reform continued to grow and the federal PCs continued to stagnate, but the 1997 election produced very much the same results. Reform won 60 seats, and I became the leader of the Official Opposition. The federal PCs increased their representation to 20 seats, but vote splitting still kept the federal Liberals in power.

By this time many of our party members, many federal PC members, and members of provincial PC parties were becoming tired of the vote splitting and losing seats by default to the Liberals because of it. The conflicting interests of the two groups were in need of reconciliation. So my colleagues and I launched what became known as the United Alternative initiative. It involved organizing a steering committee to define the common ground, ideologically and policy wise, between Reformers and the PCs and a step-by-step consultation with our own grassroots membership on ways and means to create a "united alternative" to the Liberals.

Eventually this effort produced a proposal to create a new federal party to be called the Canadian Conservative Reform Alliance, which former Reformers and Progressive Conservatives were invited to join in support of agreed-upon principles and policies.

Because this effort had been initiated by Reform and myself, many PC members were suspicious that it was simply a thinly veiled takeover initiative and were reluctant to endorse or support it. Some means had to be found to convince them that it was a sincere effort to reconcile the differences between us and establish a new, more politically effective relationship.

One approach might have been to keep compromising the principles, policies, and structure on which the alternative was to be based until it finally won acceptance. But this would have produced an unprincipled union of expediency unlikely to attract public support and still would not have addressed the suspicions of a takeover.

The other approach was for me to put the leadership of the whole enterprise on the table and to encourage several prominent personalities from the PC camp to contest it. This idea was strenuously resisted by some of my key advisors, who feared we would lose control of the whole united alternative initiative to which we had thus far given direction and had worked so hard to facilitate. But I felt that running the risk of losing the leadership was preferable to sacrificing the principles, policies, and opportunity that the united alternative initiative was designed to advance, or to allowing the whole effort to stall because of suspicions that could not be alleviated in any other way.

So, to make a long story short, I put the leadership of the Canadian Alliance on the table and encouraged two prominent provincial Progressive Conservatives from Alberta and Ontario to contest it along with myself.[162] I subsequently lost the leadership and was replaced by Stockwell Day, a former Progressive Conservative cabinet minister from Alberta. But the Canadian Alliance became a reality, and the differences between Reform and many provincial PCs were essentially reconciled.[163]

---

[162] I should make it clear that, notwithstanding the necessity of "putting the leadership on the line," my colleagues and I entered the contest with every intention of winning it and made a very strenuous effort to do so. I personally hoped that, in the end, no personal sacrifice would have to be made, although in order for the overall enterprise to succeed the prospect had to be offered.

The believer in a mediatorial position, when confronted with the demand for personal sacrifice in order to achieve reconciliation, may also hope that what God really wants is the willingness to render it and that he will provide an alternative to self-sacrifice once that willingness is established. This was the case when Abraham was confronted with the demand that he sacrifice his son Isaac (Genesis 22:1–19). It was also the hope expressed by Jesus in his garden prayer before his arrest and crucifixion, although in his case there proved to be no alternative but self-sacrifice and he ended his prayer with the words "Not as I will, but as you will" (Matthew 26:39).

[163] Another instructive example of this type of mediatorial leadership—the paradoxical sacrificing of the leadership position itself in order to unite two or more parties—is found in the formation of the United Church of Canada in 1925. This involved the attempted merger of four distinctive Protestant denominations—the Methodist Church, the Congregational Union of Ontario and Quebec, the Association of Union Churches, and a portion of the Presbyterian Church in Canada. As a merger, it of necessity involved a reconciliation of conflicting interests and positions—in this case, religious interests and faith positions deeply held by their adherents. At the time, the Methodist Church was the largest of the four denominations, and union was therefore suspected by some members of the other congregations, especially the Presbyterians, as being nothing more than a Methodist "takeover." To overcome this divisive suspicion, the Methodist general

Because the leadership of what was left of the old federal PC Party still refused to endorse or join the Canadian Alliance, the vote splitting at the federal level continued in the 2001 federal election. The Canadian Alliance remained the Official Opposition but was still a long way from forming a government. But then the leadership of both parties changed again. The new leaders, Stephen Harper for the Alliance and Peter MacKay for the federal PCs, reached the same conclusion that we had reached earlier—that to stop the vote splitting yet another entity had to be created to which both Alliance and federal PC members could come without losing face or sacrificing principles and policies that they held dear. As a result, the new Conservative Party of Canada (CPC) was created, with both Harper and MacKay having to put their leadership on the line and contest the leadership of the new entity. Both did so. Stephen Harper then emerged as the new leader of the CPC with Peter MacKay in a subordinate position, having sacrificed his leadership for the unity cause.

And so, after much effort to reconcile the conflicting interests that divided the federal conservative camp in Canada, a new, reasonably united, conservative political party was created at the federal level. The Canadian electorate found it increasingly attractive. The vote splitting stopped. The CPC formed a minority federal government in 2006 and a majority government in 2011 with Stephen Harper as prime minister.

In the Christian model of reconciliation, sacrifice, in particular on the part of those desiring the reconciliation, is an absolutely essential feature. My point in giving this lengthy recitation of the effort to reconcile conflicting interests at the federal political level in Canada is to show that some sort of sacrifice was also necessary to achieve the desired result in that instance. When the choice was between achieving unity by sacrificing the values and standards of the *initiating* party or sacrificing the personal interests of the *mediating* party, the Christian thing to do, at least in this case, was to sacrifice the latter rather than the former. I think this was easier for me to do because of my Christian understanding of reconciliation and commitment to the approach of Jesus than it would be for someone with no such understanding or commitment.

---

superintendent, S. D. Chown, who was considered to be the leading candidate to become the first moderator of the United Church, stepped aside in favour of George C. Pidgeon, moderator of the Presbyterian Church, in order to reconcile the Presbyterians to the union.

I'm sure some of my secular political friends and advisors still think I was crazy for allowing theological considerations to play any role whatsoever in deciding whether or not to risk my political leadership position in this way. All I can say is that God's ways are not always our ways, and in the end the conflicted interests were reconciled. Hopefully this illustration is helpful to others, in particular other Christians involved in reconciling conflicting interests in the public and political arenas when they are confronted with choices as to what to sacrifice—their values and principles, somebody else's interests, or their own ego-driven interests—in order to bring reconciliation about.

A RELEVANT OIL PATCH STORY

As previously mentioned, our management consulting firm became involved in trying to improve relations between energy companies and Indigenous peoples in the province of Alberta. I chaired a group consisting of representatives from a dozen companies that met once a quarter to discuss ways and means of increasing the employment of Indigenous peoples by the companies and their purchases of goods and services from Indigenous-owned businesses.

One of the member companies in this group had a heavy oil pilot plant in north central Alberta in close proximity to an Indigenous band with 3,000 band members. Relations between the company and the band were becoming increasingly strained, and it was decided that the company needed to hire someone to act as an intermediary to improve relations and resolve some of the conflicts between them.

The man in charge of this process was a hard-boiled petroleum engineer named Norm, whom I greatly respected and admired except for one trait. Norm swore like a trooper on almost every occasion and at any provocation, one of his most frequent utterances being "Jesus Christ!"

Norm asked a number of us familiar with the situation to put forward our suggestions as to what type of a person his company should be looking for to fill this mediatorial role. I suggested "someone who incorporates the perspectives and values of both sides, the oil patch and Indigenous community, and can live and operate in both worlds." I actually had someone in mind, a Metis businessman who lived in the area, who had successfully done business with the oil company for years, and who also hunted, fished, and lived with members of the band in question.[164] I presented Norm with all the reasons why this person would be the best hire if the reconciliation of the corporate interests with those of the band was the objective of the exercise. Norm also received alternative suggestions from others knowledgeable about the situation, including from his company's legal and public affairs departments.

Eventually the day came when Norm was to announce, in his usually colourful manner, his decision as to what kind of person the company should be looking for:

> "Our legal beagles think we should hire a lawyer of some sort who is familiar with the treaty rights of the band and all the legal aspects of our relationship with it. The PR people want me to hire some pretty face who will look good and convincing on TV explaining our positions if and when we get into disputes with the band. And Manning here … [Norm paused for effect] … Manning wants us to hire Jesus Christ!"

Someone else then suggested, tongue firmly in cheek, that perhaps the company should take all the candidates for the position down to the Athabasca River (which bisects north central Alberta) and hire the first one who could walk across on top of the water.

It was all said in jest, but I found it significant that somehow hard-boiled Norm seemed to recognize in a job description calling for "someone who incorporates the perspectives and values of both sides … and can live and operate in both worlds" a likeness to Jesus Christ. If the reconciliation of conflicting interests was the goal, this assessment of the type of mediator required was perhaps more insightful than he knew.

Future Applications

Our world abounds in conflicts. Conflicts between husbands and wives, parents and children, labour and management, the rich and the poor, resource developers and environmentalists, public and private interests, Protestants and Catholics in Northern Ireland, Israelis and Arabs in the Middle East, tribal groups in Africa, Islamic extremists and the West … the

---

[164] *Metis* refers to the offspring of a North American Indigenous person and a White person, especially one of French ancestry. In my experience, people of "mixed race" can often play a key role in reconciling the conflicts and tensions between the racial groups from which their own lives are derived.

list goes on and on. In every instance there is a need for the reconciliation of conflicting interests.

In Canada, the most tragic and long-standing conflict situation in need of reconciliation and healing is that involving the relationship between our Indigenous peoples and the rest of Canadian society. In recent years, the past and present status of this relationship and how to achieve reconciliation have been the subject of a massive Royal Commission study and report, public apologies by the government of Canada and Christian leaders for past wrongs inflicted on Indigenous peoples through the residential school system, and most recently by the work of the Truth and Reconciliation Commission headed by Justice Murray Sinclair.[165]

To address the reconciliation challenges presented by any and all of these conflicts, a variety of arbitration, dispute settling, peacemaking, and reconciliation processes are available for application. These processes make up the reconciliation *tool kit* available to any peacemaker and include the following:

- Separation models, in which the disputants go their separate ways. The conflict is reduced or eliminated by absence of contact, and "peace" is achieved at the price of the relationship.
- War models, in which the disputants fight it out until the strongest or the smartest prevails. The conflict is resolved, temporarily and usually with much bitterness, when one party is able to impose its will on the other.
- Dictatorial models, whereby an authority superior in strength to the disputants enforces settlements, and peace is established at the expense of freedom.
- Surrender models, in which interests and positions are surrendered by one or the other of the disputants for the sake of peace or in the hope of surviving to fight another day.
- Educational models, in which disputants, with the help of sympathetic counselling, are urged to seek accommodation through increased understanding and appreciation of their own interests and those of the other side.
- Transactional or bargaining models, such as occur in the marketplace or in labour management arbitration, whereby conflict resolution is achieved through mutually advantageous trade-offs and compromises.
- Jurisprudential models, in which the conflicts between disputants are submitted to judicial authority or independent third parties for binding arbitration.

[165] See Report of the Royal Commission on Aboriginal Peoples, Government of Canada (1996); Statement of Apology to Former Students of Indian Residential Schools by Prime Minister Stephen Harper on behalf of the Government of Canada, 39th Parliament, sess. 2, ed. Hansard, no. 110 (June 11, 2008); and Final Report of the Truth and Reconciliation Commission of Canada, Government of Canada (2015).

- Political models, which in democracies involve the submission of conflicts to a representative assembly, in which the disputants have the freedom to make their case but must submit to the will of the majority with respect to a settlement.

Whereas applications of the separation, war, dictatorial, and surrender models are ultimately destructive to the achievement of harmonious relationships, there is certainly merit in applying, where appropriate, the educational, transactional, jurisprudential, and political models to conflict resolution. For the Christian, however, is it not also our responsibility to bring the Jesus approach to reconciliation to bear on those conflicts in which we are involved either as disputants or as mediators? Is this not the approach we should gently but firmly commend to our secular friends as the model of *last resort* when other approaches to conflict resolution have been tried and found wanting?

The apostle Paul, who sought to follow Jesus' approach to conflict resolution in both its vertical and horizontal dimensions, once wrote that it models and foreshadows the method and the means whereby the Author of our existence will ultimately "reconcile to himself all things."[166] And to those of us who seek to apply it to the conflict situations in which we find ourselves embedded, there is the great hope and encouragement offered by Jesus himself: "Blessed are the peacemakers, for they will be called children of God."[167]

[166] Colossians 1:20.

[167] Matthew 5:9.

1.12 THE JUDAS WAY

THE SELF-SACRIFICIAL ACT THAT WAS AT THE HEART OF Jesus' approach to reconciliation occurred within a distinctively political context. In fact, the circumstances surrounding his arrest, trial, and execution are the most explicitly political of all the circumstances encountered by Jesus and his small band during the three years of his public work. They included political unrest in the city of Jerusalem, political scheming by his religious opponents, an unholy alliance between the ecclesiastical and political authorities, a direct encounter with Roman authority, the payment and receipt of a bribe, the mobilization of soldiers, and the mobilization of a mob—all culminating in a mock trial, an unjust verdict, and a state-sanctioned public execution.

Jesus' own conduct under these circumstances, his navigation of the faith-political interface on this occasion, and his continued pursuit of the *Jesus way* under these conditions stand out in stark contrast to the course of action that he and his followers might have pursued had they been guided by political instincts devoid of any spiritual ethic or motivation such as that which guided Jesus.

For example, what if the disciples, increasingly alarmed by the unfamiliar and threatening circumstances in which they were finding themselves, had called in Lucifer Inc., the top political consulting firm of the day, for advice on how to extricate themselves from an increasingly dangerous political situation? Or imagine if they could have acquired access to one of the top political consulting firms of our day—a firm whose principals are strategically clever and experienced but totally secular. What advice might the Jesus party have been given and how might it have contrasted with the Jesus way—the course of action Jesus actually pursued?

To illustrate the difference between the Jesus way and the course of action that might have been recommended by a top consulting firm, please allow me to engage in a fictional account of what could well have been going through the mind and heart of Judas Iscariot, the disciple who ultimately rejected the Jesus way and betrayed his master to his enemies. While the following description of *the Judas way* is fictional, it is nonetheless plausible in that Judas was in many respects the most political of Jesus' disciples and quite capable of acting as described hereafter. I believe this fictional tale to be particularly instructive to those who would seek to use Jesus for their own political ends, no matter how noble or well-intended those ends might be.

THE JUDAS WAY

Judas Iscariot, unlike most of Jesus' disciples, is not a rustic Galilean. He is from Judea and apparently well enough connected in Jerusalem to have ready access to the ecclesiastical and political authorities. Perhaps more than any of the other disciples, Judas believes that Jesus is, or at least could become, the *political* Messiah of Israel—the one who could free the Jewish people from the iron yoke of Rome just as Moses freed them from bondage in Egypt centuries before.

Judas' conception of the Messiah as a political and military leader is increasingly at odds with Jesus' presentation of himself as the son of a Father God whose ultimate mission is the reconciliation of human beings to God and to each other through the exercise of self-sacrificial love. And Judas finds it increasingly incomprehensible that Jesus should willingly sacrifice himself for the sake of establishing some ethereal spiritual kingdom rather than taking advantage of his current popularity with the public to motivate and lead them politically in a crusade against Rome. Is not Galilee, where Jesus' influence is the greatest, already more than ripe for such a revolution? Therefore, Judas (in this fictional scenario) becomes more and more convinced that he must rescue Jesus from the futility of his spiritual quest and persuade him to pursue the political mission that Jesus is ideally positioned to lead.

As Jesus and his small band make their way to Jerusalem, Judas takes one other disciple into his confidence—Simon the Zealot, formerly a member of a radical and violent political group dedicated to the liberation of the Jewish people from the Romans. Of all the disciples, Simon the Zealot is the one most likely to share Judas' perspective.

Judas says to Simon, "If Jesus continues to do and say the things he's doing and saying, the chief priests and Pharisees are going to instigate his arrest by the Romans and insist on his execution, probably by crucifixion. Jesus won't resist it, Simon. In fact, he'll acquiesce because of his personal conviction that this is his destiny. He continues to insist that his mission is to establish some kind of 'kingdom of heaven,' which neither you nor I nor most of the people either understand or want."

"But," protests Simon, "I left the Zealots to follow him. Let's continue to follow and see where he leads."

"No," says Judas vehemently. "Following him further is going to lead to disaster, not just for him but for those of us identified with him. He's going to sacrifice us along with himself. We need to rescue him from the folly of this spiritual course and persuade him to use his influence with the people to pursue the true mission of the Messiah—liberation of our people from the yoke of these cursed Romans and the restoration of Israel as the independent nation that the God of Israel always intended us to be."

"So what are you suggesting?" asks Simon.

Judas enthusiastically whispers his plan as they plod along the road to Jerusalem. "You, Simon, will restore your contacts with the Zealots. We're going to need their help. When Jesus is arrested, as he surely will be soon, he'll be shuttled between the court of the high priest and Pilate's court. Or, if worst comes to worst, between Pilate's court and Golgotha where the Romans crucify criminals. So we form two groups. One company of your Zealot friends starts a fire at the Roman stables on the outskirts of Jerusalem—something big enough and threatening enough to draw away a major portion of the garrison. At that moment, the second group—you and I among them—will attack the smaller contingent guarding or transporting Jesus. We free him and then make for Galilee as fast as we can, where the people are ready to rise up against the Romans, either in direct rebellion or in support of a subversive underground liberation movement with Jesus as the inspirational figurehead."

"But," Simon again protests, "Jesus will never go along with such a plan."

"Not initially," says Judas. "But when the prospect of crucifixion becomes real, perhaps he will. And in the end, what is he going to do—refuse to come along with us when we rescue him from certain death? He's not going to have much choice if we handle this decisively—he's going to be our political Messiah whether he wants to be or not.

"At some point we'll have to share this plan with Jesus and the others and convince them to support it. But not yet. Let's get everything in place first, and then just before the Passover we'll persuade Jesus and the rest that this is the best, the only, course of action ultimately open to us if Jesus is to fulfill his true Messianic destiny."

And so the Judas conspiracy begins to take shape. The Zealots are contacted and are more than willing to participate. Rumours of Jesus' imminent arrest are increasingly heard in the temple courtyard and on the streets. Pilate and the Roman garrison are increasingly uneasy, anticipating "trouble" as the Passover nears.

To implement his plan, Judas must get a clearer idea of exactly when Jesus is likely to be apprehended. He therefore goes to the temple authorities and indicates that, for a fee, he will betray Jesus into their hands at the right moment if they will tell him when the arrest is to occur.

"Tomorrow night, late on the Passover evening" is their answer as they give Judas the thirty pieces of silver he has demanded to make the betrayal believable in their eyes.

Pleased at having obtained this intelligence, Judas meets with Simon early in the morning of the following day to finalize implementation of the plan.

"Today is the day of decision," Judas says to Simon. "My way or his. Political action or submission to a pagan political power in the name of God-knows-what. Get a few moments with Jesus alone this afternoon, before the Passover feast. Tell him what we have in mind. Tell him it's all arranged. Plead with him to go along with it, if not for his sake then for ours and for the sake of Israel. Then let me know what he says."

Simon does as he is told. He has a brief time with Jesus alone that very afternoon and seeks out Judas immediately after.

"Well," asks Judas anxiously, "what did he say?"

"Not much," says Simon. "He thanked me for my concern for our fellow disciples and the Jewish people. And he said that tonight just before the Passover supper he'll have some words to say to us that will make clear what path he intends to follow and that we can choose to follow or not. Then he asked me a strange question. He asked, 'Do you not know me, Simon, even after I have been among you such a long time?'—as if I should already know what he is going to say and do and needn't have asked."[168]

Judas slams his fist into his other hand in frustration. "He always talks in riddles, but the time for riddles is running out. Let's see what he has to say tonight, but be prepared for a confrontation between us. It's not just his life that's at stake but ours and the future of our people."

On Jesus' instructions, preparations have been made for the disciples to eat the Passover supper together. They gather in a large upper room and are conversing quietly among themselves when Jesus enters. He bids them sit but then gets up, wraps a towel around his waist, and proceeds like a household servant to wash their feet.

As Jesus kneels to wash Judas' feet, Judas tries to avoid his gaze. But Jesus looks straight at him as he says to them all, "You call me Teacher and Lord, and rightly so, for this is what I am. Now that I have washed your feet you should wash one another's feet."

Judas seethes internally. This is not a demonstration of the leadership of a political or military Messiah. This is the talk and actions of a lowly servant. As the evening proceeds, there is nothing in Jesus' conduct or word about political action. Nothing in his word or conduct about taking up the righteous sword to liberate God's people. Nothing in his word or conduct about escaping the terrible fate that hangs above all their heads by a thread. So this is his answer. Jesus is not going to be a political Messiah. He is not going to accept the aid of the Zealots. He is not going to take up the sword or encourage his followers to do so. Jesus is not going to take advantage of Judas' carefully laid out plan. And the rest of the disciples, hanging on his every word, are going to follow him like sheep to the slaughter.

Jesus seems to sense what is going on in Judas' mind and heart, for he again looks directly at him and says, "You are clean, though not every

[168] In the Gospel record, Jesus actually put this question to the disciple Philip (John 14:9). But he could have put it to any one of the disciples. He could put it to us—Christians who have long professed to follow him and yet have not fully learned his ways.

one of you." Shortly thereafter, as they sit at the table, Jesus offers Judas a piece of bread and says. "He who shares my bread has lifted up his heel against me."

Something in Judas suddenly yields to an alien and malevolent force. A spirit that he has flirted with in the past—a spirit of hatred and loathing—now fully possesses him. Jesus has betrayed the Messianic mission he could have fulfilled; well then, Judas will betray him. Judas rises to leave. Glancing at Simon, he jerks his head toward the door, silently ordering Simon to join him. But Simon slowly shakes his head and turns back to Jesus.

Judas flees into the night to betray his one-time master to the authorities. Shortly thereafter, in confusion and remorse over what he has done, he takes his own life.

Two thousand years ago, the Jesus way of dealing with political and ecclesiastical opposition to his teachings and actions (the Jesus way of going about the ultimate task of politics, which is the reconciliation of conflicting interests), was fundamentally different than the Judas way. Jesus refused to allow himself to be used politically by others: not by the prince of this world, who urged him to seize the sword of Caesar; not by the people who followed him because he could provide them with bread; not by the political Zealots, who wanted only a political Messiah; and not even by those of his own intimate circle who mistook or rejected his mission. Judas, more than any other disciple, epitomizes the Jesus follower who in the end wanted to use Jesus for political purposes at variance with, rather than submissive to, the Jesus way.

As it was then, so it remains to this day. And Christian believers at the interface of faith and public life and those with political instincts and interests—perhaps backgrounds steeped in the conventional political wisdom of our times—need to decide like Simon the Zealot did. Will it be the Jesus way or the Judas way?

1.13 FOLLOW ME!

ONE OF THE SIMPLEST AND EARLIEST INSTRUCTIONS THAT Jesus gave to his earliest disciples was "Follow me."[169] It was also one of the last instructions he gave to Peter in calling upon him to carry on the nurturing of the disciples and the ministry of reconciliation in Jesus' name.[170] So what does this mean with respect to following Jesus in his role and conduct as a public figure?

It means that we should seek to become receiver-oriented incarnational communicators who literally embody and personify the truths we desire to communicate; who immerse ourselves in the lives and communities of those we seek to influence and serve; and who frame our communications, to the maximum extent possible, within the conceptual frameworks and vocabularies of those we address.

It means rejecting the temptation to win the support and allegiance of others solely by promising to meet their most obvious and immediate needs; rejecting the temptation to assure them that there is no human need that cannot be met by the market or the state; and rejecting the temptation to rely on the spectacular, the marvellous, the mysterious, and all the magic of image marketing and image politics to win them over.

In particular, following Jesus in the public arena means resisting the temptation to accept political power and influence whenever it is offered, no matter by whom, no matter on what terms. This does not mean that Christians should refrain from seeking public office or from vigorously endeavouring to bring their values and influence to bear

---

[169] Matthew 4:19; Mark 1:17; Luke 5:27; John 1:43.

[170] John 21:19, 22.

on public policy and lawmaking; the central thesis of this entire book on navigating the interface of faith and public life is to better prepare believers to do precisely that. What following Jesus in the public arena does mean is resisting the temptation to gain political influence on the devil's terms. It especially means resisting the temptation to try to bring about the kingdom of heaven on earth by seizing the authority and powers of the state and using them to *compel* obedience to the Christian agenda, rather than by inviting men and women to freely choose to follow and serve Christ.

Following Jesus in preparing ourselves for public service should include adherence to his ethical standard—looking not to a moral code but to a person, Jesus himself, as our moral guide; making self-sacrificial love the supreme ethic to be pursued and practised; encouraging and rewarding those who put the interests of others ahead of their own while constraining those who consistently put their own self-interest ahead of everything else; and forming or joining a moral community or fellowship—preferably a small and intimate one—where that highest of ethical standards will be practised and where we will be supported and held accountable by others for doing so.

Following Jesus at the interface of faith, public life and politics also means being willing to unlearn as well as learn; being aware of *the dark side of the moon* and avoiding the religious and political extremes that may lurk in the shadows of our theologies and ideologies; and understanding the complementary relationship between conservation and change, recognizing that change is often necessary to conserve the principled purpose of an institution or practice.

Following Jesus in public life means redirecting our personal ambitions from the service of ourselves to the self-sacrificial service of others and taking to heart his declaration that "whosoever will be chief among you, let him be your servant."[171]

Following Jesus in the public arena especially means learning to follow the great guideline he gave to his earliest followers to be "wise as serpents and harmless as doves." Above all, it means bringing to the strife-ridden arena of contemporary politics the ministry of reconciliation—the unique, otherworldly, non-coercive, self-sacrificial approach to the

[171] Matthew 20:27 (KJV); see also Luke 22:26.

reconciliation of conflicting interests that Jesus so consistently taught and so dramatically demonstrated.

AN INVITATION TO THE SECULAR READER

I have primarily directed this summary of leadership lessons from the public life of Jesus to those who have a Christian commitment. But I would like to challenge my friends who do not share my faith—and probably think I am misguided in trying to apply it as I have, however imperfectly, to the practice of contemporary politics and public service—to *directly examine* for yourselves what Jesus has to say and teach.

By urging you to directly examine his life and teachings, my plea is for you to go to the source, the best source documents we have on his life and teachings being the Gospels. I suggest that such direct examination is preferable to basing your opinions about what genuine Christianity is about on your reading of secondary sources or your personal experiences of Christian derivatives and institutions far removed in time and space from his person, life, and words.

In your mind's eye, place yourself in a village in first-century Palestine. Jesus has come to spend a few days there, and you have the chance to meet and listen to him personally. Suppose he says and does even a tenth of the things he is reported to have said and done by the Gospel writers. Then, looking you straight in the eye, he gently says, "Follow me." What would you do? In my case, hard as it is for those of us with political ambitions to follow anyone, I think I can safely say that I would have followed. But, now, what about you?

THE HONOURABLE MEMBER FROM GALILEE

Jesus was not a member of any governing council, but he came to represent deliverance from evil, restoration of fellowship with God, food for the hungry, healing for the sick, help for the poor, comfort for the lonely, freedom for the oppressed, and the triumph of life over death.

He taught all who would listen—unlearned and learned alike. He spoke of evil as a reality from which people needed deliverance. And he told of a kingdom where the ruler is not a tyrant but a loving Father and where citizenship is based not on race or wealth but on faith and love.

The common people heard him gladly, and some actually wanted him to become the honourable member from Galilee. But he said his constituency was not of this world. And when some of his more zealous supporters came by force to make him a candidate, he withdrew himself from them.[172]

He told his followers that *they* were to be his representatives—salt and light—wherever God had placed them. *We* are to be his witnesses wherever God has placed us.

So, if you are a Christian believer called to practise your faith in some public arena, perhaps *you* could be the honourable member from Galilee, representing not just your constituents, party, or particular interests but also him: on your student or municipal council, in a provincial or state legislature, in a national parliament or congress, or in whatever public arena you have been called upon to serve.

Remember what he represented: deliverance from evil, restoration of fellowship with God, food for the hungry, healing for the sick, help for the poor, comfort for the lonely, freedom for the oppressed, life over death, faith in a loving Father, and a kingdom distinguished by love.

Remember also that he especially charged his followers to be wise as serpents (not foolish) and gracious as doves (not threatening) in all their public work and representations of him.

So who will be the honourable member from Galilee in your community? Could it be you? Will it be you?

If so, will your representation of Jesus be conducted with the wisdom of the serpent and the graciousness of the dove—the only kind of representation he authorizes and honours?

---

[172] John 6:14–15.

PART 2:

LEADERSHIP LESSONS

from the Life of Moses

INTRODUCTION

THERE ARE MORE REFERENCES TO MOSES AND THE LAW of Moses in the teachings and discourses of Jesus of Nazareth than to any other leader of Israel or prophet. In his Sermon on the Mount, for example, he referenced the law of Moses eight times. In his other discourses he referenced God's dealings with Adam and Eve, Noah, and Abraham—all historical incidents described in the books of Moses. After Jesus' resurrection, he was in conversation with two of his disheartened disciples on the Emmaus road, and it was reported that "Beginning with Moses and all the Prophets, he explained to them what was said in all the Scriptures concerning himself."[173]

Moses deserves our serious attention from the standpoint of his profound influence on the life and teachings of Jesus. But as one of the best known religious and political leaders in history, Moses is worthy of study in his own right—particularly by those seeking to successfully navigate the interface of faith and public life.

From a leadership standpoint, Moses encountered virtually every trial and circumstance that a modern leader faces: fierce opposition from external opponents; the burden of overwork and the need to delegate; the challenges of executive decision-making, administration, and law making; threats to his leadership from his closest associates (arguably the most trying form of opposition a leader faces); continuous criticism and complaining from his followers; shortages of resources; the charge that he had broken his promises; outright rebellion against his leadership; the roller coaster ride between great accomplishments and profound disappoint-

[173] Luke 24:27.

ments; the strain that leadership puts on family life; and the problem of succession.

At the same time, Moses was a leader whose intimate relationship with his Creator involved a sense of divine calling or providential positioning; numerous experiences with the miraculous; a constant effort to discern God's will with respect to governance; the communication and enforcement of God-given laws and standards; lawmaking, particularly in relation to morality, mediation, and intercession; experience with the benefits, abuses, and limits to the Rule of Law; encounters with evil in all its forms; the challenge of maintaining the spirit of the laws in competition with their material and ceremonial embodiments; and the reception and interpretation of revelations of the character of God that profoundly affected both his political and spiritual leadership.

There is therefore much for anyone involved in public life, politics, and government to learn from the life of Moses. There is especially much for contemporary Christians with political interests and ambitions to learn, starting with the concept of the providential positioning of believers so that they can join with God in his work in the world.

2.1 POLITICAL INVOLVEMENT

IN DEMOCRATIC SOCIETIES SUCH AS CANADA IT IS imperative that citizens involve themselves in democratic processes and institutions—informing themselves on public issues, recruiting and supporting candidates for public office, voting in elections, running for public office, and actively engaging in public debate and advocacy. The motivations for doing so range from the unabashed pursuit of self-interest to the selfless and altruistic pursuit of the public interest.

In my view, it is particularly important that people of faith involve themselves in the politics of their community and their country. We too are citizens with political responsibilities, and if we are Christian believers we have the added faith-based responsibility to bring the salt and light of the life and teachings of Jesus to bear on all the various systems and circumstances in which we find ourselves placed.

So what principles should guide the person of faith, in particular the Christian believer, with respect to political involvement? Does the God in whom we believe involve himself in the politics of this world? Does he actually call believers to political involvement, and if so, in what ways? How does one discern a providential call to political involvement, if there is such a thing? Most importantly, how do believers avoid being deceived into believing that a call rooted in ulterior motives and ambitions is a providential calling?

In the following pages, we explore answers to these questions by examining the life of Moses—led, according to his own testimony, reluctantly and haltingly at first, by the hand of God from the palace of the pharaoh of Egypt to become the liberator, lawgiver, and leader of the Hebrew people.

This exploration is particularly relevant to the person of faith seeking to understand God's leadings with respect to political involvement. But such an exploration is also relevant to the secular reader seeking to better understand the faith-based involvements of faith-motivated political activists in our times, in particular those whose faith is rooted in the wisdom and traditions of Judaism, Christianity, or Islam.

THE PATTERN

There is a discernable pattern in the religious experience and practices of humanity that has prevailed from the dawn of time to our present age—people of faith desiring and sometimes earnestly seeking a deeper understanding of God being rewarded with a particular revelation of who God is and how he involves himself in the world and acting on that revelation in some concrete way. Our earliest ancestors seemed most conscious of God as the Creator and sustainer of life, saw him most often as active in nature and the life and death of his creatures, and feared and worshipped him as such. As we have seen, the most revolutionary aspect of Jesus' ministry was his conceptualization of God as a loving Father actively at work in reconciling human beings to himself and to each other. But in the intervening centuries perhaps the most prevalent conceptualization of God was that of a supreme ruler whose principal involvement in human affairs was political—as a warrior-king, lawgiver, and judge.

The writer of the letter to the Hebrews declared, "Anyone who comes to him [God] must believe that he exists and that he rewards those who earnestly seek him."[174] He then specifically mentioned Moses as one who "persevered because he saw him who is invisible."[175] Moses, as we will see, recorded five instances in which he received a distinct revelation of God's identity and his involvement in the world. Three of these were political involvements—God as liberator involved in freeing the Hebrew people from bondage in Egypt, God as warrior involved in delivering the fleeing Hebrews from Pharaoh's pursuing chariots, and God as lawgiver and

[174] Hebrews 11:6.

[175] Hebrews 11:27.

judge at Mount Sinai, where Moses received the Ten Commandments. But let us begin our study with Moses' early life and calling.

MOSES' EARLY CAREER AND LEADERSHIP EXPERIENCE

Moses was born into a Hebrew family, miraculously rescued as a baby from the waters of the Nile by an Egyptian princess, then nursed by his own mother, who then took him to the princess to be raised in Pharaoh's household.[176] Eventually he would encounter the call of God in a most dramatic way at a bush that was on fire but did not burn up.[177] But long before that encounter, he was providentially positioned for future political activity by virtue of the unique circumstances surrounding his birth, his early upbringing, and his cultural heritage.

Initially, Moses was providentially positioned in a highly *privileged* position—a prince of Egypt living in the household of Pharaoh. From this position, he no doubt gained an understanding of the inner workings of the Egyptian government and the strengths and weaknesses of Egypt's ruling class, including the Egyptian military—understandings that would eventually stand him in good stead in seeking to negotiate and lead the liberation of his own people.

But being providentially placed in a privileged political position also appears to carry with it corresponding obligations—in Moses' case, to use his privileged upbringing and understanding to liberate his people. Privileged providential positioning was not an unconditional blessing or an end in itself but a *means to an end*, an end that God would eventually reveal to Moses in a clear and unmistakable way.

Having found himself providentially placed in a privileged position, there was still much that Moses did not know about his calling or future mission. What Moses did see from where he stood were the injustices being done to his own people by the Egyptians and by the Hebrews to each other. In response to this, something—one might argue divine prompting—impelled him to take action, to intervene. He saw an Egyptian abusing a Hebrew slave, killed the Egyptian, and buried the body in the sand. The next day he saw two Hebrews fighting among themselves and intervened again, only to be asked "Who made you ruler

---

[176] Exodus 2:1–10.

[177] Exodus 3:1–12.

and judge over us?"[178] His crime revealed, his interventions on behalf of his people rebuffed, Moses was forced to flee Egypt and began a forty-year exile in Midian herding sheep.[179] This failure of his first attempt to exert political leadership shook to the core Moses' self-confidence as a potential liberator and leader of Israel.

IMPLICATIONS FOR US

If there is such a thing as providential positioning, as the experience of Moses indicates, it is appropriate to ask, What does *our* positioning by birth, cultural heritage, and personal circumstances suggest in terms of possible future political and spiritual activity?

In my case, I was raised in a home that was both evangelical Christian and political; my father was elected to the Alberta legislature in the midst of the Great Depression and served there for 33 years, 25 as premier. As a young person, I never experienced much difficulty in accepting the basic tenets of the Christian faith; my struggles were more with how it works out in practice and how it applies to business, science, and politics. Although my father never encouraged me to become directly active in the political sphere, I absorbed enough of politics, government, and western Canadian political history to have a sense of the most appropriate time to enter the political arena, and I eventually did so—mainly for the purpose of creating a new political movement based in western Canada and dedicated to reforming Canadian federal politics.[180]

As Christians in the Western world, relatively well endowed with resources and freedoms to practise and communicate our faith, many of us like Moses are providentially privileged. If so, what are the corresponding obligations that our privileged position confers upon us, particularly with respect to serving others less fortunate than ourselves?

Caution of course needs to be exercised in interpreting any particular providential leading from our positioning by birth, cultural heritage, or personal circumstances. For instance, there was little in the humble positioning of the shepherd boy David to suggest that he was being prepared to be king of Israel (other than that herding sheep is good

---

[178] Exodus 2:14.

[179] See Exodus 2:14–22.

[180] For more on my adventures in Canadian federal politics, see Manning, *Think Big*.

preparation for politics, as some cynics have said). Yet David became one of God's greatest political and spiritual leaders. Wisdom and discernment are needed to interpret where our positioning might—or might not—be providentially leading, but there is still great merit in personally addressing the questions that the concept of providential leading raises.

The failure of Moses' initial leadership attempt also raises several questions from a spiritual perspective. Should he have waited on God for more specific leading and instruction on the how (God's way) and the when (God's timing) of the liberation of his Hebrew brethren? Or was Moses' failed attempt a necessary step on his journey as a leader? Could it be that Moses' confidence in himself as a potential liberator and leader of Israel *needed* to be shaken to the core before God could use him in such capacities?

Applying these considerations to our own situations, how inclined are we to wait on God until we have clear direction, and how do we reconcile this need to wait with the apparent need to seize an opportunity? Second, where, what, or who is the source of *our* confidence that we can lead—a *self*-confidence that is usually deemed necessary in order to lead successfully?

There is an old saying that in politics "timing is everything." There is a time to wait patiently and there is a time to take advantage of the situation. As Brutus put it in *Julius Caesar*,

> There is a tide in the affairs of men,
> Which, taken at the flood, leads on to fortune;
> Omitted, all the voyage of their life
> Is bound in shallows and in miseries.
> On such a full sea are we now afloat,
> And we must take the current when it serves,
> Or lose our ventures.[181]

But as some wag has also observed,

> There is a tide in the affairs of men
> Which, taken at the flood, leads to certain death …
> by drowning.

[181] William Shakespeare, *Julius Caesar*, act 4, scene 3.

So how does the believer get a proper sense of God's timing for political involvement? The general thrust of the Scriptures on this point is that the believer, especially the zealous believer, is apt to rush the timing, whereas the spirit of God more often counsels patience.[182]

My own approach to discerning correct timing for political involvement, which I do not hold out as exemplary, involved sensing a long-run political opportunity on the distant horizon; questioning whether this insight might be God-given or not; and waiting for some sort of confirmation. And then, unless otherwise directed, praying for God's guidance and blessing with respect to seizing the opportunity.

MOSES' DIRECT CALLING

In addition to Moses' early positional calling, he later received what might be called a *direct calling,* as described in the story of his encounter with God at the burning bush. In this encounter Moses received direct and explicit instruction to enter the political arena.

God begins by giving Moses a special revelation of himself as the eternally present one—the "I AM."[183] As previously mentioned, this is the first of five special revelations of the nature and character of God received by Moses during his lifetime, three of which modelled for Moses what he himself was to do politically.[184]

One might conclude, therefore, that in the life of a believer a fresh revelation of the nature and character of God is a key dimension of any direct calling. In Moses' case—as in the commissioning of Isaiah—the revelation of I AM precedes the call to go and do.[185] The revelation of who God is precedes the receiving of the particular assignment.

Having revealed himself in a spectacular way at the burning bush, God then informs Moses what God is doing and what he intends to do with respect to the liberation of the Hebrew people. He tells Moses,

---

[182] Note that it was the failure to wait that doomed the leadership of Saul, Israel's first king, to both spiritual and political failure (1 Samuel 13:1–15). Consider also the counsel of David to "wait patiently" for God's direction (Psalm 37:7; see also 27:14) and the counsel of Jesus to his disciples to wait in Jerusalem until endowed for service by his spirit (Acts 1:4).

[183] See Exodus 3:4–14.

[184] God is revealed as the eternal "I AM," Liberator, Warrior, Judge and Lawgiver, and Grace. See chapter 2.2.

[185] Isaiah 6.

> "*I* have indeed seen the misery of my people in Egypt. *I* have heard them crying out because of their slave drivers, and *I* am concerned about their suffering. So *I have come down* to rescue them from the hand of the Egyptians and to bring them up out of that land into a good and spacious land, a land flowing with milk and honey."[186]

God's approach to liberating the Hebrew people is very different from Moses' first initiative in this regard. Further, Moses' reaction to the direct call of God to political involvement is not what one would expect from someone who once aspired to leadership. Moses, his self-confidence long ago shattered and further diminished by forty years of herding sheep far from any circle of political influence, professes himself to be incapable of doing what God demands and pleads with him to "send someone else."[187]

God's providential leading of Moses into political involvement involves revealing to Moses what God himself is doing and instructing Moses to join him in that endeavour. As we later see, this appears to be one of the primary ways in which God guides believers into political involvement. He first shows us more of himself and what he himself is doing and then invites or instructs us to join him in that work.

A similar pattern is evident in Jesus' explanation of his own calling:

> "My Father is always at his work to this very day, and I too am working … The Son can do nothing by himself; he can do only what he sees his Father doing, because whatever the Father does the Son also does. For the Father loves the Son and shows him all he does."[188]

IMPLICATIONS FOR US

How does God call believers to political involvement if and when he does so? By revealing to believers who he is and what he himself is already doing in the world. As a believer, how does one discern and respond to God's call to political involvement? By drawing near to God's presence and ascertaining what he is already doing—things that we may have already endeavoured to do unsuccessfully in our own strength as Moses did—and joining in.

---

[186] Exodus 3:7–8, emphasis added.

[187] See Exodus 4:1–17.

[188] John 5:17, 19–20.

With respect to receiving and responding to a providential calling to political action, I must confess to personally having had no clear sense of a direct calling to enter federal politics or to found a new political party, though I employed the usual Christian tools for attempting to discern God's will on these matters: prayer, searching the Scriptures for guidance, and consulting fellow believers. The one aspect of my own experience that somewhat corresponds to the idea that we believers get our lead as to what we should be doing in the world politically by perceiving what God appears to be doing has to do with reconciliation.

Christians believe that God is active in the world to "reconcile to himself all things" through Christ;[189] democratic politics at its highest level is also about the reconciliation of conflicting interests by non-coercive means. Therefore, seeing the political arena as an arena where God is carrying out what the apostle Paul called the ministry of reconciliation can become a calling of sorts to the Christian believer who sees the work of God and political participation in this light.

Without in any way suggesting that my own experience is exemplary or denying that there is such a thing as a direct calling to political action, my inclination, nevertheless, is to advise caution—caution demanding spiritual discernment—if one thinks that one has received a direct calling of God to act politically.

In my experience, those believers who profess to having received such a calling more often than not deceive themselves and their faith-oriented supporters. They mistake the call of personal political ambition, the call of their friends and supporters, or the call of political opportunity or necessity—all appropriately spiritualized—as the call of God.

THE CALL TO BE, AS DISTINCT FROM THE CALL TO DO

So how can one distinguish between a truly providential calling and the siren call of other leadings? The answer, I believe, lies in the broader teaching of Scripture on the need to distinguish between the call to do and the call to be.

Since leaving the active political arena and having more time to reflect on these matters than when in the heat of battle, I have been led to give much more weight to the call to *be,* as distinct from the call to *do*—the

[189] Colossians 1:20.

call to *be* a person motivated and shaped by the person of Jesus and called into an intimate relationship with him. It is out of this deeper call that the providential call to do will eventually flow. It is responding to the call to be—a person modelled after the person of Jesus—that is our greatest safeguard against self-deception with respect to the call to do.

The call to be is embedded throughout the biblical story. The apostle Peter (a man of action if there ever was one), in the light of cataclysmic predictions concerning the destruction of the current world order, did not give early believers a to-do list. Rather he said, since all these things are going to happen, "what kind of people ought you to *be*? You ought to live holy and godly lives as you look forward to the day of God and speed its coming."[190] The same call is made to us today, in spite of whatever cataclysmic predictions might be made concerning the state and fate of the world.

There is such a thing as God's *call to do*—including the call to political service—such as Moses received at the burning bush. That said, I believe such callings to be relatively rare and that great discernment is required to distinguish the true calling from the false. On the other hand, the *call to be* the kind of people God wants us to be is much more clear. This is the higher calling out of which the call to action in partnership with God will flow.

This *call to be* is most clearly described by the apostle Paul in his letter to the Ephesians and invites our wholehearted response:

> I urge you to live a life worthy *of the calling you have received.*
> *Be completely humble and gentle; be patient,* bearing with one another in love.
> *No longer be infants,* tossed back and forth by the waves, and blown here and there by every wind of teaching …
> Instead *[be truthful]*, speaking the truth in love.
> Put off your old self … [and] *be made new* in the attitude of your minds …
> Put on the new self … *be like God* in true righteousness.
> *Be kind and compassionate* to one another, forgiving each other, just as in Christ God forgave you …
> *Be imitators of God* … as dearly loved children and live a life of love, just as Christ loved us and gave himself up for us …
> *Be very careful,* then, how you live …
> *Be wise* not unwise, making the most of every opportunity …
> *Do not be foolish,* but understand what the Lord's will is …

190 2 Peter 3:11–12, emphasis added.

Be filled with the Holy Spirit …
Be thankful to God the Father for everything in the name of our Lord Jesus Christ.[191]

[191] Ephesians 4:1–2, 14–15, 22–23, 32; 5:1–2, 15–18, 20, emphasis added and some paraphrasing.

2.2 AT WORK WITH GOD

AT SOME POINT, EVERY LEADER FACES THE CALL AND responsibility to act. For people of faith, actions are undertaken and shaped by a variety of factors, including our spiritual convictions. Focusing again on the life of Moses, we now examine the fundamental relationship between God's character, his active presence in the world, and our own actions.

GOD REVEALS HIMSELF TO MOSES

In the book of Exodus Moses recorded five distinct revelations that he received from God concerning who God is and what he was doing—revelations that then guided Moses as to what he was to do as the leader of Israel. These revelations included,

- God revealing himself as the eternally present *I AM* to Moses at the burning bush.
- God revealing himself (also at the burning bush) as *liberator*—the God who has come to free his captive people from bondage in Egypt.
- God revealing himself as *warrior*—the God who fights for his people—at the Red Sea where the Egyptian army and cavalry are miraculously destroyed. In ecstasy Moses pens a victory song, rejoicing that "Both horse and driver he [the LORD] has hurled into the sea."[192]
- God revealing himself as *lawmaker* and *judge* at Mount Sinai, where Moses receives the Ten Commandments.
- God revealing himself again at Mount Sinai as the God of *love, mercy, grace, and compassion* when Moses is summoned a second time to the top of the mountain. God is not only a just lawmaker and judge; he is also the God who forgives sin, even the sin of rebellion.

[192] Exodus 15:1.

Once Moses had fresh insights into God as the liberator of Israel and God as lawgiver and judge, he was able to join in the work he perceived God to be doing. While this participation was entered into with great reluctance in the case of returning to Egypt—where his previous self-directed liberation effort had failed—it was wholehearted when it came to proclaiming and administering the law of God to Israel.

GOD AS LIBERATOR, LAWGIVER, AND JUDGE

The liberation of the Hebrew people from slavery in Egypt has been a great inspiration to people in bondage from ancient times to the present. The story is at the heart of the theology and sacred celebrations of Judaism. It inspired the victims of slavery liberated by the Wilberforce campaign in Britain and the Civil War in the United States. It has informed and inspired the civil rights movement in America and the outworking of liberation theology in Latin America. So much has been written and spoken on this theme, both theologically and politically, that I can add little to it, other than to make the following observation, which flows from Moses' representation to the Hebrew people concerning the twofold object of true liberation.

Liberation for the Hebrew people was to mean freedom *from* bondage in Egypt. But God intended it to mean more than that. It was also to mean freedom *to* something—to worship and serve God. "Then the LORD said to Moses, 'Go to Pharaoh and say to him, "This is what the LORD, the God of the Hebrews, says: 'Let my people go *so that* they may worship me.'"'"[193]

So while the work of Moses as God's partner in liberating the Hebrews *from* slavery in Egypt took only a short time, the work of Moses as God's partner in leading the Hebrews *to* worship and serve their divine liberator occupied the rest of his life.

Proclamation and administration of the law of God became the primary instrument whereby the new-found liberty of the Hebrew people was to be governed and prevented from disintegrating into license and some new form of bondage. The aspect of God's character and work that Moses most consistently represented to the Hebrew people, over the longest period of time, and under the greatest variety

[193] Exodus 9:1, emphasis added.

of circumstances was that of God as *lawgiver and judge*, the focus of the following chapter.

GOD AS WARRIOR—MOSES' FAVOURITE CONCEPTION OF GOD

As believers we are susceptible to developing a favourite conception of God to which we cling and which may even blind us to greater and more relevant revelations of God and his (and therefore our) work.

In the case of Moses, for example, it would appear that it was the revelation of God as warrior that became his favourite conception of God. This may have been because military command was part of Moses' upbringing in Pharaoh's household.[194] Or perhaps it was because Moses anticipated the future military battles that Israel would face in order to occupy the Promised Land. As a leader Moses found his greatest security in God as the one who fights for his people. It was this conception of God that lifted him to poetic heights of ecstasy after God's interventions on behalf of Israel at the Red Sea.

For Moses, however, there was a danger in holding and being guided by his preference for the "God as warrior" revelation. The danger was that it could, and did, blind him to an even more needful revelation of God's character and work—God as grace. Could it likewise be so for us?

GOD AS GRACE—THE CONCEPTION OF GOD THAT MOSES LEAST UNDERSTOOD

The fifth and last great revelation of God's character and work came to Moses when he and the people of Israel had been ordered to leave Mount Sinai and proceed to the Promised Land.[195] It began paradoxically by God declaring first what he would *not* do—"I will not go with you, because you are a stiff-necked people."

In one of his most revealing discourses, Moses then responded by pleading with God not to send Israel forth unless God's presence accompanied them. God relented and replied, "My Presence will go with you, and I will give you rest." But Moses wanted more, looking specifically

[194] According to Josephus, Moses himself once led an Egyptian military force into Ethiopia (*Antiquities of the Jews*, 2.9.2–2.11.1).

[195] See Exodus 33 to 34:7.

for assurance that God would manifest himself again as the warrior who fights for his people. He pleaded, "Now show me your glory"—glory in Moses' mind no doubt meaning the strength and glory of the warrior God who fought for his people.

God responded by saying that, yes, he would manifest his glory. He would do so, but not by a display of his warrior powers and might as Moses wished. Rather, he would show him "my goodness [grace, mercy, compassion]."

God then ordered Moses to ascend Mount Sinai a second time with two more tablets of stone, on which the law would be re-inscribed. When he did so, Moses received this incomparable revelation of the character and work of God:

> Then the LORD came down in the cloud and stood there with him and proclaimed his name, the LORD. And he passed in front of Moses, proclaiming, "The LORD, the LORD, the compassionate and gracious God, slow to anger, abounding in love and faithfulness, maintaining love to thousands, and forgiving wickedness, rebellion and sin. Yet he does not leave the guilty unpunished; he punishes the children and their children for the sin of the parents to the third and fourth generation."[196]

Sadly, this is the revelation of God that Moses seemed to have the greatest difficulty comprehending and accepting. Perhaps it was because God declared that he was even prepared to forgive rebellion—something Moses could never quite bring himself to do. While Moses never tired of reminding Israel of God the liberator, God the warrior, and God the lawgiver, what he heard and saw when he ascended Mount Sinai a second time was scarcely mentioned in his final addresses to Israel.

IMPLICATIONS FOR US: THE NEED FOR SEEING GOD AT WORK

It is helpful to reflect on our own experience of receiving and acting upon a faith-based understanding of who God is and what he is doing.

Have you ever received a fresh understanding of who God is or seen him at work as he was in the life of Moses? Did you see that realization as a call to join in that work? Seeing where God is already at work can help us to clearly discern the difference between the call to action that is

[196] Exodus 34:5–7.

rooted in faith and the call to action that is otherwise motivated and self-directed.

With respect to my own experience with Christians in Canadian politics, I would venture to say that most of us, regrettably, have *not* had any fresh understanding of God's character or activity in our country that can truly inspire or direct our personal political efforts.

In western Canada we have examples from our past: church ministers like J. S. Woodsworth and Tommy Douglas (on the left) and Christian laymen like William Aberhart and my father, Ernest Manning (on the right), all of whom were specifically inspired and led by their Christian convictions to found political movements that would address the suffering and injustices of the Great Depression.

And then there are the examples of the women who became politically active in the suffragette, prohibition, and farmers' movements in the first part of the 20th century, many drawing their inspiration and sustenance from their religious convictions and experience. Nellie McClung, one of the "Famous Five" who secured the recognition of women as "persons" in Canadian law, was also a crusading member of the missionary-oriented Methodist Church. On the gravestone of Henrietta Muir, co-founder of the National Council of Women in Canada and the Victorian Order of Nurses, are inscribed the words "Her delight was in the law of the Lord." And Louise McKinney, one of the first two women elected to a legislature in the British Empire and founder of the Women's Christian Temperance Union, was also one of the first commissioners of the newly formed United Church of Canada.

Despite all these inspiring examples from the interface of faith and politics in our past, our current generation of Christian-oriented political activists is more like Moses in Egypt *before* his burning-bush experience. We are engaged in well-intended efforts to address the challenges of the day, but rather than stemming from and drawing inspiration from a revelation of God at work, these efforts are largely self-directed and driven by other influences.

We see injustices—income inequality, gender inequality, or the intergenerational injustice of chronic deficit spending, for example—and are moved to do something to address them. But are such efforts really any different from those efforts to address such injustices that are rooted motivationally in humanism, the social sciences, and secular political philosophies?

If this assessment is correct, then it points to our desperate need for a fresh revelation of God's character and work in our time. If we are to bring anything more than human wisdom and resources to bear on addressing the ills of society we need more and clearer revelations of the nature and work of God in our time—the contemporary equivalent of those received by Moses.

IMPLICATIONS FOR US: GOD AS LIBERATOR

One of the characteristics of almost all liberation movements is their tendency to major on the *freedom from* aspect—the aspect most conducive to motivating the unfree—and neglecting the *freedom to* aspect. This is true even in the area of spiritual liberation; we evangelicals, for example, place much more emphasis on securing freedom from the bondage of sin than we do on the ends to which that freedom is to be exercised.

Surely we can learn the need for this balance from the liberation experience of the Hebrews under Moses. In the Old Testament Scriptures, fewer than ten chapters are devoted to the liberation of the Hebrews from slavery in Egypt; dozens more chapters are devoted to how they are to exercise that freedom in service to God and each other under the law of God.

Let us, therefore, place as much or more emphasis on the *freedom to* dimension of the liberation movements of our time as we place on the *freedom from* dimension. Let us place as much or more emphasis on developing the institutions and processes whereby the new liberties are to be governed as we do to dismantling those institutions and processes that hold people in bondage. Let us place as much or more emphasis on cautionary measures to prevent new freedoms from disintegrating into license as we do to removing obstacles to freedom.

IMPLICATIONS FOR US: WHAT IS OUR FAVOURITE CONCEPTION OF JESUS?

The fact that Moses appeared to have had a *favourite* conception of God raises the following questions for us as Christians: Do we have a favourite conception of Jesus that particularly influences our Christian calling and activity? Is there an aspect of Jesus' character or work that especially draws us to him?

In my case (as a politician who favours bottom-up democratic processes), it is Jesus' interaction with the public that I find most attractive. We see it as he travelled from town to town communicating his unique message, speaking persuasively to small groups of common people—occasionally making major addresses in the synagogues or to larger groups—and, of course, publicly jousting with his opponents. Anyone who has tried to build a grassroots movement or engaged in a campaign to convince large numbers of people to support a cause cannot help but admire the genius and achievements of Jesus in this regard.

But what about you? Do you find yourself particularly attracted to Jesus the teacher, Jesus the healer, Jesus the friend of the poor, or Jesus in some other role? In other words, do you have a *favourite* Jesus?

For those who are politically inclined, it may well be that our favourite picture is of Jesus as a political activist. How about Jesus driving the money changers out of the temple—a public and political act that his politically ambitious disciples greatly admired and longed to imitate?[197]

Not surprisingly, this incident brought to the minds of the disciples a relevant quotation from a psalm of David, "Zeal for your [God's] house consumes me."[198] Certainly this conception of Jesus has been attractive for Christians through the ages, from the Crusaders to members of the Moral Majority. But is this conception of Jesus as a political activist one from which politically inclined Christians today should take their primary lead?

What about political action rooted in religious zeal? While Jesus was motivated by religious zeal to purify his Father's house, he—by virtue of who he was—was able to exercise self-control over this zeal. His disciples, however, had much to unlearn and learn before they could do likewise. For example, their uncontrolled zeal to advance the kingdom would one day lead them to propose burning down a Samaritan village because its people had rejected their master.[199] Jesus had to rebuke them sternly and expressly forbid them to have anything to do with the Samaritans until they were fully imbued with his spirit.[200]

[197] See John 2:13–17.

[198] Psalm 69:9.

[199] See Luke 9:51–56.

[200] See Matthew 10:5; Acts 1:8, 8:4–17.

In my experience there is great danger when uncontrolled religious zeal is translated into political action.[201] This danger needs to be scrupulously guarded against. Most significantly, the antidote to destructive religious zeal is to be found in the very same psalm of David of which the disciples had remembered only a part. David himself knew what it meant to be consumed by religious zeal for political ends. But he was also well aware that when such zeal is not controlled by God's spirit it can lead to actions that disgrace the people of God and repel those who might otherwise seek him. Hence in that same psalm David prays, "May those who hope in you not be disgraced because of me … may those who seek you not be put to shame because of me."[202]

There is definitely inspiration and guidance for Christians who are motivated to action by the example and teachings of Jesus. But lest we become dangerously consumed by zeal for the cause, let us, like David, pray, "May nothing I do or say out of zeal for the work of Christ cause the Christian community to be disgraced or those who might seek him to be repelled because of me."

IMPLICATIONS FOR US: GOD AS GRACE

It was the fifth revelation that Moses received concerning God's character and work—that of God as grace—that he appeared least to understand or appreciate. But what about us?

Think back to your favourite conception of Jesus. If you are politically inclined it might be that of Jesus as a political activist, Jesus full of zeal, or Jesus as a man of the people. While there is value to each of these conceptions, for me, politics at the highest level is ultimately about the reconciliation of conflicting interests. If that is the case, then shouldn't the revelation of Jesus that most motivates and guides us at the interface of faith, public life, and politics be that of Jesus as the Saviour and

---

[201] John Milton's caution in this regard comes to mind. He defined a statesman as someone who has first learned the government of himself, and thereby becomes qualified to govern others. Referring to Oliver Cromwell, he wrote, "He first acquired the government of himself, and over himself acquired the most signal victories; so that on the first day he took the field against the external enemy, he was a veteran in arms, consummately practiced in the toils and exigencies of war" (John Milton, *The Poetical Works of John Milton*, ed. Egerton Brydges [London: William Tegg, 1862], lvi).

[202] Psalm 69:6.

reconciler of human beings to God and to each other? Surely it is this conception of Jesus—Jesus as the ultimate manifestation of God's grace, mercy, compassion, and forgiveness—that we should most faithfully and vigorously seek to represent in our personal relationships, in the marketplace, and in the public square.

2.3 THE RULE OF LAW

IN THE PREVIOUS CHAPTER WE EXPLORED HOW GOD leads his people into vocational tasks by giving them fresh revelations of his character and work in the world. We saw this principle in operation as Moses' life was impacted through five distinct revelations of the character and work of God. In this chapter we return to the fourth of these revelations: God as *lawmaker* and *judge*.

Throughout Moses' life, it was this aspect of God's work that he most consistently represented to the people of Israel, so much so that in later years the law of God came to be referred to as the law of Moses.[203] What, then, were the implications for Moses and the children of Israel in seeing God as lawmaker and judge? And what might be the implications for us today? The lessons learned from this revelation and its aftermath are instructive for anyone involved in the formation or enforcement of rules.

THE RULE OF LAW

The revelation of God as lawmaker and judge is most clearly seen in Moses' receiving the Ten Commandments on Mount Sinai.[204] These commandments became part of a body of divinely inspired laws that Moses would communicate to the Israelites—laws intended to govern their relationships with God and with each other. In its totality this body of law covered every aspect of the Israelites' personal, family, and national life. It was accompanied by promises of great blessings for obedience and

---

[203] For example, Joshua 8:32; 2 Kings 23:25; and John 7:23.

[204] See Exodus 19–20.

threats of dire consequences for disobedience.[205] The aftermath of this revelation is recorded in the Old Testament as a 400-year-long endeavour to establish right relationships through law.

In my opinion, this record constitutes one of the most thorough and original textbooks in all of sacred and secular literature on what can and cannot be achieved through the Rule of Law. As such, there are lessons that rule-makers and rule-enforcers of every kind can learn from studying this record, no matter where they find themselves in the community. These lessons are especially relevant to legislators, as the making of statute law and regulations is one of the chief tasks of those elected to our federal Parliament, provincial and territorial legislatures, and municipal councils.

THE BENEFITS OF LAW

One of the lessons to be gleaned from studying law in the biblical record is that whenever and wherever laws are just—and justly administered—the benefits to individuals and society are many and abundant. These benefits, seen throughout history, include the restraint of evil, the protection of human rights, order throughout civil society, and the direction of resources toward beneficial ends. In Canada, the Rule of Law is recognized in our Constitution as one of the fundamental principles on which the country itself is founded and as essential to the achievement of "peace, order, and good government."[206]

The benefits achievable through just laws justly administered align with Scripture's constant emphasis that adherence to the law of God is a means of both doing God's will and receiving his blessing. This is emphasized in Moses' last addresses to the people of Israel, in which he commanded the Israelites "to love the Lord your God … and to keep his commands, decrees and laws" because by doing so they "will live and increase, and the Lord your God will bless you."[207] The same emphasis can be seen in the Psalms: "blessed are those … who walk according to the law of the Lord … who keep his statutes and seek him with all their heart."[208]

[205] See Deuteronomy 28–30.

[206] Preamble to Canadian *Charter of Rights and Freedoms, Constitution Act 1982*, p. 1.

[207] Deuteronomy 30:16.

[208] Psalm 119:1–2.

And, of course, the benefit of maintaining the law was emphasized by Jesus himself in his Sermon on the Mount:

> "Do not think that I have come to abolish the Law or the Prophets; I have not come to abolish them but to fulfill them. For truly I tell you, until heaven and earth disappear, not the smallest letter, not the least stroke of the pen, will by any means disappear from the Law until everything is accomplished."[209]

Jesus, David, and Moses all understood the importance of law and the blessing that it can confer upon those who follow it. Jesus, in particular, also understood the limits to law and the manner in which it can be abused.

THE ABUSE OF LAW

Evil cannot abolish an instrumentality—such as the Rule of Law—that has been established by God and intended for good. Lacking the ability to do away with the Rule of Law, the age-old tactic of the evil one is to pervert it toward evil ends. This perversion can take a number of forms. For example, while one of the possible benefits of law is freedom, one of the most effective ways of suppressing a freedom is to smother it via excessive rule-making and regulation. Consider, as an illustration of this perversion, the comprehensive state regulation of religious freedom in the former Soviet Union and in present-day China.

Throughout the ministry of Jesus, he frequently addressed the abuse of law and the spirit-quenching effects of excessive legalism. For example, he vehemently denounced the practice of making law a burden rather than a blessing, rebuking the Pharisees—the custodians of the Mosaic law—for laying "heavy, cumbersome loads" on the people's shoulders and not lifting a finger to relieve them.[210]

Likewise, Jesus condemned the abuse of law through inconsistent and hypocritical practice:

> "Woe to you, teachers of the law and Pharisees, you hypocrites! You give a tenth of your spices—mint, dill and cumin [i.e., you keep the law in small matters]. But you have neglected the more important matters of the law—justice, mercy and faithfulness. You should have practiced the latter, without neglecting the former."[211]

---

[209] Matthew 5:17–18.

[210] Matthew 23:4.

[211] Matthew 23:23.

The worst abuses of the Rule of Law, however, are those where laws are deliberately harnessed to the practice of evil. Jesus himself, for example, was the victim of one of the most twisted abuses of law imaginable. In the lead-up to his crucifixion, Jesus was brought by the Jewish leaders to stand trial before the Roman governor, Pilate. Pilate was unable to find Jesus guilty of violating any Roman law and was prepared to let him go. His accusers, however, declared that Jesus was a blasphemer and that, according to Moses' law, "he must die, because he has claimed to be the Son of God."[212] The law of God was twisted to such a degree that it was used to condemn to death the Son of God.

Thus the Rule of Law—even the rule of the law of God—is a two-edged sword. It is capable of being harnessed to achieve enormous benefits but is also capable of doing enormous harm when abused. To protect the Rule of Law from being discredited, those who value and practise it must scrupulously guard against its abuse.

THE ABUSE OF LAW BY LAWMAKERS

There is another abuse of law that is particularly pernicious, as it destroys faith in the Rule of Law itself, and that is the abuse of law by those who make the law, in particular by elected lawmakers.

As mentioned, my father spent his entire career as a Canadian lawmaker. Every so often he made it a point to remind his colleagues that "those of us who make the laws and those of us who administer the laws must *keep* the laws, or we lose our moral authority to govern."

What he was particularly concerned about was the temptation of lawmakers to bend the law in their favour or to ignore rigorous administration of the law when it was politically expedient to do so.

There is an old movie entitled *A Man for All Seasons* about a Christian believer and lawmaker, Sir Thomas More, who was tempted in his time to abuse the law in precisely these two ways.[213] He resisted that temptation at the cost of his life, and his story should be a lesson and an inspiration to lawmakers of every age.

More was a man of great personal integrity and a defender of the Rule of Law who had become chancellor of England at the time when

[212] John 19:7.

[213] Sir Thomas More's story is told in the film *A Man for All Seasons* (directed by Fred Zinnemann [1966; UK: Highland Films]).

King Henry VIII wanted to replace his wife Katherine with his mistress Anne Boleyn. But the law (Roman Catholic church law) said this couldn't be done without a divorce, which the pope was reluctant to give. Henry wanted a divorce from his wife, but a law stood in the way. More's position was that the law must be upheld or changed by lawful means, but it should not be bent or broken for any cause.

More was then assailed by nobles such as the Duke of Norfolk, who wanted the law circumvented in the name of convenience—to keep the peace in the political family. Norfolk, who liked More and wanted to help him out of his dilemma, presented him with a bill *bending the rules* on the divorce question. But More refused to sign it on the ground that it violated the law.

> More: You and your class have "given in" as you rightly call it—because the religion of this country means nothing to you one way or the other.
>
> Norfolk: Oh confound all this. I'm not a scholar, I don't know whether the marriage was lawful or not but dammit, Thomas, [we've all signed this bill authorizing the king's marriage], look at these names! Why can't you do as I did and come with us, for fellowship?
>
> More: And when we die, and you are sent to heaven for doing your conscience and I am sent to hell for not doing mine, will you come with me, for fellowship?[214]

Shrewd answer! More resisted the temptation to bend or break the law for expediency's sake. But then the tempter comes at him again from the opposite direction. More, whose life was now in danger from the king and his friends, was assailed by his idealistic but hot-headed son-in-law, William Roper. He wanted More to use his powers as chancellor to go after Richard Rich (an up-and-coming politician), who was intent on winning the king's favour by accusing More of treason. Roper wanted More to defend himself and the faith, even if he must bend or break the law and abuse his powers as chancellor to do so. More argued that Richard Rich should be left alone until he broke the law, even if he was the devil himself, to which his son-in-law replied,

> Roper: So, now you give the devil benefit of law!
>
> More: Yes, what would you do? Cut a great road through the law to get after the devil?

[214] *A Man for All Seasons.*

> Roper: Yes! I'd cut down every law in England to do that!
>
> More: Oh? And when the last law was down, and the devil turned 'round on you, where would you hide, Roper, the laws all being flat? This country is planted thick with laws from coast to coast, man's laws, not God's! And if you cut them down, and you're just the man to do it, do you really think you could stand upright in the winds that would blow then? *Yes, I'd give the devil benefit of law for my own safety's sake!*[215]

More resists the temptation to bend or break the law in the name of convenience and expediency, and he resists the temptation to bend or break it for the sake of personal advantage. He seeks to uphold the law *for his own safety's sake as a believer and a citizen.*

THE LIMITS TO LAW

While the Scriptures and history have much to teach us concerning the benefits and abuses of law, I think the greatest lesson we can learn from the experience of ancient Israel with the Rule of Law concerns the limitations of law and lawmaking. This is another lesson relevant to all rule-makers and enforcers, whether they are parents in the home, leaders in the church, executives in the workplace, or lawmakers in the political arena.

As discussed, the law of God was conceived and promulgated in order to establish and maintain right relationships between Israel and God and among the Israelites themselves. The latter prophets reached a sobering conclusion regarding the success of the attempts to achieve right relations by means of law alone. They concluded that laws—even laws that were given directly from the hand of God—are insufficient in themselves to achieve righteousness and justice. Unless law is accompanied by an internal transformation—inscribed on human hearts, not merely on tablets of stone or in books of law—it is insufficient to achieve righteousness, justice, and good behaviour.[216]

It was, in part, the prophets' realization of the limitations of the Rule of Law that led them to long so fervently for the coming of the Messiah. They longed for the one whose coming Moses prophesied[217] because the Messiah would fulfill the mission of the law by becoming the means of the inner transformation required to obey it.

---

[215] *A Man for All Seasons*, emphasis added.

[216] For example, see Jeremiah 31:31–3 and Ezekiel 11:19–20; see also 2 Corinthians 3:3.

[217] See Deuteronomy 18:15.

IMPLICATIONS FOR US

What then can we learn from the experience of Moses and the Israelites with respect to the Rule of Law—its benefits, abuses, and limits? What can we learn, whether we are a rule maker in a home, church, or other organization or in a legislature or simply a citizen and member of a community?

To enjoy the benefits of law, it is essential that Christians first recognize their responsibilities as citizens to work—whenever and wherever possible—within the strictures of the Rule of Law; we should be law-abiding citizens who follow the Rule of Law. That does not mean that we should pay blind allegiance to those laws we consider unjust or ill-advised. But we should do our utmost to change rather than violate those laws—working with and within, rather than against, the Rule of Law.

There are also lessons we can learn from the outworking of the Rule of Law in Israel as we respond to it within our own Christian communities. Primarily, there is a need to acknowledge and deal with the ways in which we can abuse the Rule of Law and disrespect its limits. Rather than relying on grace and looking towards inner transformation, we far too often attempt to achieve right behaviour through rules of our own making—multiplying and strictly enforcing them, despite our creedal acknowledgement of the all-sufficiency of the grace of God.

Rules, of course, have their necessary place in guiding us through the wise establishment of boundaries. But how many young people have been turned away from following Jesus by too much law and not enough grace? Rules of worship and conduct are necessary to shape, guide, and protect a spiritual community, hence the law given to Moses for the benefit of Israel, and rules of worship and conduct for Christians today. But many people today refuse to darken a church door because all they have ever encountered there was a dry and pharisaical Christian legalism. Recognizing the limitations of the law is a step towards creating a grace-filled space in which people can seek or return to God.

Outside of our own Christian community, what might be the implications for society-at-large of these lessons from Moses with respect to the Rule of Law? In particular, to what extent have our parliaments, legislatures, and municipal councils—as lawmaking bodies—come to grips with the limitations of law?

As discussed, laws may be beneficially used to accomplish many worthwhile objectives—including the constraint of evil, the protection of human rights, the maintenance of order throughout civil society, and the direction of resources toward beneficial ends. But when legislators seek to use laws to reach far beyond such objectives—when we declare or imply that we can create a "just society," a Canada "strong and free," or a "true north" utopia simply by enacting legislation and implementing public policies—we deceive ourselves and our constituents by ignoring the limitations of the law.

In theory, of course, our legislatures could pass laws requiring each of us to love our neighbour as ourselves and requiring public servants to love their clients as themselves. But the great lesson of the Israelite story is that such laws would be of little effect and insufficient in themselves to achieve such ends. As the apostle Paul declares in his letter to the Galatians, if a law could have been framed that imparted "life" in all its abundance to Israel and humanity, then righteousness and justice would have come by the law of Moses.[218]

If the law of God was so severely limited in its ability to produce such results, why should we believe that our own laws could do so? In fact, having seen the way law can be abused, we should be warned that it is precisely those laws that reach for utopia that can most easily be turned into instruments of oppression. Such is what comes from failing to recognize the limitations of law and seeking to use it to achieve ends beyond those limits.

Should this frank and honest acknowledgement of the limits of law lead to disillusionment and the abandonment of hope for a better country? As the apostle Paul so clearly pointed out, the realization of the law's limits should lead us not to despair but instead to search for righteousness and justice in another source.[219] While Moses only dimly perceived that source, it is fully revealed to us in the New Testament as Jesus—the fulfiller of the law through the transformation of hearts. It is in him that our hope lies. "For the law was given through Moses; grace and truth came through Jesus Christ."[220]

[218] Galatians 3:21.

[219] Galatians 3:23–25.

[220] John 1:17.

2.4 THE ROLE OF THE LEADER

ALTHOUGH THE INITIAL CALL MOSES RECEIVED WAS TO lead the Hebrews out of Egypt, that task was only the start of his leadership. Through the journey in the wilderness, Moses' role shifted from being an inspirational revolutionary leader to leading a reluctant people on a depressing detour of their own making, away from and not toward the better future originally envisioned for them. As we will see, Moses was instrumental in acting as a mediator between God and the people, in the institutionalization of values and practices, and, finally, in serving the people by preparing a successor to lead after his death. At the heart of all that Moses did was the recognition that the purpose of his leadership was not self-glorification but to join in the work and service of one greater than himself.

LEADERSHIP AS MEDIATION

As previously mentioned, I've come to believe that leadership at any level invariably involves endeavouring to reconcile conflicting interests. In Moses' case this meant not only mediating disputes among the Israelites themselves but also acting as a mediator between God and his people.

Initially, of course, Moses acted as a mediator between God, the Israelites, and Pharaoh. But once the Red Sea had been crossed, Moses began to face intense criticism from the people he was leading (a topic we explore more deeply in the next chapter). Despite being freed from slavery, they resented the hardships of the desert journey toward the Promised Land and frequently demanded a return to Egypt. Most often their criticisms were directed at Moses as God's representative, forcing Moses to stand in the gap between God and his people.

For example, the Israelites refused to enter the Promised Land after receiving a negative intelligence report from spies sent to scout it out.[221] God then threatened to destroy them and start all over again by creating a new nation from Moses' descendants. But Moses interceded as a mediator on their behalf, reciting back to God the promise he had declared on Mount Sinai: "The LORD is slow to anger, abounding in love and forgiving sin and rebellion."[222]

But perhaps the most striking example of Moses as mediator occurred when venomous snakes were sent among the people in response to yet another outbreak of rebellion. Again Moses interceded in prayer for the people, and God responded by instructing him to make a bronze snake and put it up on a pole. Then Moses was told that whoever looked at the bronze snake, after being bitten, would live.[223] In the New Testament, Jesus specifically referred to this incident as analogous to his own role as a sin bearer and his mediatory death on the cross: "Just as Moses lifted up the snake in the wilderness, so the Son of Man must be lifted up, that everyone who believes may have eternal life in him."[224]

As Christians, no matter what position we occupy in society or an organization, we are called to practise the ministry of reconciliation. In doing so we are putting into practice one of the most central doctrines of our faith.[225] It is instructive to recognize that mediation was one of the central tasks of Moses' leadership and that in this regard he models leadership in the spirit of Christ.

INSTITUTIONALIZING FOR THE FUTURE

While dealing with issues at hand through mediation is an unavoidable aspect of leadership, it is also critical to prepare for the future if the values, mission, and distinctive character of the organization or community are to be sustained over the long run. Such preparation includes more than succession planning; in particular, it includes

[221] See Numbers 13:26–14:4.

[222] See Numbers 14:11–19.

[223] Numbers 21:4–9.

[224] John 3:14–15.

[225] 2 Corinthians 5:17–21.

institutionalizing those values and practices necessary to achieving long-run sustainability.

Thus—on instruction from God—Moses communicated to the children of Israel the legal, material, procedural, and ceremonial means whereby they were to worship and serve him and one another. In fact, more than sixty chapters of the Pentateuch are devoted to descriptions and instructions pertaining to how the Israelites were meant to live with respect to their treatment of one another and resolving conflicts; how they were to celebrate the Sabbath and various feasts and festivals; how they were to worship individually and communally, and the role of priests within worship; what they were to eat, and the means by which they were to stay healthy; and the various punishments and blessings for their responses to these instructions.

On the surface these laws may look like mere religious trappings. On closer inspection, however, they were about preparing the community for the future. In fact, all these regulations were means to facilitate the end of bringing glory to God through worship, obedience, and service. In order for the future to be prepared for, the correct end had to be kept as the central concern.

The historian Will Durant ruefully observed that it is the tragedy of things spiritual that they languish if unorganized but are corrupted by organization.[226] True to Durant's observation, many of the laws, structures, and ceremonies established under Moses and meant to facilitate the worship and service of God became, by Jesus' time, ends in themselves. Moses' law had become corrupted to such a degree that, in Jesus' judgment, the temple was made into a "den of robbers" and the Sabbath a wearisome burden; and the law itself was more about splitting hairs than about justice and mercy. The Rule of Law established by Moses had tragically degenerated for the most part into a dry and spiritually bankrupt legalism. It was perverted to the point where the Jewish leaders could even say to Pilate, "We have a law [the law of God], and according to that law he [the Son of God] must die."[227]

Any worthwhile pursuit—spiritual, political, economic, academic, or charitable—needs to be organized in some fashion if it is to be sustained.

[226] Will Durant, *The Age of Faith* (New York: Simon and Schuster, 1950), 768.

[227] John 19:7.

More often than not, this is the leader's responsibility. When done well, institutionalizing sustains the life and purpose of the enterprise. But far too often the means and manner of institutionalizing can quench the spirit of an organization. It takes wise leadership indeed to discern what leads to life and what leads to death. Being acutely aware of these possibilities, however, is the first step toward preventing institutionalization from eventually strangling the organization or community it is meant to sustain.

PREPARING FOR SUCCESSION

Providing a qualified successor is often one of the last and most trying tasks of leadership. This task is complicated by the fact that there will be many others with distinct ideas as to who your successor should be.

During Moses' long tenure as Israel's political and spiritual leader there were several attempts to displace him as leader: by members of his own household; by angry mobs of discontented and disillusioned followers; and even by the community leaders he himself had appointed.[228]

Instead, God had Joshua in mind as a successor for Moses. Perhaps Moses was aware of this from an early stage, as he assigned Joshua to lead the Israelites in one of their earliest battles.[229] He picked Joshua to serve as his aide at the tent of meeting where Moses met face to face with God.[230] Joshua was also selected as one of the twelve spies to explore Canaan, and on the completion of this mission only he and Caleb still believed that God could give the Israelites the land.[231] It seems that Joshua was being prepared by God long before he ever received the mantle of leadership from Moses.

Eventually, Moses was clearly directed to "commission Joshua, and encourage and strengthen him, for he will lead this people across [the Jordan] and will cause them to inherit the land."[232] By largely leaving succession and his own reputation in the hands of God, Moses left the leadership of Israel in capable hands, as Joshua went on to fulfill the mission of leading the children of Israel into the Promised Land.

---

[228] Numbers 12; 14:1–4, 10; 16.

[229] Exodus 17:9–10.

[230] Exodus 33:7–11.

[231] Numbers 13:8; 14:5–9.

[232] Deuteronomy 3:28.

THE LEADER'S LEGACY

At the end of the day, perhaps the greatest lesson we can learn from Moses is that true leadership isn't about the leader. It's about serving someone and something greater than oneself.

One of the most admirable things about Moses is that, unlike many modern leaders, he was not preoccupied in his latter years with creating a personal legacy. My father, who spent all of his adult years in politics and government, described the dangers of a leader trying too hard to shape his own legacy while still in office. "It's like trying to drive a car down the road while looking in the rear-view mirror. The most likely result will be a crash—and that will be your legacy."[233]

Moses for the most part was willing to leave not only the choice of his successor but also his legacy in the hands of God. He made no provision for members of his family, or even members of his own tribe, to succeed him. He erected no monument to himself, nor did he name any institution after himself. Even his gravesite is known only to God. He steadfastly served his people by serving the one who had called him to that service and to whom he was ultimately accountable. And what a legacy of leadership he left for Israel and for us. The books of Moses conclude with this fitting epitaph to Israel's first political and spiritual leader: "No prophet has risen in Israel like Moses, whom the LORD knew face to face."[234]

---

233 Author's personal recollection.

234 Deuteronomy 34:10.

2.5 THE CHALLENGES OF LEADERSHIP

THE PREVIOUS CHAPTER LOOKED AT THE *ROLE* OF THE leader. This chapter focuses on the *challenges* a leader invariably faces in the course of living out that role. Many of these are similar to those faced by people in positions of leadership today. They include the burden of overwork and the need to delegate; the constant encroachment of work and leadership obligations on personal and family life; and coping with a steady stream of complaints, opposition, and threats to the leader's position.

Moses was not just a political leader; he was first and foremost a spiritual leader—a man of faith to whom God had graciously revealed himself and his work. So what difference did this make in how he handled the challenges of leadership? And what lessons are there for us, as we take the necessary step of relating *our* faith to *our* calling, work, and leadership obligations?

THE WISDOM AND RISKS OF DELEGATION

The first challenge faced by Moses—like many leaders past and present—was overwork. There is always more to do than there are hours in the day. So Moses learned the wisdom of delegation. Shortly after leading the Israelites out of Egypt, Moses was visited by his father-in-law, Jethro. Having observed that Moses was overworked, Jethro urged him to delegate some of his responsibilities to officials over thousands, hundreds, fifties, and tens. Moses followed this wise advice with the apparent approval of God and the people.[235]

[235] Exodus 18:17–26; Deuteronomy 1:9–18.

Throughout his time as a leader, Moses was directed by God to further distribute the responsibilities of spiritual and temporal leadership. Notably, he established the Aaronic priesthood and the Levitical order to care for the tabernacle, an important aspect of spiritual leadership for the Israelites. He also anointed seventy elders of Israel with God's spirit to carry the burden of the people so he would not have to carry it alone.[236] One further example of Moses' delegation is how—in response to God's direction and his own inclination—Moses gave the job of scouting out the Promised Land to a task force of twelve men, one man chosen from each tribe.[237]

Many leaders, however, are reluctant to delegate and unwilling to relinquish their power, despite this being a means by which they can better serve the community they are leading. This reluctance might be due to egocentricity, personal insecurities, or a lack of faith in the abilities and motives of others—three often interrelated character flaws. While Moses had his own set of insecurities, they do not seem to have found expression in a reluctance to delegate.

Sadly, though, Moses' delegation did not always lead to positive outcomes for himself or the people of Israel. The most obvious disappointment was the betrayal of purpose by the task force Moses appointed to scout the Promised Land. This was a betrayal that led to the drastic result of Israel having to wander in the wilderness for forty years. Similarly, the community leaders to whom Moses had delegated responsibility were also those who—at the instigation of Korah, Dathan, and Abiram—later led the rebellion against his leadership and God's direction.[238] While it is often wise to delegate, there are obvious risks in doing so, and the outcomes of that delegated leadership cannot be guaranteed.

My own experience with delegation has included a reluctance to delegate because as a perfectionist I would rather do it myself and get it right than delegate the wrong task to the wrong party and then be forced to devote endless amounts of time to trying to correct the results. My observation is that when we view our co-workers as simply *functional* beings we tend to attach too much weight to whether they possess the

[236] Numbers 11:10–17.

[237] Numbers 13:1–16.

[238] Numbers 16.

functional capacity and experience required to accomplish the task, and we pay insufficient attention to whether or not they have a heart prepared for and attuned to the job.

When we view our co-workers and colleagues from a more spiritual perspective—as *human beings* and, therefore, suffering from the consequences of the Fall but also bearing in some way the image of God—we should be less inclined to lean solely on our own human wisdom in delegating and be more apt to seek guidance from him who sees the hearts of all people.

Knowing when and what to delegate, and to whom, is an integral part of leadership to which are attached both benefits and risks. It is sobering to remember that even Moses, the man of God, was not immune to ill-advisedly placing trust in those to whom he delegated authority and responsibilities and that we ourselves are not immune to misplacing our own trust when we delegate. All the more reason to seek spiritual insight and guidance in delegating responsibilities to others.

PROTECTING FAMILY LIFE

Undoubtedly one of the biggest challenges any leader faces is adequately safeguarding personal and family relations against the relentless encroachment of leadership obligations. So let us consider this challenge in the case of Moses.

Having grown up in the courts of Egypt as a prince, Moses fled to Midian after killing an Egyptian. In Midian, Moses married Zipporah, a shepherdess and daughter of a Midianite priest, Jethro. Zipporah bore Moses two sons, Gershom and Eliezer. Together, Moses and Zipporah, along with their two sons, journeyed back to Egypt. One can only try to imagine the culture shock of a shepherdess from Midian going to Egypt on a mission to confront Pharaoh!

Apparently, at some point during the conflict with Pharaoh, Moses sent his wife and sons away, back to his father-in-law, Jethro. When Jethro came to see Moses after the liberation of Israel from Egypt he brought Zipporah and their sons with him. While the Scripture records Moses' enthusiastic reception of Jethro, it says nothing at all about his reunion with Zipporah.[239]

[239] Exodus 18:5–8.

Later in the story, Moses married a Cushite woman—much to the displeasure of his sister (Miriam) and brother (Aaron)—and nothing more is said regarding Zipporah, Gershom, or Eliezer. Furthermore, although several of Aaron's sons were appointed to succeed him in the priesthood, Moses' sons are never mentioned as possible successors to his leadership.

Like many leaders, Moses' commitment to his leadership responsibilities appears to have damaged his family relationships. The same tragedy occurred with Samuel and again with David, and tragedy is definitely the right word to describe this all-too-frequent phenomenon. In Canada, the incidence of family breakup is higher among members of the House of Commons than it is among the general population.

My own experience in this area involves trying to do both—trying to satisfy the obligations to leadership and family equally and simultaneously. This is an ill-advised course because in practice the immediate and incessant demands of leadership will inexorably take precedence over family obligations, leaving one's spouse with an unequal share of family responsibilities and inevitably depriving someone—a spouse, a child, a grandchild—of needed attention, affection, and guidance.

The God we serve is first and foremost a God who treasures relationships—our relationship with him and our relationships with each other. When we sacrifice these relationships, especially the relationship with family, to other pursuits—the pursuit of wealth, power, or self-satisfaction and even such causes as public service or *doing God's work*—we are courting personal tragedy. God may call us to *self*-sacrificial service. But if that service involves involuntarily sacrificing the interests and well-being of others, especially members of our family, we need to earnestly seek his help in resolving the apparent contradiction.

It is important to ask, therefore, what safeguards are in place to ensure that your leadership commitments—whatever spheres they may be in—do not adversely affect, or even destroy, your marriage or relations with your children. This is one area where, sadly, the example of Moses is not to be emulated.

COPING WITH CRITICISM, OPPOSITION, AND THREATS

The greatest, most persistent, and most debilitating challenge of leadership that Moses experienced was coping with grumbling, complaining, criticism, opposition, and threats to his leadership from those he was attempting to lead. The Israelites grumbled about a lack of water at Marah and again at Rephidim. They complained about their lack of food in the Desert of Sin and again about their hardships at Taberah.

On several occasions the criticism and complaining about Moses' leadership turned into outright rebellion—for example, when the Israelites received the negative report from the spies sent to scout out the Promised Land and when Korah, Dathan, and Abiram challenged Moses' spiritual authority.[240] On the first of these occasions the people were even prepared to stone Moses and Aaron and replace them with leaders who would return them to Egypt—direct rebellion, not only against Moses and Aaron but also against the will and purpose of God.

In the case of threats to his own leadership, Moses did not defend himself but simply trusted in God to do so. The Pentateuch ends with Moses described as "a very humble man, more humble than anyone else on the face of the earth"—a very unusual description of a revolutionary leader.[241] And in each recorded case of Israel's grumbling and complaining to Moses about the lack of water or food, Moses took the criticism before God and sought direction from him. In each case Moses followed God's direction, and the people's needs were miraculously met.

One tragic incident at Kadesh, however, reveals a different response.[242] Again the children of Israel were bitterly complaining to Moses and Aaron about the lack of water. Moses brought the people's petition before God and was instructed to "speak to the rock before their eyes and it will pour out its water." Moses returned to the people, still bitter about their complaints, and said, "Listen, you rebels, must we [Moses and Aaron] bring you water out of this rock?" Then Moses, after seemingly attributing the forthcoming miracle to himself and Aaron rather than to God, struck the rock to bring forth water, instead of speaking to it as God had commanded. For failing to obey God's clear instructions, Moses and Aaron were severely censured. God said to Moses and Aaron, "Because you did not trust in me enough to honor me as holy in the sight of the Israelites, you will not bring this community into the land I give them."

[240] Numbers 14:1–4, 10; 16.

[241] Numbers 12:3.

[242] Numbers 20:1–13.

In many respects this is the most tragic incident in Moses' long career as a spiritual and political leader.

In sum, what can we learn from Moses' experience in dealing with the constant and intense criticism he received from the people he was called to lead, including direct threats to his leadership? Two things.

First, it is significant that Moses let God deal with direct threats to his leadership rather than trying to defend himself. This required not only admirable restraint but also a deep faith and confidence that ultimately he owed his leadership position to divine providence and that ultimately it was in God's hands, not his or the people's, to sustain or revoke it. Might those of us in leadership positions at the interface of faith and public life today come to know such a deep faith and confidence in the sovereignty of God.

Second, without trying to dodge the issue of leadership responsibility, perhaps another lesson from Moses' experience with criticism and internal opposition is not so much for the leader as it is for the followers. I can say from my own experience that constant criticism of a leader from within is more debilitating than all the attacks and criticisms from without. In Moses' case that criticism wore away at him and eventually resulted in his exasperated response at Kadesh. Consequently, it deeply and adversely affected his personal relationship with God and led directly to what he regarded as his greatest failure—his inability to personally lead the people of God into the Promised Land.

Leaders are not beyond criticism, nor should they be. But when our grumbling, complaining, and criticism undermines not only their relationship with us but also their relationship with the ultimate source of their guidance and inspiration, then we have gone too far. We need lessons in leadership, and there are plenty of those in the life of Moses. But there are also such things as godly and ungodly followership—and there are hard lessons to be learned on this front as well from the relationship between Moses and those he was called upon by God to lead.

2.6 LAST WORDS

SPECIAL ATTENTION SHOULD ALWAYS BE PAID TO HOW leaders conclude their leadership and the words they use in doing so. It is usually in their last words to their friends and followers that leaders reveal what is weighing most heavily on their minds and hearts as they look back over their careers. And it is often in these last words that they emphasize what they consider most important to pass on to the next generation with a view to the future. What they leave unsaid is often equally significant. In this concluding chapter on the leadership of Moses let us, therefore, carefully examine his last addresses to the children of Israel as recorded in Deuteronomy.

LOOKING BACK

In his last addresses, Moses said little about the miraculous deliverance of the Israelites from Egypt but instead began to rehearse the Israelite story from when they received the law of God at Mount Sinai. He recounted many significant events in the Israelites' journey: their refusal to enter the Promised Land, their wanderings in the desert, their military victories, their experiences in receiving and learning to obey the Law, and the commissioning of Joshua as their next leader.

While Moses' most significant achievement from a political standpoint was leading the liberation of Israel from slavery in Egypt, it is striking that he hardly mentions this accomplishment at all in these last addresses. Usually, liberation movements and liberation leaders have the most to say on the theme of *freedom from*—identifying and rehearsing the evils and bondage from which they have delivered their followers. Often they have far less to say about *freedom to*—identifying and emphasizing the ends toward which the exercise of the newly gained freedom of their followers is to be directed.

This is not the case with Moses. He was very clear that Israel had been liberated *from* the bondage of Egypt *in order to* worship and serve the God who had delivered them. Thus Moses' last addresses to Israel focused heavily on urging them toward the goal of worshipping, obeying, and serving God.

This emphasis in Moses' final addresses is highly relevant to us as Christian believers. We are usually quite settled and articulate on the fact that God has delivered us from our sins. But sometimes we are less settled and articulate on the purposes to which this new-found spiritual freedom is to be directed, such as living a Christlike life. Like the Israelites, we need to be often and strongly reminded to exercise our *freedom to*.

LOOKING AHEAD

Moses also used his last exhortations to turn the people's gaze towards the future by making several remarkable prophecies. Prominent among these is the promise of the coming Messiah: "The Lord your God will raise up for you a prophet like me from among your own brothers. You must listen to him."[243]

Moses also prophesied that once the Israelites were established in the land, they would desire to have a king "like all the nations around us."[244] Unlike Samuel many years later, Moses did not appear to oppose the idea of a monarchy.[245] That said, he firmly insisted that even the king is to be under the law (a concept not fully established in the Western world until the 18th century).

Furthermore, Moses prophesied Israel's future rebellion against God and the law of God—even composing a song on this theme.[246] Perhaps because of his past experience and future forebodings with respect to Israel's predisposition to rebel against God the lawgiver, Moses devoted

[243] Deuteronomy 18:15.

[244] See Deuteronomy 17:14–20.

[245] Compare Moses' relatively positive commentary on the prospect of Israel being ruled by a king, provided that king was under the law (see Deuteronomy 17:14–20), with Samuel's displeasure at Israel's request for a king and his negative commentary thereon (see 1 Samuel 8).

[246] Deuteronomy 31:14–22; 32:1–47.

much of his last addresses to Israel to reinforcing the Rule of Law.[247] This reinforcement included strong exhortations to love and obey God and the law;[248] the pronouncement of dire curses for breaking or abandoning the law;[249] and the promise of great blessings and prosperity for adherence to the law.[250] Through all these prophesies and warnings Moses directed the people toward the ultimate aim of their political and spiritual liberty—not freedom *from* the Egyptians but freedom *to* worship God.

FROM MOSES TO US

Looking back over Moses' life, certain questions come to mind that further help establish the relevance of the lessons from Moses to our lives today. First, let us ask whether Moses fulfilled the call to *do*. This was the call to join with God in delivering the children of Israel from slavery in Egypt—the call he received at the burning bush. The answer to this is obviously yes. But what about each of us? How have we received and fulfilled our own call to do—to join with God in whatever he has shown himself to be doing in our time and circumstances? That is a question we must wrestle with and revisit throughout our lives.

As we saw, however, there is a more foundational call that God makes to each of us: the call to *be*. In Moses' case this was the call to be a leader submissive to the will of God. Again, I believe Moses answered this call—reluctantly at first but admirably in later years. The impetuous Egyptian prince who once thought he could liberate Israel by himself was transformed through spiritual and political experiences into a man "more humble than anyone else on the face of the earth" and whose leadership had to be defended by God because he was reluctant to defend it himself.[251]

But again, what about us? Have we fulfilled the call to *be*—the call to be transformed by our spiritual and life experience into the likeness of Christ, who "humbled himself by becoming obedient to death—even death on a cross"?[252] Again, wrestling with this question and being faithful in our responses to it should be a key aspect of our Christian walk.

[247] Deuteronomy 12–26.

[248] Deuteronomy 11; 27:1–8; 29; 31:9–13.

[249] Deuteronomy 27:9–26; 28:13–68.

[250] Deuteronomy 28:1–14; 30; 33.

[251] Numbers 12:3. See Numbers 12, 14, 16.

[252] Philippians 2:8.

There is a subsequent question that we may ask as we reflect on Moses' life: how did he receive his sense of mission? As we have seen, Moses' sense of mission largely came through five distinct revelations of God and his work: God as the eternally present I AM, as the liberator of his people, as warrior, as lawgiver and judge, and then finally as grace.

What about us as Christians today? Have we ever received a fresh revelation of God and his work through Christ—a revelation that gives us a renewed sense of mission? Have you perhaps begun to see God anew as the Creator and sustainer of life, inviting you to join him in creation care? Or have you possibly seen God anew as the one who constrains and overcomes evil, inviting you to take ethical stands at work or in the community? Or have you been given a fresh vision of God as one who cares for the poor, the hungry, the sick, the lonely, and the oppressed and asks us to do likewise? Or have you seen God anew as the God of Grace who is reconciling all things (including ourselves) to himself and who invites us to join with him in the ministry of reconciliation? All of us need such revelations of God and his work if we are to be sustained and propelled as Christians into mission beyond our own limited capabilities.

Of course, paralleling Moses, each of us is likely to have a favoured conception of God, and we need to consider whether this is the most apt conception for us. Moses' infatuation with God as warrior limited his ability to see and work with God as grace. Is it possible that our perceptions of Jesus—perhaps as teacher, healer, or political activist—are limiting our ability to see him as the reconciler of human beings to God and to each other through his self-sacrificial death on the cross and therefore limiting or misdirecting our sense of mission?

One final question: what have we learned from the narrative of Moses and the people of Israel concerning the Rule of Law—its benefits, its potential for abuse, and its limits? If we value the Rule of Law, do we ourselves adhere to and support the law and the processes whereby our laws are made? And are we aware of the limits of rule-making—that utopia here on earth cannot be achieved by legislating, and that excessive rule-making and enforcement can quench the spirit of our children and society?

THE STRANGE OMISSION

In Deuteronomy, Moses' last addresses to Israel, he recounts his second sojourn on Mount Sinai during which he received, for a second time, the tablets of the law. But, strangely and inexplicably from my perspective, Moses makes no mention of the revelation he received on that occasion of God as grace, mercy, and compassion—the one who demands justice but forgives sin, even the sin of rebellion.

Just prior to receiving that revelation, Moses had prayed for God to manifest his presence and glory, and God responded:

> The LORD came down in the cloud and stood there with him and proclaimed his name, the LORD. And he passed in front of Moses, proclaiming,
>
> "The LORD, the LORD, the compassionate and gracious God, slow to anger, abounding in love and faithfulness, maintaining love to thousands, and forgiving wickedness, rebellion [yes, rebellion] and sin. Yet he does not leave the guilty unpunished; he punishes the children and their children for the sin of the parents to the third and fourth generation."[253]

If you or I had received such a direct revelation of God as grace, surely it would have been the highlight of our spiritual experience and we would have wanted to share it with our contemporaries and future generations! Yet Moses only mentioned this incident once in his writings, when he sought God's pardon for Israel's rebellious refusal to enter the Promised Land.[254] And he never referred to it at all in his final addresses to Israel before his death.

As previously mentioned, it may have been that Moses never fully grasped the revelation of God as grace because it was overshadowed by his more favoured conception of God as warrior. Or perhaps it was that he had a great deal of difficulty believing that God could or should forgive rebellion, which was the sin he himself had the most difficulty forgiving (understandably) given the amount of grief it caused him during his career as a leader.

Before we are too hard on Moses, what about us? As Christians, we have experienced the grace of God as manifested through the self-sacrificial life of Jesus. And so we too have received the great revelation of God as grace. As such, should that not be the highlight of our spiritual experience

---

[253] Exodus 34:5–7.

[254] Numbers 14:13–19.

that we would most want to share with our own contemporaries? Or have we allowed valid but lesser revelations and experiences to overshadow *the great revelation*—God as grace as revealed in Christ?

PART 3:
LEADERSHIP LESSONS
from the Life of David

INTRODUCTION

THE GOSPEL OF MATTHEW BEGINS BY DESCRIBING THE human genealogy of Jesus: "This is the genealogy of Jesus the Messiah, the son of David, the son of Abraham." When a blind beggar addressed him as the son of David, the beggar was rebuked by the onlookers but not by Jesus himself, who was willing to be so identified. Jesus often quoted directly from the Psalms of David, making clear on one occasion his belief that David's psalms were divinely inspired and that there was much to be learned from David's life and poetry.

From a political standpoint, of course, David was Israel's most famous king and one of history's most fascinating political figures. He was the shepherd boy who rose to prominence by slaying a giant, the warrior who fought his nation's battles, the loyal subject who suffered persecution and exile under an unjust king whom he ultimately replaced, the wise ruler who unified the fractious tribes of Israel into one kingdom, the champion of law and virtue who undermined his own moral authority by an inexplicable descent into adultery and murder, and the aging ruler who faced rebellion from within his own household and wrestled with the age-old challenge of succession. In addition to all this, he was a musician and poet who revealed his innermost thoughts and feelings through songs and poems at every stage of his long political career.

At the same time, David was a man of God, a man after God's own heart. God himself directed the prophet Samuel to anoint David king of Israel long before the nation recognized him as such. He attributed his victory over Goliath to divine aid. His own unwillingness to rebel against King Saul was because David acknowledged Saul as "the LORD's anointed." He meditated on the law of God day and night and extolled its virtues to his people. David dealt with his sins of adultery and murder by repenting in sackcloth and ashes. He suffered the consequences of his evil acts but emerged stronger in his faith than before. He led his nation in worship and aspired to build God a temple. And all his songs and poems are prayers to the God whom David feared, adored, worshipped, and served.

3.1 WHO WILL BE LEADER?

He chose David his servant
and took him from the sheep pens;
From tending the sheep he brought him
to be the shepherd of his people Jacob,
of Israel his inheritance.
And David shepherded them with integrity of heart;
with skillful hands he led them.[255]

PROVIDENTIAL LEADING AGAIN

IN STUDYING THE EARLY LIFE OF MOSES WE NOTED THAT, although he was a Hebrew, he was providentially positioned to grow up in the household of Pharaoh with exposure to the Egyptian government and military at its highest level. An outside observer, seeing Moses in that position, might well have predicted that he was destined to fill a leadership role of some kind later in life.

The early life of David, however, suggests a different aspect of providential positioning and leading. In David's case, there was very little in terms of family positioning or visible circumstances that would lead anyone, even the spiritually perceptive Samuel, to believe that the shepherd boy David could become a future king of Israel.

Like Samuel, in seeking whom God may have in mind for leadership, we need to be reminded that "the Lord does not look at the things people look at. People look at the outward appearance, but the Lord looks at the heart."[256] And what God sees and does, especially if he perceives a yielded

[255] Psalm 78:70–72.

[256] 1 Samuel 16:7.

and contrite heart, can lead a slave (Joseph) to become prime minister of Egypt, a shepherd (David) to the throne of Israel, an orphan girl (Esther) to become queen of the Medes and Persians, and a teenage exile (Daniel) to become the first minister of Babylon.

PERSONAL EXPERIENCE

In the case of my own family, which has been involved in provincial (Alberta) and federal politics in Canada since the 1930s, we have experienced both kinds of leading with respect to political involvement.

My father, Ernest C. Manning, served in the Alberta legislature for 33 years (1935 to 1968), 25 of those as premier. I was therefore born into a political family, which gave me an advantageous background from which to later enter federal politics, where I was engaged as a member of Canada's federal Parliament from 1993 to 2002.

But in my father's case, there was very little in his family background or circumstances to ever suggest a career at the interface of faith and public life, let alone a successful political career.[257]

Born on a Saskatchewan homestead on the Canadian prairies, my father's primary and formative education was received from the land. His parents were hard-working pioneers, nominally Christian but with little personal dimension to their faith. My father's formal education, received in a one-room schoolhouse, ended at grade eight. The family had only enough money to send one son (his older brother) to university, so the two younger boys had to remain on the farm to help make ends meet.

Ernest's life, however, changed dramatically in the 1920s when he and his brother ordered a crystal set radio from a mail-order catalogue and listened to their first radio broadcast. It just happened to be a religious program directed by William Aberhart, a Calgary high school principal and Christian layman who pioneered religious (and later political) radio broadcasting in western Canada.

Aberhart was an evangelical who believed in the necessity of a spiritual new birth through a personal commitment of one's life to Jesus Christ in order to be rightly related to God and to serve him in this world. As a result of Aberhart's exposition of the Scriptures, particularly John 3,

[257] For a fuller account of Ernest Manning's political career at the interface of faith and politics, see Brian Brennan, *The Good Steward: The Ernest C. Manning Story* (Calgary: Fifth House Ltd., 2008).

my father made such a personal commitment, adopting as his life's guide these words from the book of Proverbs:

> Trust in the LORD with all your heart
> and lean not on your own understanding;
> in all your ways submit to him,
> and he will make your paths straight.[258]

When Aberhart later opened an institute for the training of ministers in Calgary, my father enrolled as a student, and he soon became Aberhart's administrative assistant. By this time, the Canadian prairies were locked in the throes of the Great Depression with hundreds of farms and businesses thrown into bankruptcy and thousands of men (including many of Aberhart's former students) riding the rails in a vain search for work.

Appalled by the magnitude and duration of this economic and social disaster, Aberhart began to study the causes of the Depression. He became convinced that it could be remedied in part by applying the principles of social credit—a primitive form of Keynesian economics that maintained that a stalled economy could be kick-started by governments' expanding the money supply.

Aberhart, who always considered himself to be an educator and not a politician, began to use his radio broadcasts to encourage his listeners to form social credit study groups and to pressure the Alberta government to investigate social credit proposals. When the government proved unreceptive, these study groups decided to run candidates in the 1935 Alberta provincial election, my father being one of them.

Albertans by this time were desperate for change, and a social credit government was elected—none of whose members had ever sat in the provincial legislature before. Aberhart became the premier of Alberta, and my father became a minister in his cabinet at the tender age of twenty-six. In other words, the prairie farm boy who had responded to the call to become a minister of the gospel became a minister of the Crown. Eight years later when Aberhart died, my father succeeded him both as premier and as the director of his Christian radio ministry, renamed *Canada's National Back to the Bible Hour*.

[258] Proverbs 3:5–6.

BUT NOW, WHAT ABOUT YOU?

Not every believer acquires or is given a personal interest in the politics and governance of their local community, province, or country or feels called to become personally involved therein. But some definitely are—witness Joseph, Deborah, David, Daniel, and Esther in ancient times; or William Wilberforce and William Gladstone in the British political world; or Americans William Jennings Bryan, President James Garfield, and Senator Mark Hatfield; or the Dutch theologian and politician Abraham Kuyper; or Leonard Tilley, a Canadian Father of Confederation and New Brunswick premier; Edgerton Ryerson, founder of the Ontario education system; or William Aberhart, Ernest Manning, J. S. Woodsworth, Tommy Douglas, and several of the "Famous Five" (all women) in western Canada's political arena—to name only a few.

So what about you? Is the interest in political participation there, and where did it come from? Have you been given an interest in joining with our heavenly Father in answering 2,000 years of Christian prayer to "deliver us from the evil one"—the deliverance of human beings from injustice, illness, discrimination, environmental degradation, poverty, greed, oppression, crime, and war—deliverances that often (though not always or necessarily) involve employment of the instruments of politics, public policy, and government? Have you been given a particular interest in bringing ethical salt and light or love, joy, peace, and patience (the fruits of Christ's spirit) into such areas of human endeavour as the economy, the scientific world, the education and health-care systems, the judiciary, or the media—all of which may be penetrated and affected (though not always or necessarily) through the actions of legislatures and governments?

Is there a possibility of your becoming effectively involved politically? You may not think so, because you come from humble circumstances or a background far from the modern political arena—circumstances that appear to preclude any personal role for you in shaping your society through political action, public policy, or government. But take note of David's story, particularly its opening chapters, and take heart.

Who knows, other than God himself, what he can make of you or what he may have in store for you if your heart is open and yielded to him?

He chose David his servant
  and took him from the sheep pens;
From tending the sheep he brought him
  to be the shepherd of his people Jacob,
  of Israel his inheritance.
And David shepherded them with integrity of heart;
  with skillful hands he led them.[259]

CAUTION AND THE NEED FOR GUIDANCE

It is most important to make crystal clear that, for believers, not every inclination or *call* to become involved in politics and governance has its origins in the plan and service of God—far from it. In fact, for the believer with political interests, learning to distinguish the call of God from the siren appeals of the Tempter to personal ambition and opportunism is absolutely essential to the safe and successful navigation of the faith-political interface.[260]

Fortunately for David, the specific call to political service came to him through the wise and experienced agency of Samuel—a priest and leader who himself was a man after God's own heart.[261] Yet even Samuel had to be reminded of two vitally important considerations in recruiting believers to the work of God in the political world:

- Background, physical attractiveness, knowledge, skills, and experience—important as they are—are not the most important qualifications for such service.
- The inward condition of the human heart is the most important qualification for a right relationship with God and for political office.

More on this—the heart qualities that best qualify us for spiritually directed political action and public service—in the next chapter.

---

[259] Psalm 78:70–72.

[260] From the passage depicting the temptation of Jesus in the wilderness: "The devil led him up to a high place and showed him in an instant all the kingdoms of the world. And he said to him, 'I will give you all their authority and splendor; it has been given to me, and I can give it to anyone I want to. If you worship me, it will all be yours.' Jesus answered, 'It is written: "Worship the Lord your God and serve him only"'" (Luke 4:5–8).

[261] See 1 Samuel 2:35.

3.2 A LEADER AFTER GOD'S OWN HEART

But the LORD said to Samuel,
"Do not consider his appearance or his height …
The LORD does not look at the things people look at.
People look at the outward appearance,
but the LORD looks at the heart."[262]

TO UNDERSTAND AND LEARN FROM THE PERSONAL journey of another, particularly a journey at the interface of faith and public life, it is important to understand the historical context in which that journey began and unfolded. So let us now briefly review the context that shaped David's relationship with the priest and prophet Samuel and within which David's personal journey from the sheep pen to the throne began.

FROM THEOCRACY TO MONARCHY

Since the days of Moses, the Hebrew people had lived under a theocratic form of government. The roles of spiritual leadership and public leadership were combined, first in the person of Moses, then in Joshua, and later in the judges, of whom Samuel was the last.

Under Samuel's predecessor, Eli, the priesthood and therefore the theocracy became corrupt.[263] And although Samuel himself was a godly priest and a just administrator, his sons (like Eli's) engaged in immoral practices, and the people rejected them as Samuel's successors.[264]

---

[262] 1 Samuel 16:7.

[263] 1 Samuel 2:22–36.

[264] See 1 Samuel 8 for the story of Israel's request for a king and Samuel's response.

The children of Israel longed for a warrior-king: "Then we will be like all the other nations, with a king to lead us and to go out before us and fight our battles." Eventually they got their wish, and the story of Israel's transition from a theocracy to a monarchy—a transition in which faith and politics are inextricably intermingled—is one of the most fascinating and instructive portions of the Old Testament Scriptures for anyone operating at the interface of faith and public life today.

The transition occurred, without bloodshed, under Samuel's direction but against his better judgment. It had a profound impact on his personal relationship (and those of future priests and prophets) with Israel's future kings, especially Saul and David. It raised the issue—highly relevant to faith-oriented leaders today—of what to do when the will of the people conflicts with the leader's faith-based understanding of the will of God.

For Samuel, who firmly believed that God himself was Israel's king, the people's request for an earthly king was sacrilegious rebellion.[265] But to his immense credit, he resisted the temptation to leap to judgment based only on his own convictions and assessment of the situation. Instead, he took the request and the issue to God in prayer—no doubt agonizing prayer, as prayer over major issues with implications for hundreds of thousands of people invariably is.

God's response must have shaken Samuel to the core, for if acted upon it would turn his political and spiritual world upside down: "Listen to all that the people are saying to you; it is not you they have rejected, but they have rejected me as their king … Now listen to them; but warn them solemnly and let them know what the king who will reign over them will claim as his rights."

Reluctantly but faithfully Samuel obeyed this instruction. He had brought the issue to God in prayer, which is always the first step in trying to decide how to act on an issue at the interface of faith and politics. He had waited for a reply, not responding or acting in haste on his own initiative. Then he was told to hearken in this instance to the people's voice but to explicitly do so under protest and to make clear with prophetic insight what the long-range consequences of their actions would be. This he did also, and Samuel's warning about the expansionist and dictatorial

[265] See 1 Samuel 12:12–19.

tendencies of human government when looked to for national salvation is as relevant today as when it was given centuries ago:

> "This is what the king who will reign over you will claim as his rights: He will take your sons and make them serve with his chariots and horses, and they will run in front of his chariots. Some he will assign to be commanders of thousands and commanders of fifties, and others to plow his ground and reap his harvest, and still others to make weapons of war and equipment for his chariots. He will take your daughters to be perfumers and cooks and bakers. He will take the best of your fields and vineyards and olive groves and give them to his attendants. He will take a tenth of your grain and of your vintage and give it to his officials and attendants. Your male and female servants and the best of your cattle and donkeys he will take for his own use. He will take a tenth of your flocks, and you yourselves will become his slaves."[266]

Despite Samuel's warnings, the people still wished to proceed. When Samuel repeated their request, God replied, "Listen to them and give them a king." Samuel then proceeded to identify and anoint Saul, from the tribe of Benjamin, as Israel's first king.

SAMUEL AND SAUL

Like David, Saul came from a humble background, "from the smallest tribe of Israel and … the least of all the clans of the tribe of Benjamin."[267] When we are first introduced to him, he is hunting not for fame, fortune, or power but for some lost donkeys. His search led him to inquire of Samuel, not for spiritual or political guidance but for information on where he might find the donkeys. Humble beginnings indeed.

The record continues, "When Samuel caught sight of Saul, the LORD said to him, 'This is the man I spoke to you about; he will govern my people.'" Apparently, Samuel found this quite believable, as Saul was "as handsome a young man as could be found anywhere in Israel, and he was a head taller than anyone else."

Samuel gave Saul a message from God—that he was to be anointed leader over God's people; and that in preparation for this role, the spirit of God would come upon him and he would become a changed man.

---

266 1 Samuel 8:11–14. Samuel in effect predicts that Israel's government under its king will take at least 10 percent of the nation's gross domestic product (GDP). Today the Israeli government appropriates more than 45 percent of Israel's GDP.

267 See 1 Samuel 9–16 for the story of Samuel and Saul.

All this came to pass, and Samuel presented Saul to the people: "'Do you see the man the LORD has chosen? There is no one like him among all the people.' Then the people shouted, 'Long live the king!'"

Sadly, notwithstanding this auspicious beginning, King Saul became perhaps the most tragic character in all of the Old Testament, just as Judas Iscariot is the most tragic character of the New Testament.

At first, Saul was successful in discerning and accepting God's direction and in fighting Israel's battles, particularly with the Philistines and the Amalekites. But then on two successive occasions, he failed to heed God's specific instructions given to him through Samuel. He failed to wait for Samuel to offer the sacrifice before an engagement with the Philistines, taking on the priestly role himself. And he failed to totally destroy the Amalekites and their property as he had been instructed to do, holding on to a portion as the spoils of war.

On both occasions, Saul was deceptive in explaining what he had done (or not done) and attempted to justify his behaviour to God and to Samuel. Samuel told him he had acted foolishly and that his professed repentance was insincere and unacceptable.

As a consequence, God announced to Samuel, who conveyed the news to Saul, that he had rejected Saul as king. Saul and Samuel parted company; and "until the day Samuel died, he did not go to see Saul again." The spirit of God departed from Saul, and he was increasingly tempted and troubled by an evil spirit. (It was during this period that David entered Saul's service as a minstrel and a soldier—more on this later.)

Saul, who was once self-effacing and small in his own eyes, erected a monument to himself and his questionable victory over the Amalekites. But then, bereft of access to Samuel's guidance and God's favour, Saul descended into murderous paranoia, spiritual despair, and madness—not exactly a healthy role model for the future king, David.

CHARACTER AS A FUNDAMENTAL QUALIFICATION FOR LEADERSHIP

In the next chapter, we look at lessons to be learned from David's long and tortuous relationship with Saul before succeeding him. But long before Saul's demise, Samuel was told by God to stop mourning for him and to go and anoint a successor from among the sons of Jesse of Bethlehem.[268]

In Samuel's search for the successor to Saul, there are at least two great lessons for us as we seek to identify, recruit, and support suitable candidates for leadership in our day.

1. Outward appearances—background, physical attractiveness, knowledge, skills, experience—important as they are, are not the most important qualifications.

In our age of image politics, when being telegenic and having excellent communication skills are considered the most important prerequisites to success, this is extremely hard advice to take seriously. It seems so counterintuitive as to be almost foolish.

Even Samuel, in assessing the suitability of the various sons of Jesse for the kingship, almost repeated the same mistake he had made in assessing Saul's qualifications, i.e., putting too much faith in an impressive physical appearance. When Eliab, Jesse's first-born son and apparently an impressive figure, appeared before Samuel, Samuel's immediate thought was that "surely the Lord's anointed stands here."

> But the Lord said to Samuel, "Do not consider his appearance or his height … The Lord does not look at the things people look at. People look at the outward appearance, but the Lord looks at the heart."

To be clear, we are not being taught that such characteristics as background, physical attractiveness, knowledge, skills, and experience are unimportant. David himself had a winsome and charismatic persona. He was glowing with health and had a fine appearance and handsome features. His background as a rugged outdoorsman (which is what shepherds were) would serve him well as a soldier and during his years in exile as a hunted fugitive. David's psalms evidence an impressive knowledge of the law and of the reality of God, knowledge that he likely acquired at an early age.

But important as all these characteristics are, the lesson from Samuel's experience in recruiting David as the future king of Israel under God's direction is that they are not the most important qualifications.

[268] See 1 Samuel 16 for the story of Samuel anointing David.

2. Character—the inner condition of the human heart—is not only something most important to God; it is the most important qualification for public office.

So what did God see plainly—and Samuel only dimly at first—when he looked at David's heart?

God saw a *caring heart*. David was not the type of hired hand whom Jesus described as one who "cares nothing for the sheep."[269] Nor was he one of those self-serving and exploitive shepherds (leaders) denounced by Ezekiel: "Woe to the shepherds of Israel who only take care of yourselves! Should not shepherds take care of the flock? You eat the curds, clothe yourselves with the wool and slaughter the choice animals, but you do not take care of the flock."[270]

God saw a *servant heart, a self-sacrificial heart*. David faithfully served his father, his king, and his people. He is referred to in Scripture as God's servant—a servant king.[271] He was prepared to lay down his life for his flock, his king, his country, and his God—like the good shepherd who lays down his life for the sheep.[272] Many centuries later, the "Son of David" would also demonstrate these qualities of heart, declaring, "The Son of Man did not come to be served, but to serve, and to give his life as a ransom for many."[273]

When God looked at David's heart, he saw a *courageous heart*—courage that enabled him to defend his flock from the bear and the lion and his people from their enemies. He saw *an honest heart*, an integrity of heart that would enable David to be honest with himself and with God, unlike Saul, who was deceitful and duplicitous. In David, God saw a *faithful and loyal heart* capable of intense and prolonged loyalty to his flock, his friends (Jonathan), his king, and his God. And God saw a *patient heart*: the heart of a man who would wait on God—the posture that David frequently assumes in his psalms—rather than rush ahead impetuously on his own initiative as Saul was wont to do.

Finally, and perhaps most importantly, when God looked at David's heart he saw a *spiritually sensitive heart*—a man who could see and sense

---

[269] See John 10:13.

[270] Ezekiel 34:2–3.

[271] See Psalm 78:70–72.

[272] See John 10:14–15.

[273] Matthew 20:28.

God's presence everywhere.[274] He saw a *teachable and obedient heart*—a man who was willing to be under authority and learn to lead by first learning to follow.

CONCLUSION

You may feel that we are presenting a too idealistic picture of David and his character, and perhaps we are. David certainly had his faults, and many of these admirable heart characteristics that became evident later in his life would have been very hard for Samuel to discern in the teenage shepherd. But the main point is this: In looking for leaders—before giving your allegiance to any leader—look at the heart as God does, for character.

In seeking to identify, recruit, and support suitable candidates for leadership in our day, of course let us not ignore the importance of physical attractiveness, background, knowledge, skills, and experience. But above all, let us look for evidence of those even more important characteristics of the heart—a heart that is caring, serving, self-sacrificial, courageous, honest, faithful, loyal, patient, spiritually perceptive, teachable, and obedient to its highest calling.

---

[274] See Psalm 139:7.

3.3 THE SUBORDINATE LEADER

DAVID IN SUBORDINATION TO SAUL

WE RESUME THE STORY OF DAVID'S DEVELOPMENT AS A leader at the point where God had abandoned Saul as Israel's king and instructed Samuel to go and anoint David, a man after God's own heart, as Israel's future king.

Shortly thereafter, when Saul was troubled by an "evil spirit," one of his servants told him about David, describing him as someone "who knows how to play the lyre … a brave man and a warrior … [who] speaks well and is a fine-looking man. And the LORD is with him."[275]

David was consequently invited to enter the service of Saul on a part-time basis as a musician and an armour bearer—a rather unusual combination of responsibilities—while going back and forth from Saul to tend his father's sheep at Bethlehem.

Saul apparently had many musicians and armour bearers and paid little attention to his personal attendants. He appeared soon to forget who David was and that David was in his service. That is, until a most memorable event brought David forcibly to the attention of Saul, the army, and all of Israel.

That memorable event was, of course, the famous encounter between the shepherd boy and the giant Philistine warrior, Goliath.[276] David declared, "It is not by sword or spear that the LORD saves; for the battle is the LORD's, and he will give all of you into our hands." Empowered by his faith and against all odds from a human standpoint, David killed the

---

[275] 1 Samuel 16:14–18.

[276] 1 Samuel 17–18:8.

heavily armed giant with a stone from his sling. The Philistine army was routed and David was hailed as a national hero; the women danced and sang, "Saul has slain his thousands, and David his tens of thousands."

Because of David's popularity with the army and the people, Saul was obliged to retain him in his service and to promote him. Even Saul's own son and the heir to the throne, Jonathan, became a close friend and supporter of David's. King Saul, however, became increasingly jealous and paranoid. He resolved to destroy David, muttering darkly to himself, "They have credited David with tens of thousands … but me with only thousands. What more can he get but the kingdom?"

LIVING IN SUBORDINATION TO AN UNSTABLE AND UNGODLY LEADER

Let us now reflect for a moment on the potential for serious personal, spiritual, and political tension and conflict inherent in the employment situation in which David found himself.

Saul had been rejected by God as Israel's king, but in the eyes of Israel and of David he was still "the LORD's anointed," Israel's legitimate ruler. David was told by Samuel that he, David, was now "the LORD's anointed" and destined to succeed Saul, but David joined Saul's household and became Saul's employee and subordinate. How was David to conduct himself? Should he faithfully serve King Saul, whom God had rejected and whose behaviour was increasingly erratic and malevolent? Should he stay but start to work from within to undermine Saul until the right moment for a *coup d'état*? Should he just leave? And if so, how and when? Were there other alternatives?

WHAT ABOUT YOU?

As a Christian who has committed his or her life to God, have you ever found yourself in a subordinate employment position under the authority of a Saul—someone who apparently has legitimate and recognized authority but is ungodly, erratic, and malevolent? How do you conduct yourself? What do you do?

Suppose, for example, that you are politically inclined. You become a member of a political organization, a party, or an interest group. You feel that you have not only something to contribute but also an ability to lead, and you aspire eventually to do so. But you find yourself under the authority of the present leader, who is a Saul—unbalanced, malevolent, and increasingly suspicious of you, your potential, and your aspirations.[277] What do you do? How do you conduct yourself personally, publicly, and as a Christian?

THE SCHOOL OF SUFFERING

The life and experience of David during the first half of his life shed much light on these questions, not only for would-be leaders who find themselves in untenable subordinate positions but for anyone in similar circumstances in any organization, whether it be a company, an NGO, a university department, or a church. The commentary on this period of David's life that has been most helpful to me is that contained in a small book by Gene Edwards entitled *A Tale of Three Kings.*[278]

As Edwards observes, the God who looks at the heart and seeks leaders and followers after his own heart employs at least two very different ways of revealing and testing human hearts, including the hearts of potential or would-be leaders.

Sometimes he confers outward power and authority on an individual such as that conferred on Saul, and outward power will always reveal inner resources or the lack thereof. Certainly this was the case with Saul, who was outwardly clothed with spiritual and political authority but whose actions eventually demonstrated a total absence of the life of the spirit of God within.

However, God revealed and tested David's heart, and prepared him for his future role as king, by a very different method. David was divinely

---

[277] I have only very briefly been in this particular situation myself. As a young man, I became increasingly disillusioned with the leadership of my country's major political party leaders and therefore avoided putting myself under their authority at all. But when I became the leader of a new party founded by my friends and myself, I certainly had others under me who were discontented with my leadership—sometimes legitimately so—and aspired to replace me. This is a situation that occurs over and over again in many political organizations, companies, NGOs, and churches. As the present leader, how do you conduct yourself in such circumstances, especially if you profess to be a Christian? What are the alternatives to acting like a Saul toward those who want your job and may be prepared to go to great lengths to get it? (More on this later.)

[278] Gene Edwards, *A Tale of Three Kings: A Study in Brokenness*, reprint edition (Carol Stream: Tyndale House Publishers, 1992).

enrolled in what Edwards rightly calls "the school of suffering," suffering primarily inflicted upon him as a subordinate under the authority of King Saul.

For example,

- David was repeatedly given life-threatening military assignments by Saul in the hopes that he would fail and be killed. "I will not raise a hand against him," said Saul. "Let the Philistines do that."[279]
- Saul wreaked havoc on David's marriage and home life and sought to use David's wife (Saul's daughter Michal) as an instrument for David's destruction.
- David could not rest or be secure for a moment in Saul's presence; on several occasions Saul hurled a spear at him. Leaders like Saul are good at throwing spears.
- Saul sought to turn David's best friend, Jonathan (Saul's own son), against him, ordering Jonathan to kill David and reviling him when he refused.
- Saul sought to undermine David's source of spiritual support, accusing the priests who aided David of treason and ruthlessly slaughtering them and their families.

Thus eventually David was made an outlaw and an exile—forced out of the king's court, the army, polite society, and his own country. He was forced to wander in the desert and to live in caves and forests while Saul ruthlessly co-opted or oppressed anyone who befriended him.

Saul even used *spiritual bait* to attempt to lure David into his clutches. On one occasion, he swore an oath not to harm David. On yet another, Saul professed to repent of his homicidal intentions and even acknowledged God's will that David succeed him, only to break his word and resume the murderous pursuit of his subordinate.

LESSONS FROM DAVID'S RESPONSES: THE DOWNWARD PATH TO THE TOP

How did David respond to all of this? His responses are instructive for us if and when we find ourselves subordinate to a Saul.

David constantly refused to retaliate or to take advancement to the throne into his own hands. When spears were hurled at him, unlike most of us he did not hurl them back.

David did not decide on his own to leave Saul's company. He stayed and endured until he was driven out by Saul's decisions and actions. He

[279] 1 Samuel 18:17.

left the king's court and the army and allowed himself to be driven into exile—"until I learn what God will do for me"[280]—rather than fight for his legitimate rights and position.

On two occasions, David was in a position to take Saul's life and graduate on his own initiative from the school of suffering.[281] He was strongly urged to do so by his companions, who quoted Scripture to him in support of their advice, saying, "This is the day the LORD spoke of when he said to you, 'I will give your enemy into your hands for you to deal with as you wish.'"[282] But David refused to take Saul's life.

David decided to leave the details and timing of his succession to the throne in God's hands. When one of his fiercest and most loyal warriors, Abishai, believing it to be God's will, asked David's permission to assassinate Saul, David responded,

> "Don't destroy him! Who can lay a hand on the LORD's anointed and be guiltless? … The LORD himself will strike him, or his time will come and he will die, or he will go into battle and perish. But the LORD forbid that I should lay a hand on the LORD's anointed."[283]

DIVINE GUIDANCE WHILE IN THE SCHOOL OF SUFFERING

Throughout this entire period of his suffering under the unjust and malevolent authority of Saul, David continued to seek God's guidance, and God gave it to David. Sometimes God gave guidance directly, sometimes indirectly through the agency of others, even through David's enemies—but always just one step at a time and not in the form of some grand revelation of the path to the throne.

While on the run from Saul, David inquired of God whether he should fight the Philistines at Keilah, and God said yes.[284] David inquired again whether the Keilahites would betray him to Saul, and God said, "They will."[285] So David fled to the desert again. He inquired of God whether he

---

280 1 Samuel 22:3.

281 1 Samuel 24, 26.

282 1 Samuel 24:4.

283 1 Samuel 26:9–11.

284 1 Samuel 23:1–4.

285 1 Samuel 23:12.

should attack the Amalekites after they ransacked his encampment and carried away his wives and children. God said, "Pursue them," and David did so successfully.[286]

This is not to say that during this period David was incapable of being misguided and misled. When the Carmelite Nabal insulted David by calling him a runaway slave, David's warrior instinct took over, and he planned to slaughter Nabal's whole household. David was only restrained by the timely intervention of Abigail, Nabal's wife, and realized that God had "kept his servant from doing wrong."[287]

Finally, however, after years in the school of suffering and with no apparent release in sight, David succumbed to despair. In self-reliance, he thought to himself about the best thing to do and concluded, "One of these days I will be destroyed by the hand of Saul. The best thing I can do is to escape to the land of the Philistines. Then Saul will give up searching for me anywhere in Israel, and I will slip out of his hand."[288]

Thus, in desperation and despair, with no end to David's persecution by Saul in sight, and without any recorded seeking of God's will as on other occasions, David and his men went over to the Philistines—Israel's greatest enemy, the people of Goliath. David even prepared to march with the Philistines against his own people, a course of action that would have in all likelihood forever precluded him from the kingship of Israel.[289] But God in his mercy intervened, using the unlikely instrument of the Philistine military leaders. They deeply mistrusted David because of his past actions against them and expressly forbade him to join their forces in the battle of Mount Gilboa. It was in this battle that Saul's sons were slain and Saul himself, God's anointed, fell on his sword. He was brought down not by David and his men but by the hand of the Philistines.[290]

LIKE JESUS

There is much instruction from David's early life for Christian believers on how to act and endure if we find ourselves in a subordinate position under a boss or leader after the order of King Saul. Accept, refuse,

[286] 1 Samuel 30:8.

[287] 1 Samuel 25:39.

[288] 1 Samuel 27:1.

[289] 1 Samuel 29.

[290] 1 Samuel 31.

seek, prepare, and persevere. *Accept* that your King Saul may be in his or her position of authority, and you may be enrolled in the school of suffering, by divine appointment and for reasons you don't yet see. *Refuse* to retaliate (do not throw back spears thrown at you) in word or in deed. Treat your experience and suffering as a subordinate as preparation for advancement but do not take advancement into your own hands. Leave the details and the timing up to God. *Seek* God's guidance one step at a time and persevere. Do not be discouraged if God does not show you the big picture and master plan. Do not give in to despair and join the enemies of your King Saul in their efforts to destroy him. *Prepare* for every eventuality the best you can with the resources God has provided, including defending yourself if and when attacked, and *persevere* through whatever circumstances and along whatever path you are led until the situation is resolved.

These same lessons are taught to us by the example of Jesus, the Son of David, centuries later—an example we are enjoined by Paul and Peter to emulate:

> In your relationships with one another, have the same mindset as Christ Jesus:
> Who, being in very nature God,
> did not consider equality with God something to be used to his own advantage;
> rather, he made himself nothing
> by taking the very nature of a servant,
> being made in human likeness.
> And being found in appearance as a man,
> he humbled himself
> by becoming obedient to death—
> even death on a cross!
> Therefore God exalted him to the highest place [to the throne].[291]

> Fear God, honor the emperor … submit yourselves to your masters, not only to those who are good and considerate, but also to those who are harsh … To this you were called, because Christ suffered for you, leaving you an example, that you should follow in his steps. "He committed no sin, and no deceit was found in his mouth." When they hurled their insults at him, he did not retaliate; when he suffered, he made no threats. Instead, he entrusted himself to him who judges justly.[292]

[291] Philippians 2:5–9.

[292] 1 Peter 2:17–23.

3.4 THE INNER LIFE OF A LEADER

REVELATIONS OF THE HEART

Besides being a political and military leader, David was also a writer of poetry, a musician, and a composer of songs. Many of his poems and songs, as any reader of the Psalms will know, were expressions of his innermost fears, anxieties, and joys. Some give direct insight into what he was thinking and feeling at the time of various incidents in his life, sometimes enabling us to tell what was on the heart of this particular leader under those circumstances. Since at least some of his poems and songs apparently entered the public domain during his lifetime, they even enabled those he led (at least in his inner circle) to know what was on the heart of their leader.

In constantly giving verbal and written expression to his innermost thoughts—articulating them to God, to himself, and even to others—David stands apart from most leaders today. Contemporary politicians who write and publish serious poetry or music are extremely rare. In my recollection of my years in politics, two who come to mind are the late Václav Havel, former president of Czechoslovakia, and the late Dag Hammarskjold, former secretary general of the United Nations.[293]

Hammarskjold, who was extremely active in a political role on the world stage, is credited with saying, "I would rather live my life as though there is a God and die to find out that there isn't, than to live my life as though there is no God and die to find out there is." His diary, *Markings*,

---

[293] See, for example, Václav Havel, *Summer Meditations* (London: Faber and Faber, 1964), written while he was president of Czechoslovakia; Dag Hammarskjold, *Markings*, trans. by Leif Sjoberg and W.H. Auden (London: Faber and Faber London, 1963).

published posthumously in 1963, was described by the theologian Henry P. Van Dusen as "the noblest self-disclosure of spiritual struggle and triumph, perhaps the greatest testament of personal faith written … in the heat of professional life and amidst the most exacting responsibilities for world peace and order."[294]

Most leaders today, however, are extremely guarded even in their personal memoirs and autobiographies, rarely if ever sharing their innermost thoughts and feelings or specifically linking them to particular incidents in their careers. Certainly they are most guarded in giving expression to those thoughts and feelings during their active years for obvious reasons.

If leaders are fearful in a particular situation, the last thing they want to do is to show those fears to their followers, the media, and their opponents. If contemporary leaders are racked with uncertainty as to how to proceed in certain circumstances, they are highly unlikely to admit that uncertainty even to themselves, let alone to others. After all, isn't a leader supposed to be courageous rather than fearful, confident rather than plagued with doubts?

Not so with David. Time and time again, when he was on the run from King Saul, he poured out his heart to God, acknowledging his fear and distress but also finding strength in his faith. One example is Psalm 18. According to the ancient headnotes, "[David] sang to the LORD the words of this song when the LORD delivered him from the hand of all his enemies and from the hand of Saul."

> The cords of death entangled me;
>   the torrents of destruction overwhelmed me.
> The cords of the grave coiled around me;
>   the snares of death confronted me.
> In my distress I … cried to my God for help …
> He reached down from on high and took hold of me;
>   he drew me out of deep waters.
> He rescued me from my powerful enemy,
>   from my foes, who were too strong for me …
> Therefore I will praise you, LORD, among the nations;
>   I will sing the praises of your name.

[294] Henry P. Van Dusen, *A Biographical Interpretation of Markings* (London: Faber and Faber, 1967), 5.

WHAT ABOUT US?

Have you and I cultivated the habit of pouring out our innermost thoughts and feelings to God in verbal or written prayer on a regular basis? Surely there are good reasons for doing so.

We are invited by God himself to do so as an integral part of the development of our spiritual life and relationship with him. David said, "Trust in him at all times, you people; pour out your hearts to him, for God is our refuge."[295] Jesus invited his followers to come to him with all those fears and anxieties that can so heavily burden and oppress us, saying, "Come to me, all you who are weary and burdened, and I will give you rest."[296] Likewise, Paul in his letter to the Philippians said, "Do not be anxious about anything, but in every situation, by prayer and petition, with thanksgiving, present your requests to God. And the peace of God, which transcends all understanding, will guard your hearts and your minds in Christ Jesus."[297] Peter also advised us, "Cast all your anxiety on him [God] because he cares for you."[298]

Particularly relevant to anyone in a pressure-packed occupation is the fact that most of us very much need a safe and cathartic outlet for our emotions, especially our fears and anxieties. Otherwise, we unhealthily suppress them or vent them at the wrong time, in the wrong way, and in the wrong place.

In my own case, I acquired from my father the habit of dealing with the constant personal attacks that characterize modern politics, and the fears and anxieties they are intended to generate, by deliberately and systematically ignoring and suppressing them. This is the *develop a thick skin* approach whereby you never let any attack get to you emotionally, and you consciously suppress and avoid any emotional response. This can be quite an effective short-run coping strategy. But the danger with it is that you can become emotionally insensitive generally—insensitive to anything with emotional content or requiring an emotional response, even appeals and inputs from family and friends to whom you should be sensitive and responsive.

---

[295] Psalm 62:8.

[296] Matthew 11:28.

[297] Philippians 4:6–7.

[298] 1 Peter 5:7.

The other approach of course is to allow personal attacks to move you onto emotional ground and to respond in kind, in frustration and anger expressed physically and verbally and directed to your antagonists and their media allies. The danger in this approach, at least in the political arena, is that it is exactly how your opponents want you to react, their assumption (a valid one) being that if they can get you reacting emotionally rather than rationally, you will make serious mistakes in judgment. Some of the worst mistakes in political debates and campaigns are made when a candidate or a leader lashes out in anger and frustration at an opponent, saying words better left unsaid, doing things better left undone, and, in the public's view, *going over the top*.

I myself have used the tactic in debate of leading (some would say goading) an opponent onto emotional ground and provoking an intemperate outburst. This then allows me the comeback "If Mr. X here cannot govern his own tongue, if he cannot govern his own emotions, if he cannot govern his own temper, why should you (the voting public) trust him to govern you?"

While we do not know from the Scriptures the full extent to which David may have suppressed his fears and anxieties or how often he unwisely vented his spleen publicly in response to the taunts of his enemies, what we do know is that his primary approach throughout his life was to take it to God in prayer.[299] In a number of the psalms attributed to David, we have the example of a man of God, from shepherd to political leader, bringing the whole range of his emotional life—his fears, his frustrations, his doubts, his joys, his hopes—to the God who listens, cares, and responds in his own way and time.

You and I, no matter what public or private events and pressures stimulate our emotional life and reactions, can do no better than to follow David's example.

PRAYERS FOR PUBLIC AND POLITICAL CONCERNS

This is not the place to attempt a thorough analysis of all the subject matter of David's poems and songs. But those active in the public sphere might note the following.

[299] See Psalm 32:3–4 where David acknowledges such suppression and its disastrous impact upon him. Many of the so-called *imprecatory* or cursing psalms indicate the language he might have used. See, for example, Psalms 35, 58, 109, 140.

First, note the relatively infrequent instances of David bringing what might be considered public policy concerns to God in prayer. For instance, there is no recorded prayer by David for guidance on whether or not to expand trade with the Phoenicians or whether to raise or decrease taxes or what to do about the olive oil cartel or how best to strengthen the unity of the nation.[300]

David's overwhelming concern in his prayers was for his own safety (understandable, as his life was constantly threatened) and the protection of the nation from its enemies. You might therefore say that he certainly brought the issue of national security—the number-one concern of Israel's political and military leaders—to God. His prayers also reflect an awareness of God's concern for social justice, which likely increased and directed his own awareness of and concern for the needs of the poor and oppressed.[301] David's prayers also acknowledge the dependence of Israel's agricultural economy on God's providential provision and care.[302]

Should Christians bring public policy concerns more explicitly to God in prayer? I would answer yes, but with a caution. Yes, because we are encouraged to bring *all* our concerns to him. And yes, because for his will to be done on earth as it is in heaven, it is appropriate to seek his guidance in all spheres of human life, including those affected by public policy. It would appear, for example, that David was unwise in failing to confirm God's will as to whether or not he should conduct a national census, a public policy decision that brought judgment and grief to himself and Israel.[303]

The caution, however, is the need for great discernment in interpreting, following, and communicating God's will in such matters, given our tendency as believers to interpret our own will as God's and the complete unwillingness of modern publics to accept that spiritual considerations should have any bearing at all on public policy.[304]

---

[300] The United Kingdom of Israel would later come apart at the seams under the onerous and discriminatory taxation policies of David's son Solomon and the misguided policies of David's grandson Rehoboam.

[301] See Psalm 68:4–6.

[302] See, for example, Psalm 65:9–13.

[303] See 2 Samuel 24:1–17.

[304] I comment further on this subject in part 4 on leadership lessons from the lives of the exiles.

Second, as a Christian believer active in politics, I cannot help but read the Psalms and find individual passages that speak significantly to my political interests and concerns. I take this as an indication that God is interested in and has something to say about all our earthly preoccupations, including the political.

For example, Psalm 2 asks the question, why is the political world so hostile to genuine faith in God? Psalm 8 provides an antidote to pride—the pride that has gone before the fall of many political leaders. Psalm 19 extolls the virtue of the law—law being an occupational interest of any legislator. Psalm 22, where David expressed his feelings of abandonment, even abandonment by God himself, speaks to the loneliness of high office. Psalm 69 cautions against being carried away by religious zeal, something Christians in politics are susceptible to. Psalm 71 reflects the worries of an aging leader that his strength is failing and he may be "cast away." Psalm 78 (by Asaph) provides a spiritual-political history of Israel and prompts the question, where is the equivalent for our nation? Psalm 80 is a prayer for national spiritual revival, something our country has never really experienced. Psalm 104 speaks of God's role and ours in environmental stewardship.

And of course, for Canadians, it was a meditation by one of the Fathers of our Confederation, Leonard Tilley, on Psalm 72:8, "He shall have dominion also from sea to sea," that gave our country the name Dominion of Canada. The words of Psalm 72:1 are inscribed over the south window of the Peace Tower on Parliament Hill in Ottawa: "Give the king thy judgment, O God, and thy righteousness unto the king's son." And over the west window of the Peace Tower are inscribed the words of Proverbs 29:18: "Where there is no vision, the people perish."

My point is that there is much in the Psalms to encourage and instruct leaders, especially in our political processes, no matter what our particular interests and concerns may be.

THE DIFFICULTIES IN CULTIVATING THE INNER LIFE

Unlike David, most public leaders I know, including myself and other professing Christians, do not devote nearly enough time and attention to cultivating the inner life and the spiritual resources required to sustain it, especially during our active years. Those in active public life today find that the spiritual is constantly crowded out by external and secular pressures and inputs.

For leaders working in the public and political spheres, these pressures often originate with the media. Upon rising in the morning, the first thing many of us do is review the clippings file or online media scans to see what attacks we are subject to and what issues or developments will be disturbing the public mind that day. This is considered an absolute necessity in order to be able to respond to the media and public inquiries that are bound to follow. And then the last thing many of us do at the end of the day is watch the evening news on television, receiving yet another dose of secular anxiety-creating input capable of generating fresh worries and concerns that can last long into the night. All this type of activity has been accelerated and amplified by the growing role of social media.

One of the reasons why constantly absorbing input from the media is not conducive to the cultivation of inner resources and the spiritual life has to do with the contemporary definition of what constitutes "news." For most mass media and much of the social media, negative is more newsworthy than positive, short-run is more newsworthy than long-run, acts of violence and hatred are more newsworthy than acts prompted by love, tragedy and pathos are more newsworthy and more easily found than contentment and happiness, and controversy and conflict are far more newsworthy than agreement and co-operation.

Beginning and ending the day absorbing and reacting to these kinds of inputs is a far cry from David's meditating on the law of God day and night. And it is hard to cultivate the fruits of the Holy Spirit—love, joy, peace—when constantly feeding on media-transmitted and media-amplified hatred, tragedy, and conflict.

COUNTERMEASURES FOR CULTIVATING THE INNER LIFE

One of the things I regret is that I did not come upon Christian teaching on the "spiritual disciplines" until I was out of the political arena. I feel that a greater familiarity with these disciplines would have been of great help in maintaining my inner spiritual life and resources while in the arena.

While I realize that there is vast literature on this subject, an introduction to it that has been very helpful to me and would be helpful to anyone wanting to sustain their spiritual life under secular pressures is that provided by Ruth Haley Barton's *Sacred Rhythms: Arranging Our Lives for Spiritual Transformation.*[305]

To counter the fishbowl dimension of public life—always being open and available to demanding people and constantly in the public eye—there is the discipline of *solitude*: consciously separating oneself periodically from the madding crowd and creating space for God.

To avoid reducing the reading and study of the Scriptures to a mere intellectual enterprise akin to reading any other book, there is the discipline of *lectio divina.* The purpose is to encounter God through the Scriptures via regular preparation (*silencio*), reading short select passages (*lectio*), personally reflecting on the application of the passage to oneself (*meditatio*), responding to God based on what one has read and encountered *(oratio),* resting in the word one has received (*contemplatio*), and finally, resolving to act upon and live out the word received in the place where God has planted us (*incarnatio*).

To counter the pressures that would completely absorb us into the world, there is *prayer* itself as a spiritual discipline. This is prayer more like David's psalms; it is prayer that is akin to the inhaling and exhaling of breathing, prayer that goes beyond mere recitation and petitioning to deepen an intimate relationship with God.

To counter the all-too-easy temptation to neglect diet, exercise, and sleep, there is the spiritual discipline of *honouring the body* as a gift from the Creator and a temple of the Holy Spirit.

To counter the tendency in the secular world toward unawareness of and indifference to the presence of God and the spiritual roots of the evils that plague our personal lives and societies, there is the spiritual discipline of regular and thorough *self-examination*: the *examen of consciousness,* which awakens us to the presence of God in our daily lives, and the *examen of conscience,* which confronts us with the evils of our own lives and societies and our need for forgiveness and cleansing.

To counter the hubris of the secular world, which claims that decision-making guided solely by human wisdom is sufficient to cope with any

---

[305] Ruth Haley Barton, *Sacred Rhythms: Arranging Our Lives for Spiritual Transformation* (Downers Grove: IVP Books, 2006). I have also been aided in seeking to cultivate my inner spiritual life by Sarah Young, *Jesus Calling: Enjoying Peace in His Presence* (Nashville: Thomas Nelson, 2004).

and all personal and public problems, there is the discipline of *spiritual discernment*: learning how to seek and know the will of God and bringing it to bear wisely and graciously on the challenges that confront us.

To counter the fatigue and frustration of a world that never pauses and never sleeps, there is the spiritual discipline of *Sabbath observance*: establishing a disciplined balance between work and rest, not only periodic rest from work but learning to periodically turn off technological devices and tune out the media upon which we have become so dependent.

Finally, to counter the pressures to have our life completely defined and governed by the demands of the world, there is the amalgam of all of these into a *rule or rhythm of life* that fulfills Jesus' last great prayer for us, his followers, that we might be *in* the world as salt and light and as his ambassadors, but not *of* the world.

Did David practise anything comparable to these spiritual disciplines? Perhaps not in this systematic form; but certainly in his prayers and meditations there are abundant resources for the practice of such spiritual disciplines. It is significant that those who practise these disciplines find themselves drawn time and time again to the poems and songs of one man: David, the servant of God, whose assiduous cultivation of his inner spiritual life enabled him to survive and prosper at the dangerous and pressure-packed interface of faith and public life.

3.5 THE LEADER STUMBLES

DAVID AND BATHSHEBA

THE STORY IS A SAD ONE AND ONE OFT REPEATED SINCE. A leader at the peak of his success and known for his professed faith in God stumbles morally. David entered into an adulterous relationship with Bathsheba, wife of one of his top soldiers, Uriah the Hittite.[306] When Bathsheba announced she was pregnant, David initiated a cover-up—a cover-up that, like all cover-ups, brought even more grief than the misdeed it sought to cover.

David summoned Uriah back from the front where Israel's army was engaged with the Ammonites in the hopes that Uriah would sleep with his wife. The pregnancy would then be attributed to Uriah, and all would be well. But Israeli combat units had a rule of no sexual relations before a battle, and loyal Uriah put duty first. He refused to go home to Bathsheba, even when David got him drunk. So David sent him back to the front with a letter to his commander Joab: "Put Uriah out in front where the fighting is fiercest. Then withdraw from him so he will be struck down and die." Joab followed orders. Uriah was killed, and Bathsheba mourned for her husband. "After the time of mourning was over, David had her brought to his house, and she became his wife and bore him a son."

REVELATION AND ACCOUNTABILITY

David had everything—materially, politically, and spiritually. But he plunged himself into a personal, family, and religious crisis by violat-

[306] See 2 Samuel 11.

ing five of the ten commandments he had sworn to live by—coveting Uriah's wife and then committing theft (stealing her), adultery, murder, and bearing false witness (presenting Uriah's death as an accident of war).

"But,"—and it is an ominous *but*—"the thing David had done displeased the LORD." Fortunately for David, God had placed a man in his inner circle who was prepared to hold him morally accountable for his actions and was not afraid to speak truth to power.[307] (Would God that every leader had such a person.) The prophet Nathan was sent to confront David.

Through Nathan, God revealed the evil inherent in David's actions in an unusual way. Nathan reported to David that a traveller went to visit a rich man—a man who had everything, including sheep and cattle in abundance. But instead of taking one of his own sheep to satisfy the traveller's desire for a meal, the rich man stole a little ewe lamb from a poor neighbour who had nothing except the lamb, which was his pride and joy.

Upon hearing this report, David became incensed and declared that the rich man should make fourfold restitution for his merciless theft. Then Nathan replied, "You are the man!"

JUDGING MORALITY

By whose standards should the morality of a leader's actions and behaviour be judged? By the general moral and cultural standards of David's day and age—when women had few rights and were treated like property, and when kings had absolute power to do as they pleased—it would strike at least some of David's contemporaries as unusual that he should have any moral qualms at all or be called to account for what he had done.

And if David's actions were judged from the distant perspective of the general moral and cultural standards of our day,[308] it may strike us

[307] 2 Samuel 12.

[308] Note the danger in doing so. It was the African adventurer and author Laurens Van Der Post, reluctant to judge the morals of the ancient African bushman by the moral standards of his own day and culture, who observed, "Perhaps one of the most prolific sources of error in contemporary thinking is precisely from lifting history out of its proper

as unusual that Nathan's initial revelation of David's immoral actions focused most heavily on the fact that he had committed theft rather than that he had also committed murder and adultery—offences that in our time and culture both the secular and the religious would judge to be the more serious.

A more reliable standard for judging the morality of a leader's actions and behaviour is the standard set by a moral being superior and exterior to ourselves and independent of the general moral and cultural standards of either David's day or our own. We find that more reliable standard in the unchanging morality of our Creator, as revealed in different ways and in different circumstances to successive generations. From a moral standpoint, whether David's actions and behaviour pleased or displeased his contemporaries—whether his or our own actions please or displease us and our contemporaries—is not the point. What is important is whether or not they please God; and in David's case, they did not.

WHY?

In any event, David's immoral acts were laid before him by faithful Nathan. Then came the inevitable question, *Why*? David had everything. Why would he risk it all on an illicit love affair and the attempt at a cover-up that followed it?

> "This is what the Lord, the God of Israel says: 'I anointed you king over Israel, and I delivered you from the hand of Saul. I gave your master's house to you, and your master's wives into your arms. I gave you the house of Israel and Judah. And if all this had been too little, I would have given you even more. *Why* did you despise the word of the Lord by doing what is evil in his eyes?'"[309]

The same question has been asked a thousand times since of leaders who appeared to be at the pinnacle of their careers and influence and then risked losing it all through an illicit sexual affair—U.S. President Clinton, New York Governor Eliot Spitzer, four-star general David Petraeus, and

context and bending it to the values of another age and day" (Laurens Van Der Post, *The Lost World of the Kalahari* [London: Hogarth Press, 1958], 44).

[309] 2 Samuel 12:7–9, emphasis added.

Ted Haggard, megachurch pastor and president of the U.S. Association of Evangelicals, to name only a recent few.[310]

There are numerous modern explanations of this phenomenon, rooted, for example, in evolutionary psychology and social exchange theory.[311] Other explanations include permissive sexual attitudes generally; dissatisfaction with current relationships; unrealistic assessments of the chances of being caught; the arrogance of high office that says, "I'm the king and I can do as I please"; the loneliness and busyness of high office that erodes the ties between the leader and his own spouse and family; and the peculiar boredom of those who reach the top and seek temporary thrills through risky sexual adventures, having "no more worlds to conquer."[312]

---

[310] I am personally acquainted with several Canadian examples of this same phenomenon—divorces often rooted in unfaithfulness by politicians while in office. While I am not at liberty to discuss the personal details of the lives involved, suffice it to say that whatever immediate excitement or satisfaction may have been generated by such temporary liaisons, the consequences for all concerned are invariably tragic and long-lasting. One former member of the House, Erik Nielsen, the long-time MP for the Yukon, had the courage to frankly disclose his own experience in this regard in a memoir entitled *The House Is Not a Home* (Macmillan of Canada, 1989). See especially chapter 12, 160–164, in which he describes the devastating effects of an extramarital affair, including the tragic suicide of his wife. Nielsen concludes his narrative by offering some advice to those who aspire to elected office: "The morals and personal conduct of those in public office must always be above reproach … Do not become a commuting politician; do not tolerate separation from your family. If you do, you will lose them and learn, too late, that the House is not a home."

[311] For a contemporary discussion of this phenomenon from a behavioural-science perspective, see Alison Dagnes, ed., *Sex Scandals in American Politics: A Multidisciplinary Approach to the Construction and Aftermath of Contemporary Political Sex Scandals* (New York: Continuum International Publishing Group, 2011). See especially chapter 3 by James Griffith, "The Psychology of Risky Sexual Behavior: Why Politicians Expose Themselves." For a broader perspective that strongly emphasizes the importance of character and integrity as essential qualifications for public office, see Stanley A. Renshon, *Psychological Assessment of Presidential Candidates* (Abingdon: Routledge, 1998).

[312] A related question, worthy of further discussion, is one raised by the following observation: Why is it that to my knowledge there have been few if any media reports of illicit sexual affairs by female leaders in office such as Angela Merkel, Dilma Roussef, Cristina de Kirchner, Michelle Bachelet, Laura Chinchilla, Park Guen-hye, and Erna Solberg? Historically, we know a great deal about such female leaders as Margaret Thatcher, Megawati Sukarnoputri, Gloria Arroyo, Julia Gillard, and Helen Clarke, but nothing of this sort has ever been reported concerning them. Of all the female cabinet ministers and provincial premiers in Canada, none to my knowledge have got themselves into trouble on the sexual affair front. Why do we think this is?

But the explanation that I find most believable and most conducive to prevention and remedial action is a spiritual one: we human beings, including leaders, despite modern protestations to the contrary, are morally flawed creatures as a result of a broken relationship with the ultimate source of our being, our Creator. This deficiency in our very nature leads to thoughts and actions that, carried far enough, will mar and destroy all other relationships—with our Creator, with the physical world, with other human beings, and even with ourselves. Even those, indeed especially those, who recognize the spiritual roots of their own inclinations to evil and seek spiritual protection and deliverance through adherence to religious rules and observances are vulnerable to the desires and dictates of that nature.

And thus it was that David, the Lord's anointed, sinned and sinned grievously.

REPENTANCE AND FORGIVENESS

So what should David have done? Deny his sin and continue to cover it up, even from Nathan and God? David was wise enough from past experience to know the futility of this course of action.

> When I kept silent,
>   my bones wasted away
>   through my groaning all day long.
> For day and night
>   your hand was heavy upon me;
> my strength was sapped
>   as in the heat of summer.
> Then I acknowledged my sin to you
>   and did not cover up my iniquity.
> I said, "I will confess my transgression to the LORD"—
>   and you forgave
>   the guilt of my sin.[313]

The book of Samuel records this simple exchange between David and Nathan: "Then David said to Nathan, 'I have sinned against the LORD.' Nathan replied, 'The LORD has taken away your sin ... But ...'" Sadly and inevitably, there would be consequences (more on this later).[314]

[313] Psalm 32:3–5.

[314] 2 Samuel 12:13–14.

David acknowledged his transgressions to Nathan, but more importantly he confessed them to God. Psalm 51 is his great prayer of confession and a model prayer for all those seeking divine forgiveness and healing for offences against God. Note the nature of his admissions and petitions.

> Against you, you only, have I sinned[315]
>   and done what is evil in your sight …
> Surely I was sinful at birth …
> Yet you desired faithfulness even in the womb …
> You do not delight in sacrifice, or I would bring it …
> My sacrifice, O God, is a broken spirit;
>   a broken and contrite heart
>   you, God, will not despise …
>
> Have mercy on me, O God,
>   according to your unfailing love …
> Wash away all my iniquity
>   and cleanse me from my sin …
> Cleanse me with hyssop, and I will be clean;
>   wash me, and I will be whiter than snow.
> Let me hear joy and gladness;
>   let the bones you have crushed rejoice.
> Hide your face from my sins
>   and blot out all my iniquity.
> Create in me a pure heart, O God,
>   and renew a steadfast spirit within me …
> Restore to me the joy of your salvation
>   and grant me a willing spirit, to sustain me.

David also prayed, no doubt thinking of the fate of his predecessor King Saul, "Do not cast me from your presence or take your Holy Spirit from me."[316] This raised the question, Why was David's confession of sin accepted while Saul's was not? Why was David's violation of God's will forgiven while Saul's was not?

---

[315] While Psalm 51 is a model prayer of repentance in most respects, it is curious and somewhat disturbing that David said, "Against you [God], you only, have I sinned." In this prayer he did not acknowledge at all that he also sinned grievously against Bathsheba, Uriah, and the soldiers he implicated in Uriah's murder. Later, of course, he comforted Bathsheba (2 Samuel 12:24) and ultimately honoured her by ensuring that their son Solomon succeeded him as king (1 Kings 1:28–30).

[316] Psalm 51:11. See 1 Samuel 16:14.

When Samuel (like Nathan) confronted Saul with the fact that he had disobeyed God's commandment respecting the destruction of the Amalekites, Saul at first attempted to excuse himself but then admitted, "I have sinned. I violated the LORD's command and your instructions. I was afraid of the men and so I gave in to them. Now I beg you, forgive my sin ... but please honor me before the elders of my people and before Israel; come back with me, so that I may worship the LORD your God."[317]

The difference between Saul's confession and David's would appear to be that of frankness and sincerity. David readily acknowledged his sin without excuse, whereas Saul did not. David did not try to shift blame onto someone else, whereas Saul implied "the people made me do it," this being the second time he cited political expediency as a rationale for disobedience.[318] David did not ask Nathan to assist in providing a public cover for his transgression, whereas Saul sought such a cover from Samuel.

Genuine and open confession of sin is particularly difficult for public figures who put doing the *expedient* thing ahead of the *right* thing and who are often more concerned with the appearance than the substance of their actions. Saul's confession and repentance, marred by these factors, proved unacceptable to God, whereas David's more sincere and open confession and repentance were accepted and rewarded with forgiveness and healing.

CONSEQUENCES

If the biblical story of David were a fairy tale, it would end, notwithstanding the Bathsheba affair, by declaring that he and his family "lived happily ever after." But the David story is not a fairy tale. The sad reality of real life is that sin—the violation of right relations with God and other human beings— invariably has consequences that confession, repentance, and forgiveness may ameliorate but do not erase. So it is with us, no matter what our station in life; so it is with public figures today; so it was with David.

When David said to Nathan, "I have sinned against the LORD," Nathan replied, "The LORD has taken away your sin."[319] It would appear that God

[317] 1 Samuel 15:24–25, 30.

[318] See 1 Samuel 13:11–12.

[319] 2 Samuel 12:13.

had forgiven David even before hearing his prayer of confession and repentance. But Nathan immediately went on to declare the consequences of David's sin:

- The son to be born of his illicit liaison with Bathsheba would die. (The innocent would suffer from David's sin notwithstanding David's remorse and prayers that the child's life be spared.)
- The sword, which David had used indirectly to murder Uriah, would not depart from David's household. (David's own offspring would resort to violence as a means of addressing anything that threatened them.)
- Open sexual immorality would also plague David's household. (Just as David had secretly violated another man's wife, so his wives would one day be violated openly by "one who is close to you.")

Sadly, all of these predicted consequences of David's sin came to pass. The first son born to him and Bathsheba fell ill and died despite David's remorse, fasting, and prayers. His oldest son, Amnon, raped Tamar, the sister of Absalom, another of his sons and a potential successor to the throne. When David did nothing to discipline Amnon, Absalom took matters into his own hands and murdered Amnon in revenge. And Absalom eventually led a rebellion that nearly toppled David from his throne (more on this in chapter 3.6). During this rebellion, Absalom briefly occupied the palace in Jerusalem, where he violated his father's concubines in the sight of all Israel.

LESSONS FOR LEADERS FROM DAVID AND BATHSHEBA

Numerous lessons for leaders can be drawn from David's affair with Bathsheba, three of the most important pertaining to the impact of personal moral failings on the leader's moral authority, the need for safeguards to prevent such failings to the maximum extent possible, and the role of grace in mitigating the tragedy that such failings represent.

1. On moral authority

Leaders—whether in business, religious settings, politics, or at home—need moral authority to be effective; that is, they need authority that comes not from their position or title but from their character and the morality of their actions. It is particularly important that those of us who make the laws, proclaim the laws, and administer the laws should *keep* the laws, or else we lose our moral authority to legislate and to govern.

In David's case, perhaps the most far-reaching consequence of his sin was the loss of his moral authority within his own family and with the commanders of his army. How could he insist on high moral standards for his sons and daughters with respect to their sexual behaviour after the way he had conducted himself with Bathsheba? How could he teach them to be open and truthful when he had engaged in such a notorious cover-up? How could he urge them to refrain from violence when he had unjustly and malevolently employed the sword to dispose of one of his most loyal soldiers? And how could he insist on honesty, faithfulness, and loyalty from his army officers when they knew how they had been used to betray and murder Uriah?

In addition to the obvious spiritual reasons for avoiding immoral personal behaviour, there is an additional pragmatic reason for doing so. Since real leadership requires moral as well as legal authority, any personal action that erodes personal moral authority must be scrupulously avoided.

2. On safeguards

This is not the place for a thorough description and discussion of safeguards that might better protect leaders from stumbling morally, especially through sexual temptations and indiscretions of the type that marred David's leadership and testimony. Nor am I qualified to provide a thorough discussion of such safeguards. But let me make two relevant points.

First, there are some simple, practical guidelines for minimizing sexual temptations and exploitations—especially for those engaged in public life—that can be helpful if they are actually practised. These include the following:

- Putting the maintenance of right relationships with God and your spouse ahead of all other relationships. This includes faithfully petitioning our heavenly Father to "lead us not into temptation, but deliver us from the evil one."[320]
- Avoiding long periods of absence from your spouse and family and being at loose ends on your own after intense activity during those periods. (This is a matter of disciplined scheduling.)
- Employing, as close associates and staff, people of impeccable moral character and distancing yourself from those of loose morals.

[320] Matthew 6:13.

- Avoiding potentially compromising situations, especially with members of the opposite sex. (Billy Graham's advice to pastors about never being in a room alone behind a closed door with a parishioner of the opposite sex is relevant to political leaders as well.)
- Refraining from excessive use of alcohol or any substance or practice that impairs your judgment.
- Recognizing that sexual harassment is an illegal and immoral activity to be scrupulously avoided.[321]
- Being alert to the possibility that unscrupulous opponents, opportunists,[322] and lobbyists[323] may deliberately seek to engage you in morally compromising situations and exploit any perceived cracks in your personal integrity.

Second, on a broader societal level, it seems to me that we need to frankly acknowledge that neither the religiously rooted Victorian ethic of "thou shalt not" nor the "do as you please as long as it doesn't appear to hurt anyone" ethic of the modern sexual liberation movement have proven sufficient as a framework for governing the ethics of sexual behaviour in our time. The former has too often led to a hypocritical denial and unhealthy suppression of human sexuality, while the latter has facilitated global epidemics of sexually transmitted diseases, the commodification

---

[321] The Canada Labour Code (R.S.C. 1985, c. L-2, p. III, s. 247.1) defines sexual harassment to mean "any conduct, comment, gesture or contact of a sexual nature (a) that is likely to cause offence or humiliation to any employee; or (b) that might, on reasonable grounds, be perceived by that employee as placing a condition of a sexual nature on employment or on any opportunity for training or promotion." Such harassment is expressly prohibited by the *Canadian Human Rights Act* (R.S.C. 1985, c. H-6, p. I, s. 14).

[322] In most capital cities, there are likely to be a few unscrupulous lawyers who monitor dismissals of political staff, particularly cases where a female staffer has been dismissed by a male political employer. These staffers are then approached and asked whether there was ever any situation during their employment that might possibly be represented as "sexual harassment" and used to damage the reputation of the political employer. If there has been such a situation the political employer is then threatened with court action and damaging publicity unless an out-of-court financial settlement is agreed to, the proceeds from which are split between the lawyer and client.

[323] I recall the story of a lobbyist from Texas who came to Canada to lobby members of the Canadian Parliament and the Alberta Legislature with respect to the financing of the original TransCanada PipeLine project in the 1950s. When a young Canadian colleague suggested that it was important to research the policy positions and voting records of the members they were trying to influence, the lobbyist laughed and said, "Son, you don't understand human nature. All I need to know about an elected official is whether he has an alcohol problem, a financial problem, or a skirt-chasing problem, and I'll know how to get to him."

of sexual relations, widespread human trafficking, and an ever-expanding global market in pornography and sexual services for money.

What is needed is a more effective ethical framework for guiding sexual behaviour in the 21st century—including the sexual behaviour of leaders—and teaching conducive to that inner transformation that makes adherence to those ethics a reality in practice. In this regard, the Christian teachings on this subject I have found most helpful and commend to others are those of Dr. Charles Price, former teaching pastor of The People's Church in Toronto.[324]

3. On grace that is greater

I once heard a New Year's sermon by a New Zealand pastor, Lloyd Crawford, based on David's Psalm 23. Crawford explained how God himself is the Great Shepherd who would lead us in the paths of righteousness, restore us when we fall or go astray, and protect us in the presence of our enemies, even in the shadow of death. But working with the Great Shepherd and faithfully following behind the flock are his two great sheepdogs, "goodness and mercy." If we will follow the Shepherd, they will follow us all the days of our lives until at last we dwell safely forever in the house of the Lord.

Whether David, in the days immediately after his disastrous affair with Bathsheba, sought comfort in the words of the Shepherd Psalm that he had penned years before, we do not know. But what we do know is that, despite his sin and its tragic consequences, he was never abandoned by the Great Shepherd or his two faithful sheepdogs, goodness and mercy.

The repentant and chastened king retained his throne, and both his life and his reign knew God's continued favour and blessing. He remained devoted to Bathsheba and was eventually succeeded by their son Solomon. Centuries later, Jesus himself was not ashamed to be described as the Son of David.

There is goodness and mercy for all of us who have stumbled morally, no matter who we are or what our position, if we will trust in the grace (unmerited favour) of the Great Shepherd of our souls.

The words of the apostle Paul, written to the believers in Rome, could also have been spoken by Nathan the prophet to David the king.

[324] See Dr. Charles Price's six-part series on gender and sexuality, available at www.livingtruth.ca.

"But where sin increased, grace increased all the more."[325] And David the Psalmist, had he been able to peer far enough into the future, could have joined with us in singing,

> Marvelous grace of our loving Lord,
> Grace that exceeds our sin and our guilt!
> Yonder on Calvary's mount outpoured,
> There where the blood of the Lamb was spilled.
> Grace, grace, God's grace,
> Grace that will pardon and cleanse within;
> Grace, grace, God's grace,
> Grace that is greater than all our sin![326]

[325] Romans 5:20.

[326] Julia H. Johnston, *Grace Greater than our Sin*, stanza 1 (1911).

3.6 THE LEADER CHALLENGED—DOMESTICALLY

DAVID, A NATURAL LEADER

SCRIPTURE INDICATES THAT DAVID WAS A NATURAL leader whose leadership was readily accepted by those around him. After his victory over Goliath and his initial military successes against the Philistines, David was soon accepted as a leader by Israel's military.[327] During the long years of persecution by Saul, he became the natural rallying point around which all those disenchanted with Saul's reign gathered in increasing numbers.[328] After Saul's death, the tribe of Judah immediately accepted him as Saul's successor, but the rest of Israel did not, and a civil war broke out.[329] Because of how David conducted himself, it was not long until the rest of Israel came to the conclusion that they too should accept him as their king.[330]

Nevertheless, every leader will eventually face challenges, especially from those who aspire to be leaders themselves. In David's case, these challenges came late in his reign and primarily from within his own family, in particular from his sons Absalom (son of his third wife, Maacaa of Geshur) and Adonijah (son of his fourth wife, Haggith).[331]

---

[327] 1 Samuel 18:5.

[328] 1 Samuel 22:1–2.

[329] 2 Samuel 2.

[330] 2 Samuel 5:1–4.

[331] David had seven wives, the seventh of which was Bathsheba, who bore him Solomon and three other children. He also had nine children by his concubines (1 Chronicles 3:1–9).

DAVID AND ABSALOM: FATHER AND SON

The earliest mentions of Absalom in Scripture reveal deep personal tensions between a son and his father. These tensions occurred within the context of what today might be called a dysfunctional family, of which David was the head.[332] Because the father was a political leader and the son had political aspirations, their conflict eventually had serious ramifications, culminating in the ultimate disaster of civil war. In order to understand David's succession crisis, it is necessary to examine the family context and personal tensions between Absalom and David that lay at its roots.

As discussed in chapter 3.5, one of the most tragic consequences of David's adulterous affair with Bathsheba and his attempt to cover it up by having her husband Uriah murdered was his loss of moral authority within his own family. The prophet Nathan sadly predicted that both sexual immorality and the violence of the sword would plague David's own household—a prophecy that soon came true, with Absalom as a major instrument of its fulfillment.[333]

When Amnon, David's oldest son and his logical successor, raped Tamar, the beautiful sister of Absalom, David was furious but apparently did nothing to discipline Amnon. So Absalom took matters into his own hands, fulfilling the role that he believed his father should have filled. He invited the king and all his sons to join him at a sheep shearing. David declined to attend but gave his blessing to the event and ordered all his

---

[332] The extent to which interpersonal tensions and father-son conflicts plagued the most prominent families of the Old Testament despite their faith commitments is disturbing. Cain, the first son of Adam and Eve, killed his brother and became permanently estranged from his family. Abraham and Sarah, despairing that they would never have a son as God has promised, agreed that he should father a child through Sarah's maidservant Hagar, resulting in conflict between Sarah and Hagar and the eventual expulsion of Hagar and Ishmael from Abraham's household. Abraham's promised son, Isaac, married to Rebekah, also presided over a divided household—Isaac favoured his firstborn son, Esau, while Rebekah favoured their younger son, Jacob, who deceived his father to obtain his blessing and alienated his brother by stealing his birthright. Jacob was in turn deceived by his father-in-law, Laban (who tricked Jacob into marrying Leah when he thought he was marrying Rachel), and by his own sons when they sold Jacob's favoured son, Joseph, into slavery. And then there was the tension in David's household, culminating in Absalom's rebellion and efforts to kill his father. None of these families provide an admirable faith-based model of parent-child or father-son relations.

[333] See 2 Samuel 12:9–12; 16:20–22.

sons, including Amnon, to attend. When Amnon was "in high spirits from drinking wine" Absalom ordered his men to kill him. All the rest of the king's sons fled the scene of the crime, but it was erroneously reported to David that they too had been killed. For a brief time, David likely believed that Absalom had staged a bloody coup.

By the time the truth came out, Absalom had fled to his grandfather Talmai's court at Geshur, where he lived in exile for three years. David apparently came to understand that his failure to address Amnon's crime was the cause of Absalom's action and longed to be reconciled to him. But again David did nothing, and the rift between father and son deepened.[334]

Eventually Joab, David's military commander, knowing "that the king's heart longed for Absalom" and employing a devious strategy, secured David's consent for Absalom to return to Jerusalem.[335] But David insisted, "[Absalom] must go to his own house; he must not see my face." So Absalom lived an additional two years in Jerusalem without seeing the king. His family and political status having been in limbo for five years, Absalom appealed to Joab to serve as an intermediary between himself and his father. Joab at first refused, so Absalom set fire to Joab's barley field, which was adjacent to his own. This brought Joab to Absalom's house, where Absalom confronted Joab with the message "Look, I sent word to you and said, 'Come here so I can send you to the king to ask, "Why have I come from Geshur? It would be better for me if I was still there!"' Now then, I want to see the king's face, and if I am guilty of anything, let him put me to death."

FATHERS AND SONS

At the root of the eventual political and military contest between David and Absalom was the tension between a son and his father. While I realize that there is vast literature on the subject of father-son relations and that I am not an authority in this area, a book that has helped me better understand my relationship with my own sons and the flawed relationship between David and Absalom is entitled *From Wild Man to Wise Man: Reflections on Male Spirituality* by the Franciscan Richard

[334] See 2 Samuel 13:23–39.

[335] 2 Samuel 14.

Rohr, founder and animator of the Center for Action and Contemplation in Albuquerque, New Mexico.[336]

Rohr makes three observations directly relevant to the relationship between David and Absalom as father and son.

First, "Much of the human race experiences an immense father hunger. It is felt by women, but even more so by men. It seems the same-sex parent has a unique importance in a child's life, and *his or her absence leaves a huge, aching hole inside that is never really filled.*"[337]

Second,

> Father hunger often becomes a full-blown *father wound* … the woundedness in a man's psyche that results from not having a father—whether it is because the father has died or left the family, because the father's work keeps him absent from the scene most of the time or because the father keeps himself aloof from involvement with his children. In any event, the result is a deep hurt, a deprivation that leads to a poor sense of one's own center and boundaries, a mind that is disconnected from one's body and emotions, a life often with the passivity of an unlit fire.[338]

Third, Rohr concludes, "Without the father's energy, there is a void, an emptiness in the soul which nothing seems able to fill. All of the predictable wounds of failure and rejection wound deeply … As we grow older, we just get deeply sad. *It is sadness, but it shows itself as anger.*"[339]

Father hunger and the *father wound* that manifests itself in alienation and anger were very much present in the case of Absalom and David. In their case, it was further aggravated by the complexities of a patriarchal family with multiple wives, concubines, and numerous children by different mothers.

As an active political and military leader, David was no doubt very busy and absent much of the time. He failed to stand up for Tamar, Absalom's sister, when she was raped by David's oldest son, Amnon, a failure that Absalom bitterly resented. When Absalom hosted the sheep-shearing party to which he specifically invited his father, for whatever

---

[336] Richard Rohr, *From Wild Man to Wise Man: Reflections on Male Spirituality* (Cincinnati: St. Anthony Messenger Press, 1990, 2005).

[337] Rohr, *From Wild Man to Wise Man*, 65, emphasis added.

[338] Rohr, *From Wild Man to Wise Man*, 73, emphasis added.

[339] Rohr, *From Wild Man to Wise Man*, 83.

reason David declined to attend. When Absalom fled into exile after compensating for David's failure to discipline Amnon by having him murdered, the alienation of the son from the father was further deepened. And although we are told that "David mourned many days" and that he "longed to go to Absalom," David apparently failed to communicate any of these feelings to Absalom or to act on them.[340]

Although the Psalms would indicate that David was capable of feeling the full range of human emotions in his relationship to God, perhaps his long years as a soldier experiencing the horrors of war and personal combat had hardened him to the point where he was almost totally insensitive to the feelings of other human beings, especially those of other men. I have observed this phenomenon myself among political people (myself included) whose defence against personal attacks has been to develop a thick skin. In time, this skin can become so thick that personal, emotion-charged attacks from opponents are unable to penetrate it. Sadly, even emotion-based messages from loved ones and friends also fail to get through.

As Rohr once again observes,

> I suspect that non-weeping [i.e., insensitivity to feelings and an inability to express them] is a price that the male has had to pay for centuries of going to war … You have to split, deny and repress your feeling world to survive such ordeals. In effect, we have chosen the survival of cultural and nationalistic pretences over the survival of the male soul. Yes, men are often warlike, but they have been bred like dogs to do it, over-developing some qualities like detachment and stoicism, and repressing others like feeling, empathy and vulnerability.[341]

Returning to our story, finally after five years in which father and son did not even speak to each other let alone seek reconciliation, David summoned Absalom to the palace. Absalom bowed low to the king, and the king kissed him. But the attempted reconciliation of father to son was too little, too late. At that point, the father hunger and father wounding of Absalom, compounded by his growing political ambition, had deepened into anger and rebelliousness, which soon manifested themselves and shook the kingdom to its foundations.

---

340 2 Samuel 13:37–39.

341 Rohr, *From Wild Man to Wise Man*, 83–84.

CONCLUDING LESSONS

What can we learn thus far from the story of David and Absalom about the nature and appropriate handling of the succession issue within a business, political, or religious organization?

As a political leader, I find it highly instructive to realize that succession issues and conflicts over leadership within modern business, political, and religious organizations are often akin to family feuds—with the company, political party, or church being the family and succession involving replacement of an old and established leader (the father figure) with an ambitious up-and-coming member of the younger generation. Various other officials of the organization may also play the *mother role*, some seeking to maintain peace in the family by trying to reconcile father and son, others seeking to maintain the authority of the father to whom they are wedded, and yet others seeking to advance their preferred successor (as did Rebekah, in the case of Jacob, and the mother of James and John in Jesus' time).

What this analogy suggests is that beneath and behind the functional relations among the members of any organization, including those who lead it or aspire to lead it, lie the human and personal relationships (or lack of them) between the main characters involved. If those relationships are flawed, broken, or non-existent, succession will still occur. The old leader will eventually be replaced by a new one. But the process may well leave behind a trail of injustices, resentments, and wounds that will haunt and cripple the organization and the interpersonal relations of its key members for years to come.

Thus, we are driven again to the conclusion that so much of the life of David illustrates—indeed it is the main message of the Bible—that right relationships between ourselves and God, between ourselves as human beings, between members of a family, and between members and leaders of an organization are the all-important thing. How we achieve and maintain such relationships ought to be the primary concern of any leader if organizational success and peace, including an orderly and positive succession, are to be achieved.

In David's day, acceptance of the authority of law—God's Law—was seen as the key to achieving and maintaining such relationships. But as we have seen, there are limits to what laws and rule-making can achieve in terms of establishing right relationships even within a family, let alone a kingdom.

The day would come, however, predicted by the prophets of Israel, when a future "Son of David" would open the way to that inner transformation of human beings that writes the law of God on human hearts rather than in statute books, and whose spirit has the potential to "turn the hearts of the parents to their children, and the hearts of the children to their parents."[342] This Son of David could say what Absalom could never say, "I and the [my] Father are one,"[343] providing a model of father-son relationship vastly superior to any modelled in the Old Testament. And to those aspiring to be "chief" in their kingdoms, he would say let such be "servants of all," transmuting by their teaching and example the self-serving ambition of their politically motivated followers into self-sacrificial service.[344]

---

[342] Malachi 4:6. Note that this is the last promise of the Old Testament.

[343] John 10:30.

[344] Mark 10:44 (KJV).

3.7 THE LEADER CHALLENGED—POLITICALLY

DAVID AND ABSALOM: THE KING AND WOULD-BE KING

IN THIS CHAPTER, WE CONTINUE THE THEME OF THE leader challenged, in particular the challenge to David's leadership by his son Absalom.[345] At some point—we are not told exactly when, perhaps while he was brooding in exile from the kingdom and the king's household—Absalom decided that the old king (his father, David) should be replaced by himself. So upon his return to Jerusalem, he began to undermine David's authority. He did so by presenting himself not as a warrior and military leader equal or superior to David but rather as a leader who was particularly interested in domestic affairs—an area David may have tended to neglect, given his preoccupation with national security.

---

[345] My own experience as a political leader with the succession issue, while not to be compared in spiritual or political significance to that of David and Absalom, occurred in the context of Canadian federal politics from 1987 to 2004. Its proper interpretation would require explaining the details of the politics and personalities of that period, which is beyond the scope of this book. Briefly, however, it involved the creation of a new political party of which I became the leader, mainly by default, as few others wanted the job. This was followed by a major effort to broaden our base through the creation of two successor parties, each of which became the official opposition in the Parliament of Canada, with the last becoming the governing party. In the first transition, I lost the leadership to a provincial cabinet minister from outside our original group, who in turn lost the leadership to one of my younger parliamentary colleagues, who had also served as my first policy chief. He in turn became prime minister of Canada in 2006. For a detailed description of these events and the succession issues they entailed, see my *Think Big* and Tom Flanagan's *Waiting for the Wave: The Reform Party and the Conservative Movement* (Kingston: McGill-Queen's University Press, 1995) or Bob Plamondon's *Full Circle: Death and Resurrection in Canadian Conservative Politics* (Toronto: Key Porter Books, 2006).

Absalom got up early every morning and positioned himself on the road leading to the city gate.[346] Whenever anyone had a complaint, especially a complaint against the king and the government, he acknowledged it. He lamented, "there is no representative of the king to hear you," and added, "If only I were appointed judge in the land! Then everyone who has a complaint or a case could come to me and I would see that they receive justice."

Justice! Justice in personal and domestic affairs. Justice that the king was slow or lax to provide. Absalom no doubt spoke with fervour on this theme. Had not he himself experienced first-hand the king's failure to provide justice for his sister Tamar? And had not the king treated Absalom himself unjustly?

Moreover, Absalom combined the offer of "justice for Israel" with personal charisma and attractiveness. He was a campaign manager's dream: "In all Israel there was not a man so highly praised for his handsome appearance as Absalom. From the top of his head to the sole of his foot there was no blemish in him."[347] And as for employing the campaign tactic of kissing babies, Absalom went one better: "Whenever anyone approached him to bow down before him, Absalom would reach out his hand, take hold of him and kiss him. Absalom behaved in this way toward all the Israelites who came to the king asking for justice, and so he stole the hearts of the people of Israel."[348]

Absalom also understood the value of covering his political ambition with a devotional and religious veneer (an essential in a theocratic kingdom like ancient Israel).[349] He still professed to be David's "servant" and informed the king that he had made a vow to God while in exile that, if God should ever return him to Jerusalem, he would worship him in Hebron. (His choice of Hebron, in Judah, is significant as it is the place where David's kingship began.) The king gave his blessing for Absalom to go to Hebron to worship, saying, "Go in peace."

> Then Absalom sent secret messengers throughout the tribes of Israel to say, "As soon as you hear the sounds of the trumpets, then say, 'Absalom is king in

[346] 2 Samuel 15:1–4.

[347] 2 Samuel 14:25.

[348] 2 Samuel 15:5–6.

[349] 2 Samuel 15:7–13.

> Hebron.'" ... And so the conspiracy gained strength, and Absalom's following kept on increasing. A messenger came and told David, "The hearts of the people of Israel are with Absalom."

Thus, four years of planning morphed into conspiracy, and the conspiracy ripened into outright rebellion—a full-scale effort by Absalom and his supporters to topple David from his throne and crown Absalom the Just as his successor.

TWO PATHS TO POWER

As noted previously (chapter 3.3), the commentary I have found most helpful and true to life on the complex spiritual and political relations between Saul, David, and Absalom is that provided by Gene Edwards in his book entitled *A Tale of Three Kings: A Study in Brokenness.* Much of what follows here is a summary of Edwards' insights.

Before dealing with David's reaction to Absalom's insurrection, Edwards draws our attention to the similarities and differences between David and Absalom and their respective approaches to becoming king.

When Absalom rebelled against his father, David was about the same age as King Saul when his reign came to an end, and Absalom was about the same age as David when Saul was trying so hard to kill him. Both were driven by their respective circumstances into exile from the kingdom and the king's household; both were noticeably handsome and charismatic; and both were increasingly recognized by others as potential successors to the throne.

But here the similarities end. Whereas in his rise to power David had a spiritual mandate from the priestly prophet Samuel, there is no record of Absalom's seeking or receiving such a mandate. Whereas David was constantly respectful of King Saul's position as "the LORD's anointed" and never sought to undermine his authority no matter how many injustices Saul perpetrated against David, Absalom devoted at least four years to assiduously undermining David's authority. Whereas the discontented elements in the kingdom gradually came of their own volition to David, Absalom sought out the discontented and deliberately cultivated their discontent. Whereas David seemed to know instinctively that to foment rebellion against Saul, Israel's first king, would split the kingdom spiritually and politically, Absalom seemed to have no such inhibitions.

And whereas David's greatest preoccupation was defending Israel from its external enemies, Absalom's focus was persuading his countrymen to believe that their greatest enemy was within.

Most importantly, David steadfastly resisted the temptation to kill Saul and take the kingdom by force, even when urged by his closest associates to do so. By contrast, when Absalom's counsellor Ahithophel presented to him a plan with the specific objective to "'strike down only the king' … This plan seemed good to Absalom and to all the elders of Israel."[350]

DAVID'S REACTION TO THIS CHALLENGE TO HIS LEADERSHIP

So how did David respond to this challenge to his leadership from Absalom? Did David treat Absalom as Saul treated David—hunt him and his associates down and if at all possible kill them? In other words, did David become a Saul in order to retain his position? Or was there another way—a way consistent with how David ascended to the throne in the first place?

What was that way again (see chapter 3.3)? *Accept* that it may very well be God's will that you be replaced and that Absalom—yes, even wicked Absalom—may be God's instrument for achieving that purpose. Perhaps once again you are being enrolled in God's school of suffering for reasons you do not yet see. Treat your experience and suffering as preparation for whatever the future may hold, leaving the details and the timing up to God. *Refuse* to go on the offensive against your adversary (do not throw back spears thrown at you). Continue to *seek God's guidance* one step at a time, and do not be discouraged if God does not show you the big picture or master plan. *Prepare* for every eventuality the best you can with the resources God has provided, including defending yourself if and when attacked. And do not give in to despair, but *persevere* through whatever circumstances and along whatever path you are led until the situation is resolved.

So how does it all work out in practice? When David was advised that Absalom was marching on Jerusalem, David, the warrior-king who had fought a thousand battles, did not go out to meet him. Instead,

[350] 2 Samuel 17:1–4.

> David said to all his officials who were with him in Jerusalem, "Come! We must flee … We must leave immediately, or he [Absalom] will move quickly to overtake us and bring ruin upon us and put the city to the sword" … The king set out, with all the people following him … The whole countryside wept aloud as all the people passed by … and … moved on toward the wilderness.[351]

David was again headed to the wilderness, driven there this time by his own son as once before he was driven there by Saul.

Is David one hundred percent convinced that he is in God's will and Absalom is not? No! He instructs Zadok the priest to take the ark of the covenant, the symbol of God's earthly presence in Israel, back to the city where Absalom was in control, with these words: "Take the ark of God back into the city. If I find favor in the LORD's eyes, he will bring me back and let me see it and his dwelling place again. But if he says, 'I am not pleased with you,' then I am ready; let him do to me whatever seems good to him."[352]

On the road to the wilderness, he was confronted by Shimei, a man from Saul's clan who had never accepted David's kingship and who cursed him with these words:

> "Get out, get out, you murderer, you scoundrel! The LORD has repaid you for all the blood you shed in the household of Saul, in whose place you have reigned. The LORD has given the kingdom into the hands of your son Absalom. You have come to ruin because you are a murderer."[353]

When one of David's fighting men offered to remove Shimei's head, David restrained him, saying, "My son, my own flesh and blood, is trying to kill me. How much more, then, this Benjamite! Leave him alone; let him curse, for the LORD has told him to. It may be that the LORD will look upon my misery and restore to me his covenant blessing instead of his curse today."[354]

David did not directly retaliate against Absalom, nor was David certain of God's will respecting the challenge to his throne; but he was not passive in the face of this threat to himself and the kingdom. His entourage

---

[351] 2 Samuel 15:14–23.

[352] 2 Samuel 15:25–26.

[353] 2 Samuel 16:7–8.

[354] 2 Samuel 16:11–12.

included all his fighting men, particularly Joab, former commander of the army. His intelligence advised him that his former counsellor Ahithophel had joined the conspirators, so David prayed, "LORD, turn Ahithophel's counsel into foolishness."[355]

David also instructed one of his most trusted confidants, Hushai the Arkite, to join Absalom's council. Hushai did so and was accepted even though Absalom suspected his loyalty. When Ahithophel counselled Absalom to mount an immediate attack on David and his forces, Hushai counselled delay until Absalom could organize a larger force including all Israel. After receiving this conflicting advice, "Absalom and all the men of Israel said, 'The advice of Hushai the Arkite is better than that of Ahithophel.' For the LORD had determined to frustrate the good advice of Ahithophel in order to bring disaster on Absalom."[356]

The crisis then moved swiftly to its climax. David mustered his forces and sent them out under three commanders, Joab, Abishai, and Ittai. He offered to march with them, but the troops insisted that he not endanger himself, so he remained behind.

> So the king stood beside the gate while all the men marched out in units of hundreds and of thousands. The king commanded Joab, Abishai and Ittai, "Be gentle with the young man Absalom for my sake." And all the troops heard the king giving orders concerning Absalom to each of the commanders.[357]

Meanwhile, Absalom had crossed the Jordan "with all the men of Israel" under the command of Amasa, whom he had appointed over the army in place of Joab.[358] The battle took place in the forest of Ephraim, where Absalom's troops were routed by David's men, with over twenty thousand casualties. When Absalom tried to flee on his mule, his hair became entangled in the thick branches of an oak tree, and he was left hanging in mid-air. One of David's soldiers witnessed this and reported the situation to Joab, who rebuked him for not killing Absalom on the spot. The soldier reminded Joab of David's charge by stating, "Protect the

[355] 2 Samuel 15:31. This is David's only recorded prayer during the insurrection. Note that it is not a prayer for victory or for the destruction of Absalom but simply a prayer for foolishness on the part of Absalom's advisors.

[356] 2 Samuel 16:14. See 2 Samuel 16:5–17:14.

[357] 2 Samuel 18:4–5.

[358] 2 Samuel 17:24–25. See 2 Samuel 18.

young man Absalom, for my sake," but Joab was unmoved. He plunged three javelins into Absalom's heart while he hung from the tree. Ten of Joab's armour bearers then finished the job, and the body was thrown into a pit in the forest and covered with rocks.

Two messengers ran to bring David news of the battle. The first brought the good news, "All is well! ... Praise be to the LORD your God! He has delivered up those who lifted their hands against my lord the king." And when David asked, "Is the young man Absalom safe?" the messenger professed not to know. But when the second messenger arrived and was asked the same question, he declared, "May the enemies of my lord the king and all who rise up to harm you be like that young man."

So David was still king, delivered from the most serious rebellion ever to threaten his reign. But David, the less-than-perfect father who never really knew how to relate to his son, "went up to the room over the gateway and wept. As he went he said, 'O my son Absalom! My son, my son Absalom! If only I had died instead of you—O Absalom, my son, my son!'"

CONCLUDING LESSONS

What can we learn from the story of David and Absalom about the nature and appropriate handling of the succession issue within a business, political, or religious organization?

For me as a political leader, one of the most important lessons is that for the person of faith, there is an alternative to the route followed by Saul and Absalom—the approach that comes most naturally to us as self-centred human beings. Saul's approach was to defend his kingship to the death, employing whatever means possible—from deception to murder—to destroy his potential successor. Absalom's approach was to pursue the kingship by whatever means possible—from deception to murder—to destroy the present king and seize his throne. Saul even sought the aid of the occult to plot his course; Absalom used superficial religious observances as a means to achieve his political ends. He neither felt accountable to God for his position or his actions nor sought God's counsel.

In contrast, David's way, both to becoming king and to retaining his kingship, was rooted in his belief that the kingship is ultimately in the hands of God to dispose of as he sees fit. As Gene Edwards observed, sometimes God confers executive power upon unworthy persons—for reasons we do not understand, but perhaps to thereby reveal the true character of the person holding the office. David's role was simply and constantly to seek God's will for himself and for the kingdom, regardless of what personal advantage or disadvantage that role conferred upon him.

David would have concurred, as should we, with the declaration that the prophet and political leader Daniel made many years later to the king of Babylon: that at the end of the day, "the Most High is sovereign over all kingdoms of earth and gives them to anyone he wishes."[359] In such circumstances, as in all the circumstances of life, let us pray, "Your will be done, on earth as it is in heaven."[360]

[359] Daniel 4:25, 32.

[360] Matthew 6:10.

3.8 LAST WORKS OF A LEADER

AS DAVID ENTERED HIS LATTER YEARS, HIS TWO MAJOR works focused on preparing for the future—a characteristic of good leaders, who, even as the sun sets on their personal careers, look ahead rather than back. One of these last major works was political and involved David's preparing for his son Solomon to succeed him as king. But the other, and the one to which he devoted the most attention, was spiritual—making extensive preparations for the building of a dwelling place (a temple) for the God whom he had served all his life.

So what can we learn from the last works of David, a leader who operated at the interface of faith, public life, and politics throughout all of his adult life?

PREPARATIONS FOR THE FUTURE

At some earlier point in his career, David had promised Bathsheba—perhaps out of guilt over how he had used her and murdered her husband—that their son Solomon would succeed him as king, despite the fact that David's oldest son, Amnon, was the natural heir to the throne.[361] But apparently nothing was done to formalize this commitment, since at the time of Absalom's rebellion there appears to have been no clear plan for the orderly and peaceful succession of David as king. Not so, however, toward the end of his life. In one of his last major addresses to the officials and people of Israel, David declared, "Of all my sons—and

---

[361] 1 Kings 1:30.

the LORD has given me many—he has chosen my son Solomon to sit on the throne of the kingdom of the LORD over Israel."[362]

However, this declaration of Solomon's right of succession was not unconditional. David went on to address Solomon, saying, "And you, my son Solomon, acknowledge the God of your father, and serve him with wholehearted devotion and with a willing mind, for the LORD searches every heart and understands every desire and every thought. If you seek him, he will be found by you; but if you forsake him, he will reject you forever."[363]

Notwithstanding the clarity of God's direction with respect to the succession issue, David faced one more challenge with respect to its implementation: another rebellion fomented by yet another of his frustrated and ambitious sons, Adonijah. What makes this rebellion particularly dangerous is that this time it was supported by David's long-standing military commander, Joab.

> Now Adonijah, whose mother was Haggith, put himself forward and said, "I will be king." So he got chariots and horses ready, with fifty men to run ahead of him. (His father had never rebuked him by asking, "Why do you behave as you do?" He was also very handsome and was born next after Absalom.) Adonijah conferred with Joab son of Zeruiah and with Abiathar the priest, and they gave him their support.[364]

Although by then David was old and declining in strength and perception, he was rallied one more time by Nathan, Bathsheba, and those of his military guard still loyal to him. He ordered Solomon to be crowned king in his place; these orders were carried out swiftly and dramatically, Adonijah's support evaporated, and Solomon succeeded David as the third king of Israel.[365]

THE SUCCESSION CHALLENGE

Of all the challenges facing leaders, planning and providing for a peaceful, orderly transition to a qualified successor is perhaps the most difficult. For example, if the leader of a democratic political party and the party itself

[362] 1 Chronicles 28:5.

[363] 1 Chronicles 28:9.

[364] 1 Kings 1:5–7.

[365] 1 Kings 1:11–53.

ignore or neglect preparing for succession, they run the risk of a future leadership deficiency or crisis. But if the leader openly seeks to cultivate and prepare an outsider or the most promising of his younger colleagues for the job, that will invariably be resented by all the other aspirants to the throne, especially the most ambitious.

Hence there are benefits for any organization of having clearly understood and accepted rules governing succession. In the case of monarchies, succession is generally based on laws or conventions of heredity, which provide that the oldest living offspring of the present monarch is to be the successor. In the case of businesses, especially public companies, the selection of the next CEO is the primary responsibility of the board of directors, subject to ratification by the shareholders. In democracies, party constitutions provide for leadership reviews and selection and/or election by caucuses or party members, their choice ultimately subject to acceptance or rejection by electors.

But for those engaged in the leadership and work of God's kingdom on earth, there are two overriding questions to be answered with respect to leadership succession. Who does God desire as leader, and how is God's will in the matter to be ascertained? In my experience, the answers to the first of these questions is rarely clear, although there will always be those with various motives who will claim to know with certainty. The emphasis, therefore, must be put on carefully and prayerfully seeking God's will for ourselves and for the organization, recognizing that his ways are not our ways while acting to the best of our ability on whatever light we are given and ultimately trusting in the scriptural declaration that "the Most High is sovereign over all kingdoms on earth and gives them to anyone he wishes."[366]

SPIRITUAL PREPARATIONS FOR THE FUTURE

In the case of leaders operating at the interface of faith and public life, preparation for the future spiritually may be the greatest concern and challenge. This would appear to have been so for David.

From the days of Moses to those of David, the most important physical symbol of God's presence in Israel was the ark of the covenant, where the tablets of the law given to Moses were kept under the watchful

[366] Daniel 4:25, 32.

supervision of the Levitical priests.[367] During the priesthood of Eli, the ark was captured by the Philistines. But its presence "brought devastation on them," so the Philistines hurriedly sent it back to Israel during the time of David's spiritual mentor, Samuel.[368] For a time, it was kept at the house of Abinadab in Kiriath Jearim, but it was neglected throughout the reign of King Saul.[369] When David became king, he decided to restore its place in the worship of Israel by bringing the ark to the royal city of Jerusalem, which he accomplished after some initial mishandlings.[370] Amid much thanksgiving and celebration, the ark finally came to rest in Jerusalem, inside the tent that David had pitched for it.[371]

But "after David was settled in his palace, he said to Nathan the prophet, 'Here I am, living in a house of cedar, while the ark of the covenant of the LORD is under a tent.' Nathan replied to David, 'Whatever you have in mind, do it, for God is with you.'"[372] What David had in mind was nothing less than the construction of a house for God—a temple fit for the great God of Israel who had so guided and blessed David and his people throughout his life.

While well-intended and spiritually motivated, David's plan to build a house for God was not exactly what God himself had in mind. David explained this in one of his last addresses to his people:

> "Listen to me, my fellow Israelites, my people. I had it in my heart to build a house as a place of rest for the ark of the covenant of the LORD, for the footstool of our God, and I made plans to build it. But God said to me, 'You are not to build a house for my Name, because you are a warrior and have shed blood.'
>
> "Yet the LORD, the God of Israel, chose me from my whole family to be king over Israel forever. He chose Judah as leader, and from the tribe of Judah he chose my family, and from my father's sons he was pleased to make me king over all Israel. Of all my sons—and the LORD has given me many—he has chosen my son Solomon to sit on the throne of the kingdom of the LORD over Israel. He said to me: 'Solomon your son is the one who will build my house and my courts, for I have chosen him to be my son, and I will be his father.'"

---

[367] See Exodus 25:8–22 and Deuteronomy 10:1–8.

[368] 1 Samuel 5:6. See 1 Samuel 4–6.

[369] 1 Chronicles 13:3.

[370] 1 Chronicles 13.

[371] 1 Chronicles 15–16.

[372] 1 Chronicles 17:1–2.

David's obedience to this revelation is described as follows:

> Then David gave his son Solomon the plans for the portico of the temple, its buildings, its storerooms, its upper parts, its inner rooms and the place of atonement. He gave him the plans of all that the Spirit had put in his mind for the courts of the temple of the LORD and all the surrounding rooms, for the treasuries of the temple of God and for the treasuries for the dedicated things. He gave him instructions for the divisions of the priests and Levites, and for all the work of serving in the temple of the LORD, as well as for all the articles to be used in its service …
>
> "All this," David said, "I have in writing as a result of the LORD's hand upon me, and he enabled me to understand all the details of the plan."[373]

LESSONS

There are at least three major lessons we can draw from David's experience as a leader determined to build a "dwelling place" for God.

First, there may be aspects of our public work that regrettably preclude us from carrying out certain types of spiritual service.[374] Success in our political calling, even if God-directed and blessed, does not automatically qualify us to do whatever we have in mind to do to advance the kingdom of God. In David's case, God said to him, "You are not to build a house for my Name, because you are a warrior and have shed blood."[375]

[373] 1 Chronicles 28:2–6, 11–13, 19.

[374] For example, a modern political leader with a faith commitment, even if successful politically, will have alienated certain segments of the community who disagree with his or her ideology, policies, decisions, or actions. That alienation limits the effectiveness of that politician in personally representing the claims of Christ to those groups since, having decided that the leader is misguided politically, they will tend to assume that he is also misguided on other matters, including the spiritual. In my own case, while my secular advisors were always worried that my religious views and commitments would alienate potential political supporters, I was always more worried that my political positions and commitments would alienate potential believers from investigating the claims of Christ.

[375] 1 Chronicles 28:3. Just listing David's military exploits gives us an idea of the extent to which he was first and foremost a warrior and shedder of blood. His military exploits included numerous battles and victories over the Philistines, beginning with his defeat of their champion, Goliath, in man-to-man combat (1 Samuel 17; 2 Samuel 5, 8, 21, 23); his pursuit and destruction of an Amalekite raiding party that attacked his camp and abducted his wives and possessions (1 Samuel 30); his military defeat of the forces of the house of Saul after Saul's death (2 Samuel 2–3); his defeat of the Jebusites when he and his forces attacked and conquered the city of Jerusalem (2 Samuel 5:6–7); and military engagements and victories over the Moabites, Arameans, Edomites, and Ammonites as David expanded Israel's territory and secured her borders (2 Samuel 8, 10).

For faith-oriented leaders in public and political spheres, the fact that your role in the kingdoms of earth may impose limits on your service in the kingdom of God is a sad truth and hard to accept. In David's case, however, it was God's declaration of this reality that turned him toward making extensive preparations for others to perform the spiritual work that he himself was not qualified or authorized to perform.

Second, when it comes to the initiation of spiritual enterprises (work), David's experience reminds us that the direction and initiative for such work must come not from ourselves but from God himself. Building a dwelling place for God's presence in our homes, organizations, and society is ultimately the work of his spirit in which God invites us to join—not our work (however spiritually motivated we may be) in which we ask God to join.

As Solomon was to write, "Unless the LORD builds the house, its builders labor in vain."[376] This too is a hard lesson for leaders to accept, as two of the distinguishing characteristics of a leader are the willingness and ability to give direction and to take the initiative.

Third, and providentially, it is a combination of these two unpalatable truths—that David's military work precluded him from building the temple and that its construction was to be done at God's initiative and not his own—that gave David divinely inspired direction as to what he personally was to do both spiritually and politically during the sunset years of his life. After he sought God's direction, he was clearly instructed to focus on preparing for the future—to make preparations for his son Solomon to succeed him and to equip and mandate Solomon to build the temple.

Here then is yet another example of the scriptural principle "in all things God works for the good of those who love him, who have been called according to his purpose."[377] Its relevance for those who seek God's will for the latter portions of their lives today is the assurance that God can tell them what their past experience qualifies or disqualifies them to do in his service and what preparations they are to make for the continuance of his work among the next generation.[378]

---

[376] Psalm 127:1.

[377] Romans 8:28.

[378] In my own case, after a period of uncertainty at the end of my active political career, I became convinced that I should devote my efforts to assisting in strengthening the

SECOND THOUGHTS?

Active people nearing the end of their careers often reflect on what might have been had they followed a different path. Whether David engaged in such reflections we do not know; but if he did, he might well have wondered whether he should have focused more on the spiritual guidance of Israel than on its military and political guidance. After all, as a young man his role model for a godly leader had been the saintly Samuel, a judge and an administrator to be sure but much more a priest and a prophet. During David's lifetime, it was the prophet Nathan who had been a constant and reliable conduit between God and himself, and David might well have wondered whether he could or should have served God better had he himself been more of a prophet and less of a soldier. Or given his obvious gifts for poetry and music, whether he should have devoted himself entirely to the ministry of the arts, like his fellow psalmist Asaph, rather than to the darker arts of war and politics.

Others with both spiritual and political commitments, like the British parliamentarian William Wilberforce, have struggled with whether they have arrived at or maintained the right balance between the two. More often the fear is that they have erred on the side of allowing the demands and urgencies of the political to supplant and gradually crowd out what they might have achieved spiritually.

I have had similar thoughts myself. When I was in my early twenties, my father was premier of Alberta and the director of Canada's National Back to the Bible Hour, a national evangelical radio ministry calling on Canadians to place their faith in Christ. During the 1960s, in preparation for celebrating Canada's 1967 centennial as a nation, he promoted the idea that the centennial reflections and celebrations should include explicit recognition of Canada's spiritual heritage and the need for its revitalization. A young colleague of mine and I went on an extensive national speaking tour (not unlike an issue campaign tour) promoting this concept. Genuine spiritual revival is of course the result not of

---

knowledge, skills, ethics, and leadership capacities of the next generation of participants in Canada's political processes, including providing some guidance based on my own experience of navigating the interface of faith and politics. These activities I carried out through the work of the Manning Centre for Building Democracy (manningcentre.ca), the Manning Foundation for Democratic Education, and my role as a senior fellow of Regent College's Marketplace Institute.

human effort but of a moving of God's spirit. But I have since wondered whether continuing to promote and work for spiritual revival in Canada to the same extent and with the same energy that I later gave to promoting political reform might have been the better and more God-honouring path.

My conclusion is perhaps the same one that David might have come to if he had engaged in such retrospective reflections: there is no point in second-guessing God or yourself on the balance to be achieved between the spiritual and the political if you genuinely believe that you have been led to work at the interface between the two. Better to trust that you have been in God's plan, however imperfectly you may have understood it or followed it.

In David's case, if he erred during his career by being overly preoccupied with his military and political role in Israel, he was given a God-directed opportunity during his latter years to restore the balance by putting the majority of his efforts into preparation for the building of a dwelling place for God—the last and most enduring of David's works.

The lesson? Solomon, David's son, put it this way:

> Trust in the LORD with all your heart
>   and lean not on your own understanding;
> in all your ways submit to him,
>   and he will make your paths straight.[379]

[379] Proverbs 3:5–6.

3.9 LAST WORDS OF A LEADER

Do not cast me away when I am old;
do not forsake me when my strength is gone …
Even when I am old and gray,
do not forsake me, my God,
till I declare your power to the next generation,
your mighty acts to all who are to come.[380]

THE LAST WORDS OF LEADERS TO THEIR INTIMATES AND followers tend to reveal what is weighing most heavily on their mind and heart as they look back over their careers. And it is often in these last words that they emphasize what they consider most important to pass on to the next generation. So it was with David.

We noted (see chapter 3.8) that in his last recorded address to the officials and people of Israel, David's entire focus was on preparation for the future, both spiritual and political.[381] He declared, "I had it in my heart to build a house" for God (the temple), but God showed David that he was not the one to do so. Rather, he was to appoint his son Solomon as his successor and make all the preparations for Solomon to establish the spiritual edifice that David himself had hoped to build.

It is also worth noting that David's last major address to Israel ended fittingly in a prayer, David ever being not only the king but also the psalmist of Israel. In his prayer, David acknowledged that the kingdom and all its resources belonged to God, not men; he acknowledged that God continued to test the hearts of those who served him and that God

[380] Psalm 71:9, 18.

[381] 1 Chronicles 28–29.

was "pleased with integrity." He specifically prayed that God would shape and inspire the future desires of the people of Israel. "LORD ... keep their hearts loyal to you."

DAVID'S WORDS TO SOLOMON—HARSH WORDS

David's last recorded words to his family are almost entirely directed to Solomon and also focused on preparation for the future.[382] Much of David's final advice was positive and God-honouring, but it must be acknowledged that David's political advice was of a different spirit.

He was particularly worried that his former military commander Joab and the household of Saul would never accept Solomon as king and would seek to overthrow him. And so he instructed Solomon, "Deal with him [Joab] according to your wisdom, but do not let his gray head go down to the grave in peace." And with respect to Shimei of the household of Saul, who had welcomed Absalom's rebellion and cursed David as he fled from Jerusalem, "You will know what to do to him. Bring his gray head down to the grave in blood."

While we may be disappointed that David's last words include such malevolent advice, they serve to remind us that the biblical record is remarkably candid in how it reveals and records, for our instruction, not only the virtues and accomplishments of God's servants but also their weaknesses and failures. David was a man after God's own heart, a just and able ruler, and an inspired psalmist; but he was also a man of his times, a politician desirous of retaining power for himself and his successors, and a warrior who had shed blood.

The story of David's long relationship with Joab, ending in his advice to Solomon to have Joab killed, is both tragic and instructive. It raises some very tough questions for leaders operating in the rough-and-tumble world of *realpolitik* while also endeavouring to live in accordance with God's will and standards.

Joab served David for more than forty years.[383] They fought side by side in innumerable battles against David's and Israel's enemies. Joab risked his life protecting David from Saul and his army. David appointed him the head of his own army because Joab was the first to attack and

---

[382] 1 Kings 2. See also 1 Chronicles 28.

[383] See 1 Chronicles 11:6; 2 Samuel 11:14–17; 18:6–14; 19:1–8; 24:2–4.

conquer the Jebusite stronghold of Jerusalem to make it David's royal city. It was Joab who carried out David's orders to have Uriah killed so that David could possess Bathsheba and who helped with the cover-up. It was Joab who defended David against the most serious threat to his kingship—the armed rebellion led by Absalom. It was Joab who gave David sound advice to prevent the army from deserting when David showed more grief over Absalom's death than he did appreciation for the army's victory. And it was Joab who cautioned David not to invoke God's wrath by conducting an unwarranted census of Israel's fighting men.

Yet, Joab was treacherous and violent to excess.[384] He not only shed blood in fighting Israel's wars but he shed "innocent blood." Against David's wishes, he murdered Abner, King Saul's general who sought to make peace. Also against David's wishes, he murdered Amasa, the commander of Judah's army. And it was Joab who struck down David's son Absalom in defiance of David's order to "Be gentle with the young man Absalom for my sake."

So the question arises, does a morally upright leader like David nevertheless need a Joab—someone who, in order to protect or advance the interests of the leader and the kingdom, will do the things that the leader's own conscience and convictions will not allow him to do himself? Did Elizabeth I need a Walsingham, her principal secretary and spymaster, to eliminate her dangerous enemies, by fair means and foul, in order to secure and empower her reign? Did Abraham Lincoln need the services of those unscrupulous political henchmen who bribed and bullied undecided congressmen into voting for the constitutional amendment that abolished slavery in the United States?

Joab does what David cannot bring himself to do personally, murdering Uriah and eliminating Absalom as a threat to the throne; yet is not David morally culpable for Joab's actions on his behalf?

Surely the answer to this question is yes; the leader is morally responsible and accountable for the actions of his or her subordinates in such instances. And if those actions are immoral and contrary to one's understanding of God's will for human conduct, then the sooner those persons are removed from positions of influence, rather than continuously relied upon, the better. Perhaps David eventually came to this realization,

[384] See 1 Kings 2:31–34; 2 Samuel 3, 20, and 18:5.

although late in the day. Unless Joab was removed from his position of influence, his capacity for treachery and violence would ultimately destroy Solomon and the kingdom. Hence David's harsh advice to Solomon to "Do not let his gray head go down to the grave in peace."

DAVID'S WORDS TO SOLOMON—GODLY WORDS

To his credit, however, most of David's last recorded words to Solomon constitute positive and godly instruction. They include the command to build the temple in accordance with all the plans and preparations that David had made. "Consider now, for the LORD has chosen you to build a house as the sanctuary. Be strong and do the work."[385]

But the primary emphasis of David's last words to Solomon is twofold: First, take care of the spiritual condition of your own mind and heart. "Acknowledge the God of your father, and serve him with wholehearted devotion and with a willing mind ... If you seek him, he will be found by you; but if you forsake him, he will reject you forever."[386]

And second, like Moses in his last charge to Israel, David calls upon Solomon to adhere to the law of God as revealed to Israel. The future king of Israel, who will make and enforce laws, is himself to be under the law.

> "Be strong, act like a man, and observe what the LORD your God requires: Walk in obedience to him, and keep his decrees and commands, his laws and regulations, as written in the Law of Moses. Do this so that you may prosper in all you do and wherever you go and that the LORD may keep his promise to me."[387]

I personally find it remarkable that this concept—that those with the highest political authority are themselves to be subject to the Rule of Law, a concept that was only embraced many centuries later after a long and painful struggle by the Western democracies—should have been so strongly and consistently insisted upon by Moses and David, the greatest lawgiver and greatest king of ancient Israel.

LAST WORDS

There are seven verses in 2 Samuel 23 that are announced as "the last words of David."

[385] 1 Chronicles 28:10.

[386] 1 Chronicles 28:9.

[387] 1 Kings 2:2–4.

"The inspired utterance of David son of Jesse,
  the utterance of the man exalted by the Most High,
the man anointed by the God of Jacob,
  the hero of Israel's songs:
"The Spirit of the Lord spoke through me;
  his word was on my tongue.
The God of Israel spoke,
  the Rock of Israel said to me:
'When one rules over people in righteousness,
  when he rules in the fear of God,
he is like the light of morning at sunrise
  on a cloudless morning,
like the brightness after rain
  that brings grass from the earth.'
"If my house were not right with God,
  surely he would not have made with me an everlasting covenant,
  arranged and secured in every part;
surely he would not bring to fruition my salvation
  and grant me my every desire.
But evil men are all to be cast aside like thorns,
  which are not gathered with the hand.
Whoever touches thorns
  uses a tool of iron or the shaft of a spear;
  they are burned up where they lie."[388]

In these verses, David attributed his words to the spirit of God speaking through him. He declared that a ruler is to be a blessing to his people when he rules in righteousness and the fear of God. He also asked a question in the negative that I reframe in the positive. It is a question that all of us, whether we are thinking of the welfare of our own lives and homes or the welfare of a city, province, or nation, should ask and answer for ourselves: Is my house right with God? Once again, as throughout his lifetime, the necessity of right relationships—positive and peaceful relations that David rarely achieved within his own household but strove to achieve within the kingdom—was foremost on his mind.

LEARNING FROM DAVID

As we close these lessons in leadership from the life of King David, it is appropriate for each of us to ask what aspects of David's experience are most relevant and meaningful to us personally.

[388] 2 Samuel 23:1–7.

Is it the evidence of providential leading in David's early call into God's service and the encouragement that comes from knowing that God can take a shepherd boy from the sheep pen to the throne of a kingdom if that is God's will?

Is it the importance that God attaches to character, the inner condition of the human heart, as a qualification for service in his kingdom and in the kingdoms of this world? If God attaches such importance to character in recruiting leaders, should not we do the same?

Is it the realization that for the man or woman after God's own heart there is a downward path to the top—a path that may well involve years of subordination to cruel and unjust superiors and leading through the school of suffering but that in the end fully prepares us for self-sacrificial service to God and to others?

Or is it the revelation of David's inner life and personal relationship to God as expressed in his poems and hymns that is most meaningful and relevant to our lives? Does not David's example strongly encourage us to pour out *our* innermost thoughts and feelings to the shepherd of our souls and to devote more of *our* attention to the cultivation of *our* inner lives?

Since none of us is without sin—all of us falling short of God's moral standards—is it the sad but instructive story of David's moral failings with respect to the Bathsheba affair that speaks most directly to our own condition? Is there not both instruction and encouragement for us in David's acknowledgement of his failings, his heartfelt repentance, and his subsequent experience of forgiveness, cleansing, and grace?

Or is it the lessons in relationships, exemplified and taught by David's life, that stand out for us as we contemplate his life and ours? What importance and priority do we attach to *getting right* our relationship to God, our families, and other human beings?

And as we approach our sunset years and the temptation to retire into self-indulgence, does David's use of those years to prepare his family and his people for what lay ahead speak most critically and powerfully to those of us of the self-centred *me* generation?

LAST WORDS TO YOU—A REFLECTION ON PSALM 143

In my case, as much as I have studied and profited from the lessons taught by David's career, it is his psalms and the revelation of his inner life that

I find most inspiring and instructive. One psalm in particular, Psalm 143, has been a source of comfort and guidance, especially in my post-political years.

It begins with a petition for God's help and a frank acknowledgement of the moral imperfection of the petitioner, who, perhaps like many of us in leadership positions in our homes and organizations, was in a position to impose legal and moral demands on others:

> LORD, hear my prayer,
>   listen to my cry for mercy;
> in your faithfulness and righteousness
>   come to my relief.
> Do not bring your servant into judgment,
>   for no one living is righteous before you.[389]

Next follows an admission of need and a cry for relief from spiritual and mental depression, the immediate cause of which is not disclosed but which those of us who have suffered personal or political reversals know all too well.

> The enemy pursues me,
>   he crushes me to the ground;
> he makes me dwell in darkness
>   like those long dead.
> So my spirit grows faint within me;
>   my heart within me is dismayed …
> I spread out my hands to you;
>   I thirst for you like a parched land.
> Answer me quickly, O LORD;
>   my spirit fails.
> Do not hide your face from me
>   or I will be like those who go down to the pit.[390]

Finally, this inspirational psalm ends with a list of six profound petitions that, if granted, would restore God's servant to spiritual health and well-being no matter what circumstances he or she may be called upon to endure.

---

[389] Psalm 143:1–2.

[390] Psalm 143:3–4, 6–7.

> Let the morning bring me word of your unfailing love,
> for I have put my trust in you.
> Show me the way I should go,
> for to you I entrust my life.
> Rescue me from my enemies, O LORD,
> for I hide myself in you.
> Teach me to do your will,
> for you are my God;
> may your good Spirit
> lead me on level ground.
> For your name's sake, O LORD, preserve my life …
> for I am your servant.[391]

Is not this the great lesson from the life of David most applicable to ours? David chose to put his trust in God, to lift up his soul to God, to hide himself in God, and to claim God as his own. As a consequence, the morning truly did bring David word of God's unfailing love. David truly did receive knowledge of God's will and the way David should go. He was time and time again delivered from the "enemy" of his soul. And in the end, notwithstanding all the ups and downs of his political and spiritual life, he was guided by God's spirit onto *level ground*—personally, politically, and spiritually.

[391] Psalm 143:8–12.

PART 4:

LEADERSHIP LESSONS

from the Lives of the Exiles

INTRODUCTION

IN THIS SECTION WE EXAMINE LESSONS THAT CAN BE learned from the lives of believers who came to leadership positions in societies and political systems that for the most part were hostile to their values and beliefs. While Jesus made few references to these leaders in his public discourses, in one sense he had more in common with them—people like Joseph, Daniel, Esther, Ezra, and Nehemiah—than he did with Moses and David in that he, like they, found himself imbedded in a culture and political system—that of imperial Rome—that was at best indifferent and at worst hostile to his faith.

In Jesus' case, he was literally a member of a minority within a minority both politically and religiously. As a Galilean he was a member of a regional minority within the Jewish political community, which was in turn a tiny minority within the Roman Empire. As the leader of a new religious movement, he was a minority within the broader religious community of the scribes and Pharisees, who were in turn a faith-based minority within the polytheistic and pagan society of Rome.

Moses and David were servants of God who exercised political leadership in a community—Israel—where their faith was generally shared by the people they were called to lead. But Joseph, Daniel and his friends, and Esther were servants of God who rose to positions of leadership in societies and political systems that were hostile to their faith. Their circumstances were therefore more analogous to the situation of Christian believers today who attain positions of leadership in the secular societies of our time—societies that, if they tolerate religious faith at all, relegate its expression to the private sphere and seek to purge its presence and influence from the public square.

Lessons in leadership taught by the experiences of Joseph, Daniel, and Esther—serving from a minority position in a hostile majority culture and walking the difficult line between co-operation and compromise—are therefore particularly relevant to believers who attain positions of leadership in the materialistic, humanistic, and secular societies of today.

Ezra and Nehemiah, while they were first and foremost leaders of God's people, had the unenviable task of trying to restore the life and vitality of a defeated and discouraged faith community immersed in a hostile environment. Their experience is especially relevant to spiritual leaders today who seek to carve out a spiritual homeland and rebuild spiritual institutions from a minority position under conditions hostile to faith.

4.1 THE SOVEREIGNTY OF GOD

FAITH IN THE SOVEREIGNTY OF GOD

BELIEF IN THE SOVEREIGNTY OF GOD IS BELIEF IN GOD'S supremacy—that all things are under his rule and control and that nothing happens without his direction or permission. It is the belief in the God "who works out everything in conformity with the purpose of his will" and who declared to Israel through the prophet Isaiah, "What I have said, that I will bring about; what I have planned, that I will do."[392]

For the ancient Israelites it may have been relatively easy to believe in the sovereignty of God when they were living in their own land under the law of God, triumphing in battle over their pagan enemies, worshipping God in their own way, and living under the rule of kings whom they believed to be "the LORD's anointed." But this faith in God's supremacy was shaken to its foundations when Israel was conquered by the Assyrians and Judah by the Babylonians, when their rulers were executed or led away in chains, when the temple was desecrated and destroyed by a foreign army, and when the survivors of these disasters became exiles in foreign lands whose rulers and people were hostile or at best indifferent to the beliefs and practices of the people of God.

The question "How could God allow ...?"—the question believers and skeptics alike invariably ask in times of trouble and calamity—gnawed away at the very foundations of their faith. How could one believe in the sovereignty and supremacy of God after these calamities? And even if one retained one's faith in God, how could one practise it in environments so indifferent or hostile to it?

[392] Ephesians 1:11 and Isaiah 46:11.

Thus arose the sad lament of the believer in exile, "How can we sing the songs of the LORD while in a foreign land?"[393]

THE EXILE OF THE MODERN BELIEVER

Persecuted Christian minorities living in Muslim countries or under militantly atheistic regimes such as those in North Korea and China can readily identify with the situation of the Jewish exiles in Babylon. But so can contemporary Christian believers living in the materialistic, humanistic, and secular societies of the Western world.

At one time the Christian faith occupied a respected and influential position in these societies. Today it is increasingly banished to the private sphere or at worst attacked and declared irrelevant and antithetical to progress in education, science, law, the arts, the media, business, and politics.

In the political realm in Canada, it is now considered taboo to speak of your own most deeply held religious convictions, or those of your constituents, in the House of Commons or the provincial legislatures, notwithstanding the declarations of our *Charter* that "Everyone has the following fundamental freedoms: (*a*) freedom of conscience and religion; (*b*) freedom of thought, belief, opinion, and expression."[394]

Ironically, the preamble to that *Charter* actually begins with the phrase "Whereas Canada is founded upon principles that recognize the supremacy of God and the rule of law." But when this phrase—"the supremacy of God"—has been appealed to as relevant to moral issues before the courts, it has been dismissed as "a dead letter" and irrelevant to the secular Canada of today.

In a 1999 child pornography case before the BC Court of Appeal, the judge dismissed moral arguments rooted in the *Charter*'s recognition of the supremacy of God with these words:

> "I accept that the law of this country is rooted in its religious heritage. But I know of no case on the *Charter* in which any court of this country has relied on the words Mr. Staley invokes [i.e., principles that recognize the supremacy of God]. They have become a dead letter and while I might have wished the contrary, this

---

[393] Psalm 137:1–4 states, "By the rivers of Babylon we sat and wept when we remembered Zion. There on the poplars we hung our harps, for there our captors asked us for songs, our tormentors demanded songs of joy; they said, 'Sing us one of the songs of Zion!' How can we sing the songs of the LORD while in a foreign land?"

[394] *Constitution Act, 1982*, c. 11, p. 1, s. 2.

> Court has no authority to breathe life into them for the purpose of interpreting the various provisions of the *Charter* ... The words of the preamble relied upon by Mr. Staley can only be resurrected by the Supreme Court of Canada."[395]

Note that the judge not only dismisses arguments based on a Christian conception of morality but does so in language as offensive as possible to Christians—pronouncing the supremacy of God to be a "dead letter" capable of "resurrection" only by the Supreme Court.

As for the Supreme Court of Canada, in a 1993 case dealing with physician-assisted suicide, Chief Justice Lamer declared Canada to be a "secular society" in which the court was not obliged to be guided in any way by "theological considerations."

> "Can the right ... to choose suicide, be described as an advantage of which the appellant is being deprived? In my opinion, the Court should answer this question without reference to the philosophical and theological considerations fuelling the debate on the morality of suicide or euthanasia. It should consider the question before it from a legal perspective ... while keeping in mind that the *Charter* has established the essentially secular nature of Canadian society."[396]

And so as contemporary Christians, many of us find ourselves asking the same questions that perplexed the Jewish exiles in foreign lands centuries ago. How could a sovereign God allow this to happen? How can one continue to believe in the supremacy of God in such circumstances? And from a practical standpoint, even if we retain our faith, how can and should we practise it in indifferent or hostile environments?

For answers to these questions, let us look to the experience of the Jewish exiles and the initial leadership given to them by the prophet Jeremiah.

JEREMIAH'S LETTER—EXPANDING THE EXILES' CONCEPTION OF THE SOVEREIGNTY OF GOD

Jeremiah as you may recall was the prophet who ministered from about 626 to 586 BC and witnessed the destruction of Jerusalem and the temple in 587 BC. He prophesied the destruction of Judah as a nation and the exile of the Jewish people to Babylon as a result of their alienation

---

395 *R. v. Sharpe*, BCCA [1999] 416, p. 79–80.

396 *Rodriguez v. British Columbia (Attorney General)*, SCC [1993] 3, S.C.R. 519.

from God by sin. But he also ministered to the exiles with messages of instruction concerning how they were to live in their new circumstances and provided messages of hope for the future.

> This is the text of the letter that the prophet Jeremiah sent from Jerusalem to ... the people Nebuchadnezzar had carried into exile from Jerusalem to Babylon ... "This is what the LORD Almighty, the God of Israel, says to all those I carried into exile from Jerusalem to Babylon: 'Build houses and settle down; plant gardens and eat what they produce. Marry and have sons and daughters; find wives for your sons and give your daughters in marriage, so that they too may have sons and daughters. Increase in numbers there; do not decrease. Also, seek the peace and prosperity of the city to which I have carried you into exile. Pray to the LORD for it, because if it prospers, you too will prosper.'"[397]

Note the radical proposition that Jeremiah advanced—that the LORD Almighty says that *he*, not Nebuchadnezzar, is the one who had carried them into exile from Jerusalem to Babylon. In the same letter he repeated this assertion twice: "Seek the peace and prosperity of the city to which *I [the God of Israel]* have carried you into exile ... Therefore, hear the word of the LORD all you exiles whom *I* have sent away from Jerusalem to Babylon."[398]

Just as God's people were in his hand when they were in the Promised Land singing psalms by the river Jordan and under the authority of divinely anointed kings, so were they still in his hand while exiled to a foreign land, in mourning by the rivers of Babylon, and subject to foreign kings, who were also ultimately under God's authority. In other words, the first prerequisite for God's people to survive and serve him in exile conditions was an expanded belief in the sovereignty of God.

JEREMIAH'S LETTER—INSTRUCTION ON HOW TO LIVE FAITHFULLY IN EXILE

The exiles were then given God's instructions through Jeremiah on how to live faithfully in exile.

---

397 Jeremiah 29:1, 4–7.

398 Jeremiah 29:7, 20, emphasis added.

1. Settle down and build

Settle down, build houses and families, and engage in productive work (agriculture, in this case) that you may increase in number and not decrease.

2. Pray

God is reachable by prayer from Babylon just as he was from Judea. Pray specifically for the peace and prosperity of the place where God has relocated you so that you may prosper from its prosperity.

3. Disregard false spiritual advice

You are to disregard the voices and visions of false and immoral prophets who counsel you to act contrary to these instructions.

This is apparently a reference to false prophets like Hananiah, whose confrontation with Jeremiah is described in the chapter preceding Jeremiah's letter to the exiles.[399] Hananiah, like Jeremiah, prefaced his instructions to the exiles with "This is what the LORD Almighty, the God of Israel, says." But in effect he told the exiles there was no need to settle down in or to pray for Babylon. Their exile, he told them, would be temporary because "within two years" God would "break the yoke of the king of Babylon" and bring them back to Judah. Hananiah's advice to the exiles was similar to that of self-proclaimed prophets today who instruct Christians *not* to involve themselves in the societies, environments, and places where God has placed them, because the return of Christ is imminent. It is particularly significant that Jeremiah appeared to be more concerned about the exiles being led astray by false prophets from among their own religious community than he was about them being led astray by the influence of the Babylonians.

4. Trust the promises

Lastly, God, through Jeremiah, sought to restore the courage and morale of the exiles by challenging them to trust in his promise for their ultimate spiritual and political restoration.

> This is what the LORD says: "When seventy years are completed for Babylon, I will come to you and fulfill my good promise to bring you back to this place. For

[399] See Jeremiah 28.

> I know the plans I have for you," declares the LORD, "plans to prosper you and not to harm you, plans to give you hope and a future."[400]

LESSONS IN LEADERSHIP

In the following chapters we look at lessons that can be learned *from* the leadership of the exiles in the hostile spiritual and political environment in which they found themselves. But in Jeremiah's letter we have an example of leadership being provided *to* the exiles by the prophet. What then would be the equivalent leadership message *to* believers living in exile among the materialistic, humanistic, and secular societies of today?

If those in positions of spiritual leadership were to draft letters under the inspiration of the Holy Spirit to believers embedded by the sovereignty of God in the business, academic, media, science, trades, or political communities of today, what might those letters say?

Or if those in such leadership positions were to draft letters analogous to those of the apostle Paul—written to the small first-century Christian communities embedded by the sovereignty of God in larger, hostile societies—what might be the focus and content of a letter to the believers in the academy, to the believers in the business community, to the believers in the media, to the believers in the science community, or to the believers in the political community of today?

A LETTER TO BELIEVERS IN THE POLITICAL COMMUNITY

In the vast literature of Christendom there are volumes of commentary and instruction relevant to believers embedded in all the various functional constituencies of today's world. But I must say that when I was in active politics I was never aware of receiving or reading a "Letter to the Believers in the Political Community" as explicit and instructional as the letter sent by Jeremiah to the believing exiles embedded in Babylon.[401] In retrospect, if I had, it might have read something like the following:

---

[400] Jeremiah 29:10–11.

[401] From 1967 to 1987, I was peripherally and sporadically involved in provincial and federal politics in the province of Alberta. But from 1987 to 1993, I was fully involved in the creation of a new federal political party, the Reform Party of Canada. And from 1993 to 2002, I was the federal member of Parliament for Calgary Southwest in the Canadian House of Commons.

This is what the Lord Almighty says[402] to all those he has carried into a hostile political environment:

Recognize and believe that you are where you are not by your own efforts or design or by those of your adversaries but by my grace and sovereignty.[403] Therefore, conduct yourself as one who lives politically in a country founded on principles that recognize the supremacy of God even if the politicians, media, judges, and citizenry of your country do not.

Settle down there, build and plant.[404] Settle down in the constituencies, in the parties, in the interest groups, in the political offices, in the parliaments, legislatures, and municipal councils of that country—wherever I have led you politically—and be a constructive influence there. Seek a "better country" while serving the country where I have placed you.[405]

Expand my influence there by wisdom and graciousness[406] and by persuasive example, so that your numbers do not decrease but increase because others are attracted to you and your positions. Be salt and light.[407]

Seek the enlightenment and peace of the political community—serving where possible as truth tellers[408] and reconcilers of conflicting interests.[409]

Pray for the political community, for your opponents, and for all those in authority, that it may be well with you and the community at large.[410]

---

[402] In making any such assertion, the writer of the letter needs to be absolutely sure that the words written are God's words and not merely those of the writer, i.e., they must be scripturally based in every respect.

[403] As Daniel communicated to Nebuchadnezzar, "the Most High is sovereign over all kingdoms on earth and gives them to anyone he wishes" (Daniel 4:25).

[404] See Jeremiah 29:5–6.

[405] Membership in the Order of Canada, Canada's highest civilian order, is accorded to those who exemplify the order's Latin motto, *desiderantes meliorem patriam*, meaning "they desire a better country," a phrase taken from Hebrews 11:16 (KJV).

[406] This is the great guideline that Jesus gave to his earliest followers before sending them out to do public work in his name: "be ye therefore wise as serpents, and harmless as doves" (Matthew 10:16 [KJV]).

[407] At the very outset of his teachings in the Sermon on the Mount, Jesus instructs his followers to be salt and light, performing good deeds before others (publicly) that will cause them to praise God (Matthew 5:13–16).

[408] Not only are believers to "think about" whatever is true, but we are also to be "speaking the truth in love" (Philippians 4:8–9; Ephesians 4:15).

[409] At its highest level, politics, especially for those in government, is about the reconciliation of conflicting interests. In the Christian doctrine and teaching on the ministry of reconciliation through the exercise of self-sacrificial love, we have Christ's example of how to reconcile conflicting interests at the deepest level (2 Corinthians 5:17–21).

[410] 1 Timothy 2:1–3 states, "I urge, then, first of all, that petitions, prayers, intercession and thanksgiving be made for all people—for kings and all those in authority, that we may live peaceful and quiet lives in all godliness and holiness. This is good, and pleases God our Savior."

Pray that my kingdom may come and my will be done on earth as it is in heaven.[411]

Disregard the voices and visions of false prophets who counsel you to retreat into a private sphere, isolating yourself from the political community in a false holiness. And reject the counsel of the zealots who urge you to arbitrarily impose your beliefs on others. This is not the way of my grace, which invites rather than compels acceptance of me and my truth.

Be strong and courageous, trusting in my promise to someday make the kingdoms of this world my kingdoms.[412]

Be assured that I have plans to prosper you (as I define prosperity) and not to harm you, plans to give you hope and a future in the places where you are and to which I lead you.[413]

APPLICATION

One of the God-given tasks of some of the believers reading this may well be to draft and communicate such leadership letters, declaring the sovereignty of God in and over all those diverse places in this present world where God has planted his people.

And is it not the responsibility of those of us so planted to receive such instruction and act in light of the expanded conception of the sovereignty of God that such letters proclaim?

---

411 Jesus taught this prayer in the "Lord's Prayer" (Matthew 6:9–13).

412 See Revelation 11:15.

413 See Jeremiah 29:11, the great promise spoken by Jeremiah to the believing exiles in Babylon.

4.2 PROVIDENTIAL POSITIONING AGAIN

"And who knows but that you have come to your royal position
for such a time as this?"[414]
(Mordecai to Queen Esther when the Jews in Medo-Persia
were threatened with genocide)

"Your Majesty ... acknowledge that the Most High is sovereign over all
kingdoms on earth and gives them to anyone he wishes."[415]
(Daniel to King Nebuchadnezzar of Babylon in interpreting the king's dream)

IN PARTS 1, 2, AND 3 OF THIS WORK WE EXAMINED THE providential positioning of Jesus, Moses, and David in order that they might join in with God in his work in the world.

Like Samuel, in seeking to ascertain whom God may have in mind for leadership, we need to be reminded again that "the LORD does not look on the things that people look at. People look at the outward appearance, but the LORD looks at the heart."[416] And what the Lord sees and does there—especially if he perceives a yielded and contrite heart—can not only lead a prince of Egypt (Moses) to become a liberator of slaves and a shepherd (David) to the throne of Israel but can also lead a slave (Joseph) to become vice-ruler of Egypt, an orphan girl (Esther) to become queen of the Medes and Persians, and a teenage exile (Daniel) to eventually become the first minister of Babylon.

[414] Esther 4:14.

[415] Daniel 4:24–25.

[416] 1 Samuel 16:7.

"FOR SUCH A TIME AS THIS"

All three of these believers—Joseph, Esther, and Daniel—attained high office and political influence in the non-believing societies in which they found themselves. It is significant, however, that it was major disasters and calamities, not far-sighted planning and ambitious ladder-climbing, that led them to their positions of influence.

In the case of Joseph, an impending famine, and his God-given ability to interpret Pharaoh's predictive dream concerning it, led Joseph to his political position. And his God-given wisdom in managing the response to that national calamity—storing up grain in advance of the famine and utilizing its distribution to secure ownership of the land for Pharaoh—maintained him in his position and increased his influence even more.

In the case of Daniel, it was again a God-given ability to interpret an obscure but predictive dream, of the king of Babylon, that gained him his position of influence. He was then able to use that influence to save Babylon, at least in part, from the wild excesses to which Nebuchadnezzar was inclined, including the wholesale execution of his advisors, few if any of whom shared Daniel's faith.

And in the case of Esther, the "such a time as this" for which she was providentially positioned in Medo-Persia was a time when the exiled Jewish people were threatened with genocide—a threat that Esther's positioning and influence with King Xerxes enabled her to avert.

A 20TH CENTURY EXAMPLE

So does God still work in this way—using disasters and calamities often brought on by humanity's fallen nature and propensity for greed and violence—to lead believers toward positions of public service and political influence?

I believe he does. In fact, one could argue that this is one of the chief mechanisms of providentially positioning believers in this world. Who knows but that *you* are being led to political involvement and public service for such a time as this?—the "such a time as this" being one of the contemporary economic, social, or political crises of our times, affecting many people, very few of whom may share your personal faith convictions.

For example, in western Canada—one of two regions in our country (the other being Quebec) that tends to innovate politically by creating new political movements and parties—it was the Great Depression of the 1930s that led a number of professing Christians into positions of political prominence.

J. S. Woodsworth was a Methodist minister and proponent of the social gospel who publicly sided with rioting workers during the great Winnipeg General Strike of 1919.[417] Together with Tommy Douglas, a Baptist minister, and others, he eventually formed a social democratic political party, the Co-operative Commonwealth Federation (CCF), which later became the present-day New Democratic Party (NDP). The CCF/NDP became strong advocates of social justice, campaigning strenuously for old age pensions, unemployment insurance, and universal medical insurance coverage.

Another but similar example involves the Social Credit Movement in Alberta, the other major western Canadian political party spawned by the Depression. As previously described (chapter 3.1), it was led by Calgary high school principal and Christian layman William Aberhart, who pioneered Christian radio broadcasting on the Canadian prairies in

---

[417] Woodsworth left the Methodist church over its emphasis on individual salvation while neglecting, in his judgment, the deplorable social and economic circumstances in which so many of those individuals lived. It was said that if you dropped Woodsworth's Bible on the floor it would open by virtue of frequent reference to Luke 10, the parable of the Good Samaritan—a man who loved his neighbour as himself, even someone of another race and religion—to whom Jesus pointed his hearers, saying, "Go and do likewise."

During the strike, which became quite violent, Woodsworth was charged with seditious libel for a speech he wrote and published using verses from the book of Isaiah as a text. The indictment read in part, "That J. S. Woodsworth … unlawfully and seditiously published seditious libels in the words and figures following: 'Woe unto them that decree unrighteous decrees, and that write grievousness which they have prescribed; to turn aside the needy from judgment, and to take away the right from the poor of my people, that widows may be their prey and that they may rob the fatherless,' (Isaiah 10:1–2). 'And they shall build houses and inhabit them; and they shall plant vineyards, and eat the fruit of them. They shall not build and another inhabit; they shall not plant and another eat; for as the days of a tree are the days of my people, and mine elect shall long enjoy the work of their hands.' (Isaiah 65:21–22)" (*The King vs. J.S. Woodsworth: Indictment for Publishing Seditious Libels, Six Counts, and Speaking Seditious Words* [Winnipeg: The Defense Committee, Nov. 4, 1919]).

the 1920s, focusing on the personal salvation aspects of the gospel and his interpretation of the prophetic Scriptures.[418]

During the Depression the training institute for ministers that Aberhart founded operated a soup kitchen to serve the poor and unemployed. In the long lineups that formed outside it, he began to see former public-school students of his whom he had sent off to be teachers, doctors, and lawyers. But now they were riding the rails by the thousands, from city to city, searching in vain for work. The experience impelled Aberhart and his supporters, my father among them, into politics.[419]

Whether or not one agrees with the political positions of Woodsworth and Douglas, Aberhart and Manning, or their respective interpretations of the Scriptures, there is no question that their faith-based responses to an economic and social disaster, the Great Depression, prompted their actions and propelled them into positions of influence.

WHAT ABOUT YOU AND RECEIVING DIRECTION FROM CONTEMPORARY CRISES?

If God still works in this way—using disasters and calamities that are often the product of humanity's fallen nature—to lead believers toward positions of public service and political influence, what about you?

Could it be that *you* are being led by your Christian convictions to some such involvement by one of the many economic, social, and political crises that afflict our current world, regardless of whether the people of your community, province, or country share your personal faith convictions?

---

[418] It was said that if you dropped Aberhart's Bible on the floor it would open to John 3 and Jesus' admonition to Nicodemus that he could not enter or serve the kingdom of God unless he was "born again" of God's spirit from within. Later commentators on these two religious streams that crossed the Canadian prairies in the 1920s and 1930s have pointed out that if you put the vertical shaft of personal salvation and the horizontal crossbar of the social gospel together, you have the cross—the great symbol of the Christian faith and a more inclusive picture of the life and teachings of Jesus.

[419] For a more thorough description of this period and the activities of William Aberhart and Ernest C. Manning, see Brian Brennan, *The Good Steward: The Ernest C. Manning Story* (Markham: Fifth House, 2008).

The Challenge of Combatting Human Trafficking

In chapter 1.9 we reviewed lessons to be learned from the campaign to abolish slavery within the British Empire—a campaign led to a great extent by committed Christians like William Wilberforce. But what about modern day slavery, which has reached crisis proportions? The modern day perpetrators of human trafficking are enslaving more human beings today—especially vulnerable women and girls—than did the slave traders and slave owners of the 18th century. Could it be therefore that your growing awareness of this modern day crisis is your providential calling to engage in a 21st century equivalent of the Wilberforce Campaign, freeing the modern day victims of human trafficking in the name of Christ?

The Challenge of Caring for the Sick

Our world is periodically wracked by health crises—the AIDS disaster that began in Africa and is now worldwide; Ebola outbreaks on that same continent; the SARS outbreak of 2003, which provided Canada with a foretaste of what a pandemic-like health crisis might be like and how to deal with it; and the increases in cancer cases, hereditary diseases, and end-of-life health issues that lead so many today to despair of life despite all the advances of modern medicine. Such crises challenge individuals, communities, governments, and societies to conduct medical research, to engage in health-care education, to pursue preventative and supportive private initiatives and public health-care policies, and of course to engage directly in the administration and delivery of medical care for the ill.

Could it be that, for some Christian believers, a personal and acute consciousness of and concern for these health-care challenges constitutes providential leading—a providential call to become personally and actively involved in meeting the health-care needs of others in the spirit of Christ? The New Testament abounds with stories of Jesus and his disciples being confronted with the needs of the sick and being directed by the Holy Spirit to respond to them with compassion and care. The history of the Western world includes numerous accounts of Christian believers who were confronted with health-care crises and out of their faith convictions risked their own health in order to respond to the needs of others.[420] Could it be that a condition of our times of which you are acutely conscious is a health-care crisis that you are being led to address in some way? And could it be that God is putting to you the same question he posed to Esther long ago through Mordecai, "Who knows but that you have come to your royal position"—a position of awareness of a need and the opportunity to help—"for such a time as this?"

The Challenge of Environmental Stewardship

Our world, including your local community, is increasingly faced with serious environmental challenges—the increasing degradation of soil, water, vegetation, and atmospheric conditions as a result of our insatiable appetite for goods and services and the means we employ to satisfy that appetite.

Could it be that for you as a Christian believer an increasing consciousness of and concern for environmental degradation constitutes providential leading—a providential call for you as a believer to act: to constrain your own demands for goods and services in the spirit of Christian self-sacrifice; to rediscover environmental stewardship and creation care as a spiritual obligation to our Creator and his creation;[421] and to participate in issue and electoral campaigns to raise environmental conservation and responsible resource stewardship on the agendas of local, provincial, and national governments?

---

[420] Historians documenting the rise of Christianity in the Roman Empire have noted that it was the active and compassionate response of Christian believers toward the victims of the plagues (likely smallpox) that wracked the empire in the 2nd and 3rd centuries—in contrast to the response of pagan leaders and physicians who tended to flee the scene—that increased the appeal of the Christian faith among the general population. To quote Charles Moore, "During the plague of Alexandria when nearly everyone else fled, the early Christians risked their lives for one another by simple deeds of washing the sick, offering food and water, and consoling the dying … [They] not only took care of their own, but also reached far beyond themselves … In an era when serving others was thought to be demeaning, the 'followers of the way,' instead of fleeing disease and death, went about ministering to the sick and helping the poor, the widowed, the crippled, the blind, the orphaned, and the aged. The people of the Roman Empire were forced to admire their works and dedication. 'Look how they love one another' was heard on the streets" (Charles Moore, "Pandemic Love," *Plough Weekly* (blog), http://www.plough.com/en/topics/faith/discipleship/pandemic-love).

[421] My own family's growing awareness of creation care as a Christian obligation has found expression through my wife Sandra's participation as a member of the board of A Rocha Canada—a Christian stewardship organization working in conservation, environmental education, and sustainable agriculture.

In other words, could it be that a condition of our times of which you are acutely conscious is environmental degradation—a condition that you are in a position to address in some way? Who knows but that you have come to that position for such a time as this?

The Challenge of Conflict Resolution

It is also true that our modern world abounds in conflicts—economic, social, environmental, cultural, and political. But could it be that the existence of conflict in whatever circumstances you find yourself again constitutes providential positioning—a providential call for you to exercise at a human level what the apostle Paul called the ministry of reconciliation, serving as a self-sacrificial mediator of conflicting interests after the example of Jesus?[422]

In many respects, democratic politics at its most profound level is all about the reconciliation of conflicting interests by non-violent means. During my time in Canada's national politics one of the greatest and most worrisome conflicts facing the country was on the national unity front, with a growing portion of the political class and population of the province of Quebec desiring to secede from the Canadian federation.

My own awareness of this challenge—secession challenges being among the most dangerous crises that can afflict an established state—began in the 1960s and led me to study secession crises in other times and countries, especially federations,[423] and the various ways of dealing with them.[424] By the 1980s, growing discontents in western Canada were

---

[422] See 2 Corinthians 5:17–21.

[423] In particular, I focused on studying the most prominent and disastrous secession crisis to afflict a major federation in the 19th century, namely the secession of the southern states from the American Union, which triggered the American Civil War. My focus was not on the war itself but on the 30-year period preceding it and the various legislative, judicial, and political means employed in attempts to resolve the conflict between North and South by peaceful means.

[424] See 1 Kings 11–14 and 2 Chronicles 10–12. It should be noted that the Old Testament itself contains a detailed and instructive account of a secession crisis, namely the secession of the northern tribes of Israel from the United Kingdom established by Saul, David, and Solomon. This crisis, precipitated in part by the heavy taxes imposed by Solomon to finance the building of the temple and his palaces, and the ill-advised reaction of his son Rehoboam to Israel's demands for relief, had dire consequences for both Israel and Judah—civil war, religious apostasy, and eventually military defeat of the divided kingdom by the Assyrians and the Babylonians.

leading to the creation of an embryonic secessionist movement in the west as well, which, had it succeeded in gaining momentum, would have put intolerable strains on the federation and the national government, no matter who formed it. It was to address the underlying factors that were fuelling the western separatist movement—fiscal and economic mismanagement by the federal government and institutional indifference and unresponsiveness to legitimate western interests—that my colleagues and I formed the Reform Party of Canada, with the slogan "The West Wants In."[425]

Our general approach was to give strong but responsible voice to western discontents while proposing reforms to the federation as a constructive alternative to tearing it apart. We subsequently elected a significant number of members of Parliament and were active in the House of Commons and on the national unity front when the Quebec secession crisis was brought to a head in 1995 by a province-wide referendum in Quebec on whether that province should secede or not. The referendum was won by the No side (no to secession) by the narrowest of margins, and legislation, originally proposed by one of our members, was put in place to better equip the federal government to deal with secession crises of this type should they ever arise again.[426]

During all this time I must confess that as a Christian believer participating in the politics of my country I was not particularly conscious that I and my Christian colleagues in Parliament might have come to our positions of influence, however modest that influence may have been, by providential leading for "such a time as this." During this period we received many briefs and representations from all sorts of interest groups on how best to deal or not deal with the unity crisis. But I cannot recall receiving any from the faith community or Christian organizations that sought to specifically apply the Christian teaching on reconciliation to Canada's unity crisis in any practical way. In retrospect, however, Mordecai's question was surely relevant to our case—Who can tell but that we were brought to our particular positions for such a time as this?

[425] See Manning, *Think Big*.

[426] The 1995 referendum results were No 50.6 percent, Yes 49.4 percent. The margin of victory was 1.2 percent. Bill C-20, commonly called the *Clarity Act*, passed into law in 2000. See S.C. 2000, c. 26.

Christian believers who find themselves in positions of influence in such conflict situations in the future should be more acutely conscious of the possibility and direction of such providential positioning—positioning for the express purpose of playing a reconciling role.[427]

FROM MACRO TO MICRO

Finally, it is important to recognize that the crises that may eventually lead to political involvement and influence need not always be macro crises as described earlier. They may be micro crises—crises in the lives of individuals whom we encounter every day—the crises of individual and personal deprivation, poverty, sickness, abuse, alienation, loneliness, persecution, and bad choices.

Moses' first step toward his political role as the liberator of Israel from slavery in Egypt began with a personal incident in which he saw an Egyptian abusing a single Hebrew slave and felt compelled to intervene.

Toward the end of his earthly ministry Jesus spoke of the providential positioning of believers in the kingdom-that-is-to-come and linked that positioning to how we as his professed followers respond when confronted with these micro crises in the lives of others.

> "When the Son of Man comes in his glory … All the nations will be gathered before him, and he will separate the people one from another as a shepherd separates the sheep from the goats. He will put the sheep on his right and the goats on his left. Then the King will say to those on his right, 'Come, you who are blessed by my Father; take your inheritance, the kingdom prepared for you since the creation of the world. For I was hungry and you gave me something to eat, I was thirsty and you gave me something to drink, I was a stranger and you invited me in, I needed clothes and you clothed me, I was sick and you looked after me, I was in prison and you came to visit me.' Then the righteous will

[427] Some uncertainty as to whether we as believers have been providentially positioned to play a role in such situations is probably a good thing, guarding us against arrogant presumption and driving us to pray, consult the Scriptures, and seek the advice of fellow believers as to the course we should take. It is significant that Mordecai's counsel to Esther on this subject was given not in the form of a declaration as to her duty in the situation in which she found herself but in the form of a question: "Who knows but that you have come to your royal position for such a time as this?" Who knows? Presumably God knew, but it was up to Esther to decide whether and how to respond. And if she did not act, Mordecai was convinced that God would still achieve his purposes. "For if you remain silent at this time, relief and deliverance for the Jews will arise from another place, but you and your father's family will perish" (Esther 4:14).

> answer him, 'Lord, when did we see you hungry and feed you, or thirsty and give you something to drink? When did we see you a stranger and invite you in, or needing clothes and clothe you? When did we see you sick or in prison and go to visit you?' The King will reply, 'Truly I tell you, whatever you did for one of the least of these brothers and sisters of mine, you did for me.'"[428]

Jesus was speaking of our personal responses to these personal crises in the lives of individuals we encounter. But if laws, public policy, public expenditures, and other actions of governments can have anything to do with alleviating the causes or effects of deprivation, poverty, sickness, alienation, loneliness, persecution, and bad choices, it may well be that God will also use such encounters to lead some of us toward playing a political role in shaping collective responses to such micro crises, just as he did with Moses and has done with others of his politically involved followers down through the ages.

In one sense, engaging in economic, social, and political crises—whether on the macro or micro scale—is counterintuitive. Our natural instinct is to avoid, even to flee, situations characterized by conflict, hatred, injury, uncertainty, despair, darkness, and sadness. But could it be, as it was in the case of believers in exile in times past, that it is these very conditions that constitute our providential calling to involvement? Rather than avoiding them, we are to engage with them, praying the prayer known as the Prayer of St Francis of Assisi:

> Lord, make me an instrument of your peace,
> Where there is hatred, let me sow love;
> where there is injury, pardon;
> where there is doubt, faith;
> where there is despair, hope;
> where there is darkness, light;
> where there is sadness, joy.

As a believer in the providence of God but living in *exile* in a hostile world, whatever your position in time and relation to the crises and tragedies of our age, both small and great, who can tell but that you have been brought to that position for such a time as this?

[428] Matthew 25:31–40.

4.3 DELIVERANCE FROM EVIL

"Lead us not into temptation, but deliver us from the evil one."[429]
(Jesus to his disciples in teaching them how to pray)

Do not be overcome by evil, but overcome evil with good.[430]
(the apostle Paul to the Christians in Rome)

WHILE THE CONTEST WITH EVIL IS A FEATURE OF THE Christian experience no matter what our environment, its institutionalization and dominance is more likely to occur in societies that deny its existence and spiritual roots. It is therefore particularly important that believers living in exile in environments and societies hostile to faith and the things of God have a thorough understanding of the nature of evil, how it works, and God's provisions for deliverance from its tactics and stratagems.

THE TRANSFORMATION OF GOOD INTO EVIL

I once read a commentary on the nature of good and evil by a German pastor who had survived the horrors of the Second World War. It is deeply relevant to any Christian believer but especially to those involved in and active at the interface of faith and public life, and particularly those in politics.

He was reflecting painfully on the evil of the Nazi regime—its capacity to amplify and give licence to humanity's tendency toward prejudice, hatred, cruelty, brutality, and violence. But in retrospect what

---

429 Matthew 6:13.

430 Romans 12:21.

horrified him even more was its capacity to take that which was good and admirable in human beings—the industriousness of the German people and the idealism of German youth, for example—and twist even those elements to diabolical purposes.[431]

The twisting of that which is good into something evil and destructive of human life is a major theme of both the Old and New Testaments. For example, in the Old Testament story of the Fall, that which was pronounced by God himself to be "good"—the creation itself—became cursed when the first human beings succumbed to the temptations of the evil one.[432] In the New Testament record of the trial of Jesus, the law of God, given as an instrument of righteousness and justice, was cited by Jesus' accusers in support of their demand that he, the Son of God, be crucified.[433]

If as Christians we find ourselves in the presence of such a transformation—evil fastening itself to something good and twisting it to destructive ends—it is no exaggeration to say that we are in the very presence of Satan (evil in its most virulent form) and need to be not only on guard but also in the forefront of resistance.

FROM GOOD TO EVIL IN THE LIFE OF JOSEPH AND OF ISRAEL

Joseph, for example, was a son much loved by his father, Jacob—a good thing. But this good thing was somehow seized upon by the forces of evil and twisted, only slightly at first, into favouritism, which in turn begat jealousy and resentment among his brothers. Joseph at an early age also had a gift for prophetic dreaming—a good thing, a God-given gift that would later commend him to the pharaoh of Egypt. But while he was an adolescent the forces of evil were able to take two of his prophetic dreams

[431] "This is, after all, the ghastly mystery of the terrible twelve years in which we were dealing with this dark power in Germany, years in which the devil proved himself to be a master of every ruse and camouflage. In those years that lie behind us he did not appeal to the *base* instincts of our people, but challenged the sacrificial spirit and devotion of men. He caught hold of youth at the point of their idealism and their love for their country and, posing as an angel of light, played his diabolic games with the best attributes of our people" (Helmut Thielicke, *Life Can Begin Again: Sermons on the Mount*, trans. by John W. Doberstein [Minneapolis: Fortress Press, 1963], 5).

[432] Genesis 1–3.

[433] John 19:7.

that predicted that he would someday rule over his family and induce young Joseph to share them unwisely and arrogantly, further feeding the smouldering fire of jealousy and resentment among his brothers. Eventually that fire blazed into hatred, attempted murder, and the sale of Joseph into slavery. Evil affixed itself to that which was initially good in the life of Joseph and twisted it to evil and destructive ends—rendering him a slave in exile in Egypt.

Israel and Judah provide a second example. They were once part of a united kingdom, worshippers of the one true God and heirs to his promises. They were ruled by David, a man of God, whose two greatest desires toward the end of his reign were to be succeeded by a God-honouring son (Solomon) and to build a great dwelling place (the temple) for God. These were good things—noble, spiritual, and conducive to life and happiness. But once again the forces of evil insinuated themselves, subtly at first but shrewdly and tenaciously, into the religion and politics of the kingdom.

The desire and willingness of human beings, and the Israelites in particular, to "worship" made them vulnerable to the attraction of the gods of those around them. Not only did the people succumb to this attraction, but Solomon himself was eventually led astray to worship the gods of his many wives. In addition, Solomon's desire to bring glory to God by building a magnificent temple soon morphed into a desire to build magnificent palaces for the Lord's anointed—Solomon himself. The location of the temple and Solomon's palaces in Jerusalem, in Judea, and the onerous taxes levied on the whole kingdom to pay for them led to charges of favouritism and resentment among the northern tribes. This in turn blazed into open rebellion and civil war during the reign of Solomon's son Rehoboam. It also led to religious apostasy as the leaders of the northern tribes sought to provide an alternative place and form of worship to that provided by the temple and priests in Jerusalem. As a result, God's people became divided and weakened spiritually, politically, and militarily—easy prey to the Assyrians and Babylonians, who eventually conquered both Israel and Judah and led their people into exile and slavery. Evil insinuated itself into that which was initially good and redirected it to evil and destructive ends.

GOOD TO EVIL IN OUR DAY

In our own day, examples of this phenomenon also abound. The search for truth, meaning in life, and harmonious relationships through the search for God—genuine religion in its broadest sense—ought to be a boon and a blessing to humanity in the here and now as well as in the world to come. In Canada, for example, many of the foundation stones of our health, educational, and social-welfare services were laid by people whose faith led them to self-sacrificial service to others. And it was faith in God that enabled many of my parents' generation to endure the hardships and terrors of the Great Depression and the Second World War.

But far too often the search for meaning and meaningful service in life through religious faith has been perverted and twisted to become a force for evil—a source of tyranny, persecution, religious wars, and the present-day jihads of religious extremists. It has gone from good to evil on the religious front, something terribly discouraging to the sincere believer and driving millions away from God rather than toward him.

In the political world, the pursuit of freedom down through the ages has brought the blessings of religious, intellectual, political, and economic liberty to millions in what are now regarded as free societies. But it is also true that freedom, especially freedom exercised without responsibility, can be carried to extremes so that liberation movements—from the Renaissance, the Reformation, and the French Revolution to the sexual liberation movement of the 20th century—can also be transformed into new tyrannies and new sources of suffering.

Science and technology, benevolently developed and used, have been enormous forces for good, increasing the lifespan and improving the health and well-being of billions of human beings. But it is also a sad reality that virtually every major scientific and technological advancement—from the discovery and harnessing of fire and gunpowder to nuclear fission and fusion to the discovery and manipulation of the genomes of living organisms—can also be harnessed to the science of warfare and the destruction of human life.

With respect to the provision of health care, education, and social services—efforts vital to the well-being of millions of people—bureaucracy is the predominant organizational structure adopted for their management and delivery. But that very same organizational form can also become an instrument for harm—stifling freedom and initiative, reducing human beings to mere names or numbers in a file, and dividing responsibility among so many levels and agents that no one accepts responsibility or can be held accountable for the effectiveness or morality of outcomes.

It is as if great good, through faith, freedom, science, and bureaucracy, and great evil, through the abuse and perversion of the same, are opposite sides of a very thin coin often balancing precariously on its edge. And, depending on the intentions and strength of those in positions of influence at a particular point in time, just a small nudge is all that is required for that coin to fall good-side-up or evil-side-up, with great blessing or great tragedy as the inevitable result.

PERSONAL APPLICATION

So what about us? If there truly is such a diabolic thing as good being twisted into evil, is it not important for us to identify and examine the instances in our own lives and work where the forces of evil may have fastened on to things that are inherently good and twisted them into something bad? Perhaps it is our conviction of sin turned into depression and paralyzing feelings of worthlessness; our passion for the things of Christ morphing into intemperate zeal that repels rather than attracts others; our desire to succeed and set a good example twisted into self-promotion and workaholic behaviours; or our desire to do and see others do things right pushed into obsessive perfectionism and criticism of others.

The challenge is to be alert to the possibilities and realities of good being twisted into evil so that we seek God's help in guarding against and resisting such transformations. We truly need to pray frequently and earnestly as Jesus taught us, "Lead us not into temptation, but deliver us from the evil one."[434] The good news, explored in the next chapter, is that it is at these very points of spiritual vulnerability—in ourselves, our work, or the institutions of which we are a part—that God's grace can begin its work of prevention and counter-transformation.

---

[434] Matthew 6:13.

4.4 THE COUNTER-TRANSFORMATION OF EVIL INTO GOOD

"You intended to harm me [by selling me into slavery in Egypt],
but God intended it for good to accomplish
what is now being done, the saving of many lives."[435]
(Joseph to his brothers)

THE GOOD NEWS OF THE CHRISTIAN GOSPEL WRIT LARGE is that there is a counterbalance to *evil* from *good.* In the providence of God, "where sin increased, grace [the unmerited favour of God] increased all the more."[436] Evil can be overcome with good. It can even be transformed into good, and God's servants have an integral part to play in working with him to bring about such counter-transformations.

The most striking example of this phenomenon in the Christian narrative is the transformation of the cross—a cruel instrument of torture and death—into an instrument for achieving the forgiveness of sins and the salvation of humanity through Christ's sacrificial death upon it.

When we find ourselves in the presence of such a counter-transformation we are in the very presence of God—goodness personified and in its purest form.

EVIL TO GOOD IN THE LIFE OF JOSEPH

Joseph, as we have already seen, experienced the good life of a privileged son in a God-blessed family being transformed by the evil actions of his brothers into the life of a lowly slave in a foreign land.

---

[435] Genesis 50:20.

[436] Romans 5:20.

But the greatest and most inspirational aspect of Joseph's life is that he also experienced the counter-transformation—evil transformed into good—with that transformation being the dominant and lasting influence in his life.

As a slave in the household of Potiphar, he rose providentially and by virtue of his God-given ability and diligence to be put in charge of the entire household. When he was unjustly accused of attacking Potiphar's wife, he suffered yet another crushing reversal as he was cast into prison. In the prison, again providentially and by virtue of his God-given administrative ability and trustworthiness, he was put in charge of other prisoners. There he met two servants of Pharaoh, his cupbearer and baker, who had been imprisoned for their faults. Joseph correctly interpreted their dreams, and the cupbearer was restored to his position in Pharaoh's household. But the cupbearer forgot Joseph, who continued to languish in prison until Pharaoh was also troubled by a dream, which none of his advisors could interpret. The cupbearer then remembered Joseph, who was summoned from prison to interpret Pharaoh's dream of an impending famine. When Joseph did so and proposed the policy that would safeguard Egypt from that disaster, he was promoted to the position of vice-ruler of Egypt. When his brothers came to Egypt to buy food, he revealed himself to them, rescued his entire family from starvation, resettled them in Egypt, and gave this remarkable testimony to the work of God in transforming evil into good:

> Then Joseph said to his brothers, "Come close to me." When they had done so, he said, "I am your brother Joseph, the one you sold into Egypt! And now, do not be distressed and do not be angry with yourselves for selling me here, because it was to save lives that God sent me ahead of you … to preserve for you a remnant on earth and to save your lives by a great deliverance. So then, it was not you who sent me here, but God" … "You intended to harm me, but God intended it for good to accomplish what is now being done, the saving of many lives."[437]

In Joseph's life, his abilities and ambition for leadership and his gifts for prophetic dreaming and interpretation were initially seized upon by evil forces and used against him with tragic and destructive results. But then came the more powerful and lasting counter-transformation; God in his mercy and providence took those same abilities, ambitions, and gifts

[437] Genesis 45:4–7; 50:20.

and redirected their manifestation and use for good, to "the saving of many lives."

THE ROLE OF BELIEVERS IN EFFECTING COUNTER-TRANSFORMATIONS

It seems to me, therefore, that believers occupying positions of influence in the non-believing, secular, and materialistic societies and systems of today should be especially alert to the following:

- The distinct possibility that the good with which they may be associated could be transformed into evil in their areas of influence.
- God's call to be on guard against and resistant to such transformations and to co-operate with him in resisting them.
- God's working to effect counter-transformations—good from evil—and to join with him in such work.

Certainly, those of us who live as believing exiles in societies indifferent or hostile to our faith—as Joseph, Daniel, and Esther did—have ample opportunity to exercise these three roles.

My illustrations of those opportunities and possible responses are primarily drawn from my experiences as a management consultant and an elected politician living and working in the largely secular society that Canada has become. But hopefully the sharing of them will suggest similar opportunities and responses to you no matter what your position or field of work.

PREVENTING AND COMBATTING THE ABUSE OF FREEDOM

In Canada, our *Charter of Rights and Freedoms* affirms, "Everyone has the following fundamental freedoms: (*a*) freedom of conscience and religion; (*b*) freedom of thought, belief, opinion, and expression, including freedom of the press and other media of communication; (*c*) freedom of peaceful assembly; and (*d*) freedom of association."[438]

I personally believe that Christians should be in the forefront of championing freedom, in particular the freedom of conscience and belief on which religious and political freedom depends. I am also of the view that freedom is indivisible; a threat to one freedom, such as

[438] *Constitution Act, 1982*, c. 11, p. 1, s. 2.

freedom of conscience, is a threat to all freedoms, and therefore to be resisted.

But as Christian believers acutely conscious of humanity's fallen nature and propensity for evil, do we not also have a special role to play in recognizing the potential in ourselves and others for abusing freedom—exercising freedom irresponsibly and toward destructive ends—and the need to prevent and combat such abuses?

For example, I am a believer in the freedom of economic enterprise, and when I was in the management consulting business I had ample opportunity to assist clients in the energy sector in the exercise of that freedom. But as a Christian believer I was also acutely conscious of the potential for individuals and corporations to abuse freedom of enterprise and the opportunities afforded by free markets. Gradually, I found my consulting practice led, by this awareness rather than by design, into assisting energy companies to responsibly discharge their obligations, not only to customers and shareholders but to the communities in which they operated and the environment from which they extracted resources.

But if there is one area where we as believers need to be especially alert and active with respect to preventing and combatting the abuse of freedom, it is with respect to abuses of religious freedom. I am convinced that the greatest threat to religious freedom in our society comes not from the academic and political challenges to faith from atheists and secularists but from abuses of religious freedom by religious people themselves. Such abuses provide critics, governments, and other institutions with the public support and justification for actions to suppress or circumscribe all religious thought and expression. By abuses of religious freedom I mean the use of deceit, coercion, and threats and acts of violence to achieve religious ends—as when children, women, or minorities are oppressed in the name of religion; when abortionists or gays or physicians engaged in euthanasia are threatened with violence in the name of religion; or when non-believers and believers of whatever stripe are made the objects of religious vendettas or jihads. None of these tactics are the way of Jesus, who never coerced anyone to follow or obey him but rather invited people to choose to follow and obey by the exercise of their own free will.

SAFEGUARDING SCIENCE FROM UNETHICAL USES

Suppose one is thoroughly convinced of the merits and benefits of science and is in a position of managing or directing public resources in support of scientific research and development. As believers, acutely conscious of humanity's fallen nature and propensity for evil, do we not also have a special role to play in calling attention to the potentially *dark* side of science—its application to unethical ends—and the need to safeguard against such applications? Performing such a role should not be presented or seen as anti-science but as assisting in the protection of science from applications that discredit it.

Consequently, when I was in Parliament, and later a member of the board of governors of the Canadian Council of Academies, I strongly supported the idea that major science projects—for example, those involved in the study and manipulation of the human genome—should be subject to Economic Environmental Ethical Social Legal (EEESL) studies and constraints.[439] Such studies seek to determine the implications of scientific research and development projects in these areas and propose measures to avoid misuse and to mitigate negative consequences.

As a member of the Standing Committee on Health in our Parliament, I was also involved in hearings on the application of the latest scientific techniques to assisted human reproduction through enhanced in vitro fertilization and stem cell research. This provided an opportunity to address the perennial question as to what extent the state should encourage and support scientific experimentation, the results of which may lead to serious harms as well as benefits. My colleagues and I sought, for example,

---

[439] Recognition, within the scientific community itself, of the need for such studies arose out of retrospective reflection and regret concerning the ethical implications of the development of nuclear science, which made possible the creation of the atomic bomb. Following the Second World War, the US Department of Energy specifically monitored the genetic implications for persons exposed to nuclear fallout, which in turn led to the project to sequence the human genome. This time provision was made for 5 percent of the budget of the Human Genome Project to be committed to the Ethical, Legal and Social Implications (ELSI) Research Program to foster basic and applied research on the ethical, legal, and social implications of genetic and genomic research for individuals, families, and communities. It is significant that Dr. Francis Collins, co-director of the Human Genome Project and a strong supporter of such studies, is a practicing Christian. See Francis S. Collins, *The Language of God: A Geneticist Presents Evidence for Belief* (New York: Free Press, 2006).

to have a provision written into Canada's *Assisted Human Reproduction Act*[440] stipulating that where there was a definable conflict between that which is scientifically possible and that which is ethically preferable, it should be the ethical course of action that prevails.[441]

APPLICATION

You may not be embedded in or involved with an energy company or scientific establishment, but you are no doubt embedded in or involved with some organization or institution—a school, a hospital, a union, an interest group, a political party, or a business of some sort where you are employed.

And if that is the case, could it be that your role as a believer is to be alert to instances in the life and work of that institution where the forces of evil are fastening on to things that are inherently or potentially good and twisting them into something bad? Perhaps it is the pursuit of returns on investment turned into exploitation or environmental degradation, bargaining power morphed into intimidation, communications twisted into the spin and the lie, or the pursuit of organizational efficiency and effectiveness that destroys human relationships that needs to be explicitly recognized and resisted.

And no matter what our role in society, do not all of us as professing Christians have a responsibility to guard against the abuse of religious freedom, in particular by the overzealous members of our own faith communities? The psalmist David was discharging this responsibility when, conscious of the *zeal that consumes*, he prayed, "May those who hope in you not be disgraced because of me … may those who seek you not be put to shame because of me."[442]

Let us continue to pray, as Jesus instructed, "Lead us not into temptation, but deliver us from the evil one," especially the attempts of the evil one to turn even our faith toward means and ends that will discredit the way to God in the eyes of those who so desperately need to find it. Above all, let us seek to become instruments of the grace of God in effecting the counter-transformation of evil into good.

---

[440] *Assisted Human Reproduction Act* (S.C. 2004, c. 2).

[441] Manning, et al., *Regulating Assisted Human Reproduction.*

[442] Psalm 69:6.

4.5 THE GOOD AND EVIL OF BUREAUCRACIES

THE SCRIPTURES HAVE LITTLE TO SAY ABOUT THE governance and administrative systems of Egypt, Babylon, and Medo-Persia in which exiles like Joseph, Daniel, and Esther found themselves embedded. But there can be little doubt from the historical accounts of these empires that bureaucratic organization of some sort was a feature of those systems and that dealing with the potential of bureaucracies for both beneficial and malevolent behaviour must have been a constant aspect of the experience of the believing exiles embedded in them.

For example, the administrative machinery over which Joseph presided must have been elaborate and immense in order to collect and store all the grain from Egypt's seven years of good harvests, to redistribute it during the lean years, and, in the process, to systematically establish Pharaoh's ownership and control over virtually all the physical and human resources of Egypt.

With respect to Babylon, besides a large and formidable army, the administration in which Daniel and his friends came to hold high office included a vast array of satraps, prefects, governors, advisors, treasurers, judges, magistrates, and provincial officials.[443]

And in Medo-Persia, not only did the administration consist of "satraps, governors and nobles of the 127 provinces stretching from India to Cush," but even the ruler's harem of which Esther became a reluctant member was elaborately and hierarchically organized.[444]

---

[443] Daniel 3:2; 6:1–3.

[444] Esther 8:9 and 2:8–9.

Notwithstanding the potential of complex military and governmental organizations for doing harm, Joseph, Daniel, and Esther were able to use their positions within them for preventing evil and doing good—in Joseph's case, for saving of many lives from famine; in Daniel's case, for saving the lives of Nebuchadnezzar's many advisors and officials from the uncontrolled fury of their king; and in Esther's case, for saving the lives of her own people from genocide.

PROTECTING CLIENTS FROM BUREAUCRATIC ABUSE

But now flash forward through the centuries to our day. If you are a believer embedded in a large public or private organization you will likely be practising the outworking of your faith in a bureaucratic environment. And if you are a politician and legislator dealing with health, education, social welfare, childcare, senior care, and other related services of the welfare state, bureaucracy will be the principal organizational and delivery mechanism to which you must relate. Such bureaucracies are capable of providing essential and beneficial services to large numbers of people and of achieving much good, but they are also capable of unknowingly and unintentionally doing harm.[445]

Let us, therefore, explore more specifically how believers embedded in such organizations, or responsible for their creation and management, can prevent harm and safeguard bureaucratic organizations from their *dark* side. That dark side includes the potential to do real harm to those whom bureaucracies are intended to help because of how such organizations transmit information and divide responsibility.

BUREAUCRACIES AS INFORMATION SYSTEMS

My earliest exposure to the nature of bureaucracies occurred in the 1960s while my father was premier of the province of Alberta. My thinking on this subject was very much influenced at the time by the doctoral thesis of a friend and colleague, Dr. Erick Schmidt. Erick, a committed Christian, was a special consultant to the executive council (cabinet) of the government of Alberta.

---

[445] The focus of this chapter is primarily on protecting those served by public sector organizations from bureaucratic abuse. But many of the observations made and measures recommended for mitigating the bad and facilitating the good in public bureaucracies are equally applicable to private-sector bureaucracies such as are to be found in large corporations and NGOs.

Erick's doctoral dissertation was entitled "The Morphology of Bureaucratic Knowledge."[446] It drew upon much of the classical literature on bureaucracy, on insights based on modern systems analysis and cybernetic theory, and on Schmidt's practical experience with the Alberta government bureaucracy. It analyzed bureaucratic organizations, with their layers and layers of boxes, each reporting to the box above it, as information systems. These systems transmitted information on people, resources, and situations upward to decision makers and transmitted decisions, orders, and policy guidelines downward through middle management to frontline workers.

Schmidt's contention was that these bureaucratic structures transmitted certain types of information accurately, for example, concrete information on things that could be measured and quantified, such as how many barrels of oil were produced per day by Alberta's oil fields. But these same structures could not transmit other types of data accurately at all—for example, subjective data pertaining to values, feelings, emotions, relationships—precisely the information you need to humanely provide effective services to people, especially people with special needs like the very young, the old, the poor, and the sick.

According to Schmidt's thesis, not only do bureaucratic information systems have trouble transmitting to decision makers and workers the information they need in order to care humanely and efficiently for people with special needs, but those systems actually filter out much of the required information and substitute other less relevant, even dangerously misleading, information only because it can be objectified and quantified. This is why caring systems organized in a bureaucratic fashion not only tend to reduce people to files and numbers but in the extreme can become so inhuman in their functioning that they become a menace rather than a help to the very people they are supposed to serve.

Schmidt went on to predict specific people-damaging incidents that might occur later in the 1970s to Albertans being served by Alberta's health, education, child-welfare, penal, and social-welfare bureaucracies—incidents that would occur not because of any lack of professionalism or dedication on the part of Alberta's civil servants but because of the

---

446 Erick Schmidt, "The Morphology of Bureaucratic Knowledge" (PhD diss., University of Alberta, 1975).

nature of bureaucracy itself and its inherent inability to handle people with care. That same decade, a journalist with the *Edmonton Journal*, Wendy Koenig, distinguished herself with a series of reports on precisely the types of incidents that Schmidt had predicted.

The question therefore arises (which I attempt to answer in a moment), what can believers embedded in or responsible for the management of such bureaucracies do to avoid or mitigate this potential for harm due to the manner in which bureaucracies process information?

THE BUREAUCRATIC DIVISION OF RESPONSIBILITY

Long before Dr. Schmidt penned his thesis, the great Russian author Leo Tolstoy arrived at similar conclusions through artistic and spiritual insights documented in *Resurrection*, the one great novel he wrote after his religious conversion. Prince Nekhlyudov, the hero of the novel and a surrogate for Tolstoy himself, has just witnessed the death from sunstroke of two political prisoners in the care of the Russian legal and penal system. But he is unable to identify anyone who is responsible for what he regards as their murder, other than the system itself, which assumes no responsibility. And so he concludes,

> "All this happened … because all these people—governors, inspectors, police-officers and policemen—consider that there are circumstances in this world when man owes no humanity to man. Every one of them—Maslennikov [the governor], the inspector, the officer of the escort—if he had not been a governor, an inspector, an officer, would have thought twenty times before sending people off in such heat and such a crowd; they would have stopped twenty times on the way if they had noticed a man getting faint and gasping for breath—they would have got him out of the crowd and into the shade, given him water and allowed him to rest, and then if anything had happened they would have shown some pity. They did nothing of the sort: they even prevented others from helping; because they were thinking not of human beings and their obligations towards them but of the duties and responsibilities of their office, which they placed above the demands of human relations. That is the whole truth of the matter … If once we admit, be it for a single hour or in a single instance, that there can be anything more important than compassion for a fellow human being, then there is no crime against man that we cannot commit with an easy conscience."[447]

---

[447] Leo Tolstoy, *Resurrection*, trans. Rosemary Edmonds (New York: Penguin Books, 1966), 447–8.

For a number of years I always reread Tolstoy's *Resurrection* at Easter. But the truth of his observations and their relevance to the operations of bureaucracy in modern times came home to me with particular force while I was doing community development in the Slave Lake region of northern Alberta in the 1970s and became personally aware of what came to be known as the Wabasca Baby tragedy. The facts of this case are as follows.

In April 1973, Joan Belinda Manybears, the three-month-old daughter of Lillian Manybears, became ill of an infection at her home in the First Nations community of Wabasca, 250 miles north of Edmonton, Alberta. Her mother took the infant to the nursing station in Wabasca, where it was recommended that she be transported to the nearest hospital in Slave Lake. An ambulance was summoned to transport Belinda to the Slave Lake Hospital, where, upon examination, it was recommended that the ambulance continue on to a hospital in Edmonton.

By the time the driver reached the town of Westlock just north of Edmonton, it was clear that the baby was in serious distress. The driver stopped at the Westlock Hospital, but, sadly, it was too late, and Belinda was pronounced dead. The ambulance driver was then instructed to proceed to the Royal Alexandra Hospital in Edmonton, where the provincial coroner was based, so that he could perform an autopsy. The autopsy was performed without the permission of the mother and, due to an administrative oversight, without securing the services of a mortician to prepare the body afterward for burial. The body of the child was subsequently placed in a cardboard box and returned to Slave Lake, where it was then delivered back to the mother by ambulance with little or no explanation of what had transpired.

Needless to say, the mother was horribly shocked to receive the dead body of her baby in this condition and in this way. When news of the incident became known, there was a media storm, followed by public outrage and demands in the Alberta legislature for a public inquiry.

The Minister of Health and Social Development at the time, the Hon. Neil Crawford, responded by requesting that the Alberta Hospital Services Commission make inquiries and report regarding the handling of the body of the infant.[448] In July of 1973 the commission duly reported that all the activities carried out in connection with the incident were "in accordance with accepted standards" and that no particular individual, institution, or procedure could be held responsible for what had happened.[449]

Its chief recommendation was a bureaucratic one, that changes should be made to the applicable regulations, to which the province responded with a bureaucratic prescription, an Order in Council prescribing ten pages of revisions to the Provincial Board of Health Regulations Respecting Preparation and Transportation of Dead Bodies, Funerals, Interment, and Disinterment.[450]

When the Wabasca Baby tragedy became the subject of media stories and debate in the Alberta legislature, dozens of people asked the same question: How could this happen? Couldn't one person in the system—a nurse, a doctor, an administrator, the coroner, the ambulance driver—have seen what was happening or might happen and intervened so that a grieving mother would not receive the dead body of her baby in a cardboard box delivered like a package from FedEx?

The best answer and the clue to the prevention of such atrocities by caregiving bureaucracies are not to be found in the debate in the Alberta

---

[448] The commission was directed to ascertain the following: (1) What treatment services were provided at Slave Lake, Edmonton, or elsewhere, to the infant child from, on or about April 25, 1973, until her death? (2) Following the death of the infant child, whether the conduct of persons responsible for handling the dead body was in accordance with the existing standards of conduct in the province of Alberta. (3) Whether in the opinion of the Alberta Hospital Services Commission existing standards of conduct in the province of Alberta conform with a contemporary sense of propriety and respect for the deceased.

[449] In particular, the Commission reported on July 25, 1973,

- The activities and procedures carried out by the hospitals and staff members were in accordance with accepted standards in Alberta.
- The conduct of persons responsible for handling the dead body was in accordance with the existing standards of conduct in the province of Alberta.
- The body was handled properly in that it was placed in a new container which is manufactured and recognized as being "purpose designed" for the temporary transportation of small bodies.

[450] It states, "the Provincial Board of Health Regulations, Division 26, Regulations Relating to Funerals and to the Preparation of Dead Bodies for Interment, Cremation, and Transportation be reviewed and clarified, in particular that section 26–5–5 be made more explicit and designate the levels of responsibility as they apply to health-care facilities, morticians, or relatives claiming bodies."

legislature or amendments to the regulations for the handling of dead bodies but again in Tolstoy's faith-based explanation of such tragedies, paraphrased as follows:

> All this comes from the fact that all these people, professional and well-meaning as they may be—health-service administrators, nurses, doctors, coroners, ambulance dispatchers, and drivers—are placed in circumstances where human relations are not necessary between human beings. All these functionaries were obliged to think not first and foremost of a mother and child and their duty toward them but rather of the requirements of the positions they held ... It is only necessary that people should hold bureaucratic positions; that they should be persuaded that there is a kind of business called government service that allows people to treat other people as things without having human brotherly relations with them; and that they should be so linked together by this government service that the responsibility for the results of their deeds should not fall on any one of them individually. Without these conditions, human tragedies like this would be impossible in our times. It all lies in the fact that people think there are circumstances in which one may deal with human beings without love.[451]

APPLICATION TO YOUR SITUATION

If you are a believer living in this society hostile to your faith and embedded by the providential guidance of God in a bureaucratic system—particularly a public-service bureaucracy ostensibly dedicated to providing essential services to needy people—perhaps you are there to help protect that bureaucracy from its dark side and ensure that it functions as an instrument for good rather than as a source of unintended harms.

Consider, therefore, what you can do to perform that role to the best of your God-given ability and strength. Your starting point is to pray for the wisdom and prophetic insight required to better understand the organization in which you are embedded; to perceive the nature of bureaucratic systems from a spiritual perspective, as did Schmidt and Tolstoy; and to resolve to be vigilant in guarding your bureaucracy against its dark side.

[451] Author's paraphrase of Leo Tolstoy, *Resurrection*, 447–8.

4.6 SAFEGUARDING PUBLIC BUREAUCRACIES FROM DOING HARM

WE HAVE PREVIOUSLY OBSERVED THAT THE WORKING environment for Joseph, Daniel, and Esther—believers in exile in foreign and hostile environments—was that of the huge and bureaucratic administrations that characterized the governing structures of the great empires of Egypt, Babylon, and Medo-Persia. We noted that such organizations have potential for doing both good and evil and that the exiles played an important role in promoting the good and constraining the evil. That in turn led us to examine, from a spiritual perspective, the *dark* side of the large public bureaucracies of today and the opportunities and obligations of believers embedded therein to enhance their potential for good and to safeguard them from their potential for harm.

This examination was in no way intended to denigrate the capacity of well-organized public bureaucracies for doing good—for effectively rendering essential services to large numbers of people. That capacity for doing good, however, will be enhanced by the adoption of measures to prevent such bureaucracies from doing harm. Let us therefore now examine in some detail the measures that are available to us to prevent well-intended public-service bureaucracies from doing harm—to prevent evil from arising from good. I see this safeguarding, especially by believers embedded in such systems, as essentially a spiritual undertaking, co-operating with the work of God in *delivering us from evil.*

ANTIDOTES AND PREVENTATIVE MEASURES

Are there antidotes to the vulnerabilities and predispositions of bureaucratic organizations to do harm, measures that those in positions to direct or safeguard bureaucratic operations can employ and that believers in such positions should champion and practise? My experiences with bureaucracies, particularly as a Christian believer, management consultant, and legislator, suggest the following.

1. Be reluctant to consign the care of human beings solely to bureaucracies

As Christians, instructed by God to personally and collectively care for the poor, the sick, the lonely, and the oppressed, we should be reluctant in the first place to assign, without reservation or the serious consideration of alternatives, the care of human beings, especially vulnerable human beings, to state-run social-welfare bureaucracies.[452] When we see injured human beings lying by the side of life's road, Jesus' instruction to us is to follow the example of the Good Samaritan, who first of all offered personal attention and care, rather than defaulting to the position of letting somebody else (in our case, the state) take care of them.[453]

At one time, of course, the Christian church was the primary institution in many countries, including Canada, for providing care to the most needy members of society. In modern times that function has been transferred, to a large extent, to governments. While there are certainly benefits to that transfer and it is unlikely ever to be reversed, as believers we need to be more constantly and personally proactive on the front lines of social service—offering alternative, more personalized care as individuals, families, churches, NGOs and social enterprises whose care commitment is rooted in the life and teachings of Jesus.

As leaders, supportive of public-service bureaucracies but sensitive to their dark side, before we automatically assign the care of any vulnerable class of persons to large, impersonal care systems, we ought first to inquire whether or not there are smaller, more personal and more humane caregiving alternatives and how these might be given greater opportunity and resources to provide that care.[454]

[452] See Matthew 25:31–46.

[453] See Luke 10:25–37.

[454] Canada's *Constitution Act* assigns to the provinces responsibilities for "The Establishment, Maintenance, and Management of Hospitals, Asylums, Charities, and Eleemosynary Institutions in and for the Province" (BNA 1867 91 [7]). Note that *eleemosynary* is an old word literally meaning "almsgiving," the same word used by Jesus in his Sermon on

For example, as our population ages and special care for the old and dying becomes an urgent priority, the creation and support of end-of-life home care and community-based hospice care programs and facilities by faith-based and other local groups should be encouraged, not prevented, by public policy and social legislation. Such programs and facilities are especially required as alternatives to people dying in large and impersonal health-care facilities where the beds are urgently needed for others and where physician-assisted suicide is now sanctioned by Canadian law.

2. Bring the top to the bottom

An increasing number of private-sector service organizations are requiring top and middle managers to spend more time on the front lines, where they must meet face to face with real customers and share the experiences of frontline workers. Therefore, let us strongly encourage, even compel, the top and middle management of social-welfare bureaucracies to regularly and substantially meet with their frontline employees and their clients so as to receive first-hand information and awareness of needs and conditions that will never be accurately transmitted through bureaucratic information channels.[455]

3. Respect and encourage the exercise of freedom of conscience by bureaucratic caregivers

If we are going to ask those embedded in bureaucratic care systems to be more humane and relational in their conduct and delivery of services, then we need to give them more freedom to follow the dictates of their own consciences—those inner compasses that, if spiritually sensitive, alert us to evil and draw us toward the good.

---

the Mount (Matthew 6:1–2 [KJV]). But since most Canadian charities want the right to issue tax-deductible receipts for charitable donations, it is the federal government, specifically the Canada Revenue Agency, that has largely assumed responsibility for defining and regulating Canada's charitable sector. Federal laws governing charities are long overdue for a complete overhaul, as has been done in the United Kingdom, separating the definition and regulation of charity from the federal finance department and expanding the capacities of charities, including religious institutions, for example, through facilitating the formation of social enterprises and the use of social impact bonds.

[455] Exhortations for Christians to behave in this way are to be found, for example, in Paul's description of our "calling" in Ephesians 2 and the example of Jesus described in Philippians 2:5–11.

For those drafting legislation, or establishing, supporting, or modifying public services delivered by bureaucracies, explicit attention should be given to the inclusion of *conscience* or *non-participation* rights,[456] which entitle public employees, for reasons of conscience, to refrain from participating in ethically questionable activities that employment by that bureaucracy may otherwise dictate.[457] It is true that such provisions will raise supervisory and equity problems for the managers of such services and the courts. But accepting and dealing with such problems is preferable to denying those employed by public bureaucracies, especially frontline workers, their rights to freedom of religion, conscience, thought, belief, opinion, and expression as guaranteed by the *Charter*.

4. Encourage greater freedom of action for bureaucratic caregivers

Saying that we respect and encourage freedom of conscience if we do not also permit and encourage people to act according to their consciences

---

[456] For example, private member's bills have been introduced in several provincial legislatures that would prohibit an employer from refusing to hire, advance or promote or to threaten, discipline or dismiss a health-care professional because the health-care professional is not willing to take part in or to counsel any health-care procedure that offends a tenet of the health professional's religion or the belief of the health professional that human life is sacred. See http://www.assembly.ab.ca/ISYS/LADDAR_files/docs/bills/bill/legislature_24/session_4/20000217_bill-212.pdf.

In the federal Parliament, similar private member's bills have also been introduced that would criminalize the coercion of health-care practitioners into taking part in medical procedures that offend the practitioner's religion or belief that human life is inviolable. See http://www.parl.gc.ca/HousePublications/Publication.aspx?Language=E&Mode=1&DocId=2333614.

For a related discussion of "conscience rights" in relation to euthanasia and physician-assisted suicide, see the factum (pages 5–7) of The Christian Medical and Dental Society of Canada and The Canadian Federation of Catholic Physicians' Societies in the 2014 Carter (assisted suicide) Supreme Court of Canada hearing: http://www.scc-csc.gc.ca/WebDocuments-DocumentsWeb/35591/FM120_Internener_Christian-Medical-Dental-Society_and_Catholic-Physician-Societes.pdf.

[457] In Canada, the case for allowing "conscience rights" to be recognized and enforced in particular legislation would appear to be strongest when it rests on linking conscience to explicit religious beliefs, protected by the *Charter*, and being able to demonstrate the sincerity with which the adherent holds and practises those beliefs. See the Supreme Court of Canada decision in *Syndicate Northcrest v. Amselem*, SCC [2004] 47, in dissent, M. Bastarache (L. LeBel, and M. Deschamps concurring).

is hypocritical and a contradiction in terms.[458] For frontline workers employed by bureaucracies, there is a need to provide more room for them to step outside their bureaucratic role from time to time in order to follow the dictates of their consciences and to act humanely rather than bureaucratically toward those in their care.

I realize of course that encouraging such independent behaviour on the part of bureaucrats can again create a major challenge for supervisors and can be open to abuse (more on how to curtail abuse in a moment). But I am prompted to encourage such allowances nonetheless as a result of experiences like the following.

Back when I was in the management consulting business, our firm was engaged to conduct a socio-economic impact assessment of a heavy oil plant being proposed by Imperial Oil for construction in the Cold Lake area of northeast Alberta. Our assignment was to assess the potential impact of the proposed plant on seven Indigenous bands in the area (six Cree bands and one Chipewyan) and to propose measures to mitigate negative impacts and maximize potential benefits.

I had some experience with Cree bands and personally knew some of the Cree band leaders in the area. But I needed someone to improve my understanding of the Chipewyan people. Knowing of my need, a friend introduced me to a Metis woman, part Chipewyan, named Ernestine Gibot. Ernestine advised me about the Cold Lake Chipewyans and eventually became a good friend—the best First Nations friend I ever had. As she opened up about her own life, including her spiritual beliefs, she gave me new insights into the operations of the ubiquitous social-welfare system that Canada has established for its Indigenous people.

This is not the place to tell Ernestine's lengthy and heart-wrenching story in detail, but the following aspects of it are relevant to this

---

[458] I once encountered this contradiction in a conversation with a senior official of the Chinese Communist Party when I drew her attention to the obvious contradiction between provisions in the Chinese constitution guaranteeing freedom of conscience and belief while the government continued to suppress religious expression and activity. She replied, without apparently seeing any contradiction in her reply, "In this area, the Chinese people are free to believe whatever they want; they just can't talk about it or act upon it."

commentary on the nature of bureaucracies and how to render them more beneficial to those they are intended to serve.[459]

At the age of forty-nine, with little formal education, no money, no friends at hand, no experience of city living or employment, and a drinking problem, Ernestine decided to leave her life in the northern Alberta bush as the abused wife of a Metis trapper and start over in the large and strange city of Edmonton.

It then took seven years of wandering around within the bureaucratic maze of services available to Indigenous people in Edmonton after Ernestine first arrived until she got a self-sustaining job, first as a "consultant" with our firm and soon after as a teacher's aide in an inner city school.

The path Ernestine followed took her to such agencies and destinations as the Charles Camsel Hospital; Poundmaker Lodge (an alcoholism treatment centre); provincial and city welfare offices; the Department of Indian Affairs; Hilltop House (a residence for First Nations women); numerous bars, hotels, and liquor stores; the courthouse; the city jail; several Catholic churches; the Edmonton Housing Authority; the Native Friendship Centre; the Alberta Native Communications Society; the Native Counselling Service; and the Alberta Vocational College.

By retracing Ernestine's steps and discussing them with her, I learned four things about the nature of the complex network of bureaucratic helping systems established to serve Canadian First Nations peoples:

- Sometimes it delivered certain services effectively—in particular health care and occasionally emergency financial support, accommodation, and training.
- It failed to provide personal guidance at critical times or to offer encouragement, incentive, and meaningful links to employers.
- The few individuals within the system who actually helped Ernestine were individuals she would not have met if she hadn't been in the system.
- Most importantly, in order to truly help Ernestine, these individuals often had to step outside their professional roles and act on their own initiative, rendering services above and beyond those called for by their job descriptions and sometimes in violation of the system's rules.

---

459 Ernestine Gibot's story has been well told by Robert Collins, former editor of *Imperial Oil Review*, in "The Long Hard Road of Ernestine Gibot," *Reader's Digest* (October 1984).

This was the case, for example, with her doctor and her priest, who told her, "We shouldn't really be saying this, but you must leave the north and leave your husband or you'll be dead within a year." It was also the case with two social workers who treated Ernestine as a friend, meeting with her after hours and against regulations rather than simply treating her as a client. And it was the case with the employment counsellor who referred Ernestine to me, even when our firm was not on the agency's approved list of potential employers. (After all, what management consulting firm would possibly hire a mid-fifties Indigenous woman with a grade 4 education?)

It is experiences like this that led me to address the question of what could be done to shorten the tortuous path through the bureaucratic maze that the Ernestines of our country must travel to escape the ravages of their past. It is experiences like this that lead me to encourage greater freedom of action for frontline caregivers employed by bureaucracies and responsible for serving those Ernestines.

5. Accept greater responsibility and accountability for the exercise of your freedom of conscience and action

With greater freedom must come a greater acceptance of accountability and responsibility. Hence policy, legislation, and regulations allowing for the exercise of greater freedom of conscience and action by frontline caregivers employed by bureaucracies must be accompanied by the provision of mechanisms to ensure greater accountability and acceptance of responsibility for outcomes.

In the private sector, these include the requirement for independent audits of corporate performance (not only financial audits but, increasingly, social and environmental audits), the institution of whistle-blowing mechanisms within companies to facilitate the reporting of illegal or unethical actions, and the provision of financial liability and penalties for deliberate or inadvertent actions that injure others.

Would there not be merit, therefore, in strengthening and broadening the audit requirements for public-service bureaucracies and unions to include social as well as financial audits? Would there not be merit in expanding and strengthening the provision of whistle-blowing legislation and mechanisms to public bureaucracies and public-service unions, just as such safeguards were instituted in greater measure following the gross violations of marketplace freedoms by corporations leading to the financial meltdown of 2008?[460] And would there not be merit in partially and selectively withdrawing the immunity of the Crown and public servants from legal action when their activities and those of public agencies do demonstrable harm to citizens and their interests?[461]

APPLICATION TO YOUR SITUATION

If you are a Christian believer embedded in a bureaucracy of any kind, could it be that you are there in part to provide an understanding of the nature of bureaucratic systems from a spiritual perspective—serving to protect that bureaucracy from the inadvertent expression of its dark side and to enhance its potential for good?

Suppose you are a believer providentially embedded in a government as a legislator, policy maker, or administrator, operating in a society hostile to your faith but challenged to meet the needs of some vulnerable segment of society. Could it be that you personally are there by divine appointment to

---

[460] In 2002, a private member's bill was introduced in the Canadian House of Commons entitled *The Whistle Blower Human Rights Act*, which would "respect the protection of employees in the public service who make allegations in good faith respecting wrongdoing in the public service." It failed to pass but was followed in 2005 by the passage of the *Public Servants Disclosure Protection Act* (S.C. 2005, c. 46), which is now law and forms the basis of federal whistle-blowing protection. Provincially, all jurisdictions except British Columbia, Newfoundland, and Prince Edward Island have some form of whistle-blowing legislation in place. In the US, section 806 of the *Sarbanes Oxley Act* contains significant protection and support for corporate whistle-blowers—these provisions generally being stronger and more far-reaching than those provided by Canadian legislation.

[461] For a recent analysis of this issue, see http://lawreformcommission.sk.ca/Crown_Immunity_Report.pdf. This is a 2013 report of the Saskatchewan Law Reform Commission re: clarifying and modifying the law concerning Crown immunity. In this report, the authors note, "Many observers agree that a rule of construction that presumes immunity for the Crown is broader than necessary to meet the objective of governing effectively. Particular concern has been raised that the doctrine's continued operation cannot be reconciled with the expanded role of the Crown … As Dickson C.J. wrote for the majority of the Supreme Court of Canada in 1983: '[The doctrine of Crown immunity] seems to conflict with basic notions of equality before the law. The more active the government becomes in activities that had once been considered the preserve of private persons, the less easy it is to understand why the Crown need be, or ought to be, in a position different from the subject'" (8; quote from *R. v. Eldorado Nuclear Ltd.*, 2 S.C.R. [1983] 551).

- Insist that other caregiving alternatives be considered before automatically consigning persons in need to large, impersonal, bureaucratic care systems?
- Provide leadership by example through your willingness to frequently visit the front lines and expose yourself to the conditions and experience of frontline workers and those whom they serve?
- Be that ethical salt and light of which Jesus spoke; to listen to that still small voice of your spiritually sensitized conscience and to follow its dictates?
- Personally accept responsibility for some of the outcomes of the bureaucracy's operations for which the bureaucracy itself will rarely accept responsibility, even at personal cost to your reputation, income, and career?

Will you do so even if that leads to opting out of some unethical activity and risking a career-limiting clash with the self-serving ethics of the system? Are you even willing and prepared on occasion to step outside your job description and system role to relate to some needy person on a personal and human level, as dealing with a neighbour bearing the image of God rather than with a client or a mere name in a file for whom you have a statutory obligation to serve?

In recognizing and accepting such perspectives, roles, and responsibilities as believers in exile within bureaucratic systems, my prayer would be that we be conscious—as I believe that Joseph, Daniel, and Esther were conscious—that we are called to such positions by the God whom we serve. If so, our role is to join with him in ensuring that harm is prevented and good prevails, to the benefit and saving of many lives.

4.7 DILIGENCE AND EXCELLENCE

JOSEPH, DANIEL, AND ESTHER WERE BELIEVERS LIVING in exile in societies, political systems, and bureaucracies hostile to their faith who nevertheless came to occupy high political offices and render exceptional public service. So what were the characteristics of their lives that stand out as most essential to

- The retention and deepening of their faith under such circumstances?
- Their influence and effectiveness as leaders under such circumstances?

My principal conclusions are that it was their diligence in adhering to certain spiritual practices that was highly instrumental in preserving their faith and that it was their God-given and God-directed commitment to excellence in service that made them so effective and influential. These conclusions then lead me to ask,

- How diligent are we, as believers living in societies hostile to our faith, in attending to those spiritual practices and disciplines that will preserve and deepen it?
- How committed are we to equipping ourselves to serve with excellence in positions of public service in societies and situations indifferent or hostile to our faith commitments?

In raising and addressing these questions I do not mean to imply that we can maintain our spirituality or achieve excellence in God's service by our own efforts alone. Surely it is God himself who is active in preserving and strengthening the faith of those he has positioned in faith-testing situations, and it is he who ultimately equips us for excellence in service under such circumstances. But at the same time we need to do our part—to avail ourselves of those means that he has provided for us to maintain and strengthen our relationship with him and to serve with excellence in whatever position he has chosen for us.[462]

DILIGENCE

It would appear from the scriptural record that Daniel and his companions were consistently faithful and diligent in their adherence to certain spiritual practices—prayer, fellowship with one another as believers, and the dietary requirements of the Mosaic law—despite enormous cultural and political pressures to abandon such practices for those more acceptable to their Babylonian peers and superiors.

While still teenagers, Daniel and his companions were forcibly enrolled in a three-year program to immerse them in the language and literature of the Babylonians. At the completion of this program they were to be examined by the king himself as to whether they were fit to enter his service. Then as now, *you are what you eat* is true both physically and intellectually. Daniel and his companions resolved not to defile themselves with the king's food and wine, perhaps also symbolic in their minds of not defiling themselves with the products and intoxicants of a pagan culture. They persuaded the king's officials to make their diet and its impact upon them the test of their worthiness for continued education and service. They passed the test with flying colours, preserving and strengthening their spiritual identity in a strange and hostile cultural environment by diligently adhering to the dietary provisions of the Mosaic law.[463]

Sometime later, Daniel's companions again risked their very lives by their diligent adherence to the first and second of the Ten Commandments.[464] They refused, even upon the threat of being thrown into a fiery furnace, to bow down to and worship the golden statue that Nebuchadnezzar had erected on the plains of Dura.[465] They refused to

---

[462] As the apostle Paul reminded the early Christians (believers embedded in the hostile cultures of their day), leaders in God's kingdom are called upon and equipped to govern diligently (Romans 12:8) and to both think and practise whatever is true, noble, right, pure, lovely, admirable, praiseworthy and excellent (Philippians 4:8–9).

[463] Daniel 1:3–21.

[464] See Exodus 20:3–5.

[465] Daniel 3.

have any other gods before God, and they refused to bow down to or worship any idol.

Daniel and his companions were especially diligent in maintaining their prayer life. They prayed together for the wisdom required by Daniel to interpret Nebuchadnezzar's dreams.[466] Daniel himself developed a spiritual practice that he apparently followed no matter what regime he was serving and what restrictions it placed on religious worship.[467] When faced with a law forbidding the worship of anyone but King Darius, "he went home to his upstairs room where the windows opened toward Jerusalem. Three times a day he got down on his knees and prayed, giving thanks to his God, just as he had done before."[468]

In the case of Esther, her diligence took the form of faithful and consistent adherence to the inspired advice of her mentor Mordecai, even to the point where such adherence endangered her position and life.[469]

In the case of Joseph, Scripture tells us nothing about his spiritual practices in Egypt. Yet after years of immersion in the Egyptian political and religious system he demonstrated in later life greater understanding of the purposes and ways of God than his brothers who had never physically departed from the household of faith. Whatever spiritual disciplines Joseph practised must have been learned at an early age before he was sold into slavery in Egypt. Perhaps, ironically, his faith was more vigorous than his brothers' precisely because of how it was tested and tried in a hostile environment while theirs remained a hothouse faith.

WHAT ABOUT US?

For many of us, even if we have been raised in professing Christian homes and environments, our spiritual practices, after making an initial commitment to follow Jesus, can easily dissipate into little more than sporadic Bible reading, sporadic prayer (mainly at meals), and sporadic church or fellowship-group attendance, punctuated with occasional intensifications when trouble of some sort—health, financial, marital, etc.—drives us back to God.

---

[466] Daniel 2:17–18.

[467] Daniel served in high office under the Babylonian Nebuchadnezzar, Belshazzar his successor, Darius the Mede, and Cyrus the Persian.

[468] Daniel 6:10.

[469] Esther 2:10–11, 20, 22; 4:1–17.

But such nominal religious practices are simply not adequate to sustain us under any kind of prolonged testing in a hostile spiritual environment. They are certainly not adequate to sustain our presence as salt and light at the interface of faith and modern day business, science, media, politics, or culture.

In earlier chapters on the life of David, we noted the constant attention David gave to his inner life as reflected in the Psalms. And at the risk of repetition, I cannot stress emphatically enough for those endeavouring to live out their faith in hostile cultural environments, especially hostile political environments, the importance of disciplined and diligent attention to

- *Solitude* as an antidote to constantly being in the public eye and under media scrutiny.
- The practice of *lectio divina* as a counterbalance to reading or viewing hundreds of pages a week of secular material.[470]
- *Prayer* as an alternative to the incessant communications buzz of media-dominated political discourse.
- *Honouring the body* as a counterbalance to the intense physical and time demands of public life.
- *Self-examination*, including the *examen of consciousness and conscience*, as a counterbalance to the preoccupation of image politics with manufactured and artificial appearances.
- *Spiritual discernment* as an alternative to perceiving and analyzing issues and problems solely from a secular and temporal standpoint.
- *Sabbath observance* as a means of establishing a disciplined balance between work and rest, including turning off the technological devices and media that so dominate the lives of those in the public arena.
- Integration of all the above into a *rule* or *rhythm of life* distinctly different from the rhythm of contemporary public life.

EXCELLENCE

The scriptural record leaves very little doubt that, despite many distractions and obstacles, Joseph, Daniel, and Esther were very, very good at the political and administrative work they were positioned and

[470] The purpose is to encounter God through the Scriptures via regular preparation (*silencio*); reading short select passages (*lectio*); personally reflecting on the application of the passage to oneself (*meditatio*); responding to God based on what one has read and encountered (*oratio*); resting in the word one has received (*contemplatio*); and finally, resolving to act and live out the word received in the place where God has planted us (*incarnatio*).

called upon to do. For example, if outside auditors had been called in to perform third-party evaluations on Joseph's service to Potiphar, his management of the prison, and his organization and management of the great Egyptian Grain Exchange, they would have reported that he did all these things excellently.[471] Scripture states, "the LORD was with Joseph and gave him success in whatever he did."[472]

Likewise in the case of Esther, it was not only her beauty but also the shrewdness and excellence of her conduct under the guidance of Mordecai that made her the most influential member of King Xerxes' harem.[473]

Daniel also performed so excellently that he was constantly promoted over his Babylonian peers, to the point where the only grounds that they could find for attacking him and his service was on the basis of his faith.[474]

WHAT ABOUT US?

As believers, especially those of us embedded in political organizations and systems indifferent or hostile to our faith, are we excellent at what we do? Do others see us as exceptional and excellent performers? Through diligence in our spiritual practices, do we consciously and faithfully seek God's wisdom and guidance to enable us to do our work excellently? If the performance auditors were to interview our peers, would they grudgingly be obliged to say, "He/she holds certain religious views and engages in religious practices I don't understand or agree with, but I must admit he/she is very, very good at ..."?

If we are in political or public administration positions, is this the reputation we have—a reputation for excellence in public service? And if not, why not?

As a founder of several political parties and as a member of the Canadian Parliament, I became convinced that very few of us in the partisan political arena have undergone the kind of rigorous preparation and training that is required to do our jobs excellently. To become a barista at a Starbucks coffee bar, one is required to take more than 20 hours of training. But one can become a lawmaker in Canada's Parliament

---

[471] Genesis 39:2–6, 21–23; 41:38–43.

[472] Genesis 39:23.

[473] Esther 5:1–3; 8:1–3.

[474] Daniel 6:1–5.

or any of our legislatures without one hour of training in lawmaking. One can become an elected representative of the people in any of our democratic assemblies, including our municipal councils, without one hour of preparation or training in what democratic representation really involves. How can such lack of preparation possibly result in excellence with respect to legislating or democratic representation, let alone policy-making or public administration?

In light of this need, after I left Parliament my friends and I established several organizations and training programs for strengthening the knowledge, skills, ethics, communications capacities, and leadership skills of participants in Canada's political processes, especially those with whom we have some ideological rapport and influence.[475] While this is not the place to elaborate on these organizations or programs, the main point I wish to make is that it is especially important for those of us entering the political arena with a Christian commitment to undertake such preparation and training, including training in how to navigate the interface of faith and public life wisely and graciously. Why? So that whatever public service we may have opportunity to render, it will be judged by our God, our peers, and our fellow citizens as excellent and a credit, not a discredit, to our faith in Christ.

[475] For more information on these organizations and programs, visit manningfoundation.org and manningcentre.ca. Of particular interest might be our seminars on navigating the faith-political interface and lessons from Wilberforce on the conduct of advocacy campaigns with moral dimensions.

4.8 CO-OPERATION AND COMPROMISE

BELIEVERS LIVING IN EXILE SUCH AS JOSEPH, DANIEL, and Esther—embedded in political systems and societies hostile to their faith yet effective in their political roles—must have had to integrate to some extent with those foreign cultures and co-operate in many respects with the political systems in which they served. At the same time, they remained faithful to God and did not cross the line where co-operation becomes compromise and the starting point of unfaithfulness and spiritual decline.

So what can we—believers embedded today in cultures and organizations indifferent or hostile to our faith, especially those of us operating at the interface of faith and public life—learn from their experiences? To what extent can we co-operate in order to be effective and influential for good? And what are the convictions and practices to which we must hold without compromise if we wish to retain our spiritual identity and a right relationship with God?

Of course it must be recognized that Joseph, Daniel, and Esther were literally "enslaved" in Egypt, Babylon, and Medo-Persia. So one might argue that they had little choice but to integrate and co-operate to a very large extent with the dictates of the cultures, laws, and rulers of those nations. Nevertheless, it is worth noting the particulars of their integration and co-operation as specifically mentioned in Scripture, so that we can compare and contrast them with the particulars on which they refused to co-operate or to be compromised.

CO-OPERATION IN EGYPT

In the case of Joseph, he fit in so well with the household of Potiphar and the administration of the prison in which he was unjustly incarcerated that in each instance he was entrusted with more and more managerial responsibilities. Eventually he even won the confidence of Egypt's supreme ruler through correctly interpreting Pharaoh's dream and prescribing a policy to cope with the famine that it prophesied. Pharaoh then rewarded him by putting him "in charge of the whole land of Egypt" and giving him the Egyptian name Zaphenath-Paneah.[476] He also provided him with an Egyptian wife, Asenath, the daughter of a priest of On (the Egyptian centre of sun worship), with whom he had two sons.

By the time Joseph re-established contact with his brothers, he dressed like an Egyptian, spoke like an Egyptian, had an Egyptian family, and acted so much like an Egyptian that they failed to recognize him as either a Hebrew or a member of their own family. On the basis of all external appearances, an outside observer might well have concluded that Joseph had allowed himself to be completely assimilated by the Egyptian culture and political system, in the process losing virtually all of the distinctives that would have marked him as a God-honouring member of the household of faith.

CO-OPERATION IN BABYLON

In the case of Daniel and his friends, they were specifically enrolled as impressionable teenagers in a three-year educational program designed to immerse them in the language, traditions, and practices of their Babylonian captors. At the end of their training they were interrogated by the king himself to determine whether they were fit for royal service. The fact that they not only completed this training but also passed the exam with flying colours would indicate that they must have absorbed and mastered a great deal of the culture and politics of Babylon at an early age.[477] Note also that at the very beginning of their training they were given Babylonian names—the message no doubt being "You are no longer Jews; you are Babylonians now."[478] Daniel in particular was given

[476] Genesis 41:41–45.

[477] See Daniel 1:1–20.

[478] "The chief official [Ashpenaz] gave them new names: to Daniel, the name Belteshazzar; to Hananiah, Shadrach; to Mishael, Meshach; and to Azariah, Abednego" (Daniel 1:7).

the name Belteshazzar, which may have been particularly offensive to him since it was the name of Nebuchadnezzar's god.[479]

According to Scripture, Daniel and his friends were, for the most part, successful in managing their relations with Babylonian rulers and in administering the public affairs and offices for which they were made responsible.[480] Successful management and administration in such situations requires a solid understanding of and identification with the political, bureaucratic, and cultural milieu in which one is operating. It also requires a willingness and ability to work co-operatively with subordinates, peers, and superiors. These Jewish exiles distinguished themselves from Babylonian and other foreign functionaries by the excellence of their public service. So thoroughly had Daniel and his compatriots adapted to the society and government of which they had become a part that, apart from their faith, it appears unlikely that an outside observer would have found much else to distinguish them from their public-service colleagues.

CO-OPERATION IN MEDO-PERSIA

The orphan exile Esther rose to the position of queen of the Medes and Persians. Of all the exiles, it is she who carried "co-operation" with her captors to the greatest extent, for the ultimate purpose, unknown to her at the beginning, of rescuing her people from genocide. Not only was Esther an orphan and an exile in captivity, but she was a woman at a time and in a culture where women were treated as the property of men.

When King Xerxes dethroned and banished Queen Vashti for defying his authority, his nobles proposed an elaborate beauty contest to select her replacement. Esther won the favour and approval of everyone she encountered, including the king himself, who selected her as his new queen.[481]

To attain this position, Esther had to completely and utterly subordinate herself to the mores and dictates of the culture, the kingdom,

---

[479] Daniel 4:8.

[480] Daniel 2:48–49; 3:30.

[481] Modern readers of Vashti's story in Esther 1 might admire her more than Esther. It is Vashti who defies Xerxes' effort to treat and exploit her as a sexual object and who loses her position and influence as a result. Esther, on the other hand, submits to the male-imposed dictates of the harem but in the end uses her beauty and charm to win the favour of the king and save her people.

and the harem. As an exile and a woman she had no choice. Rather than instructing her to retain or display her identity as one of God's people, Mordecai ordered her to keep her Jewish identity a secret. Of all the prominent exiles in Scripture, Esther was the one most totally absorbed into the foreign culture in which she found herself.

WHERE TO DRAW THE LINE BETWEEN CO-OPERATION AND COMPROMISE

Where and how to draw the line between co-operation and compromise is of course a highly relevant issue for Christian believers embedded today in a political and governmental environment unsympathetic to our faith. In fact there are still many Christians who do not believe it is possible to work within such hostile environments *without* compromising one's faith. Hence they refrain from involvement in politics and government altogether and are highly suspicious and critical of professing Christians who do.

So, where and how did these believers in exile draw the line between integrating with the hostile foreign environment in which they found themselves embedded and compromising their faith and relationship to God?

Here are five major examples from the experience of the exiles.

1. Worship of the one true God

Daniel and his fellow exiles drew the line with respect to the object of their religious worship. They refused, at the risk of their lives, to forsake the worship of the one true God; they refused to bow down in worship or to direct their prayers to an earthly king. In particular, they refused to worship the state when it sought to claim the total allegiance of their minds and hearts.

Shadrach, Meshach, and Abednego, when ordered to bow down and worship the golden image of Nebuchadnezzar on the plains of Dura, simply refused, even when the king threatened to throw them into a fiery furnace. Their refusal was expressed in polite but emphatic terms and contained a declaration of faith in God's ability to deliver them notwithstanding their uncertainty as to whether he would actually do so:

> "King Nebuchadnezzar, we do not need to defend ourselves before you in this matter. If we are thrown into the blazing furnace, the God we serve is able to deliver us from it, and he will deliver us from Your Majesty's hand. But even if he does not, we want you to know, Your Majesty, that we will not serve your gods or worship the image of gold you have set up."[482]

When they were miraculously delivered from the fiery furnace, they earned this testimony regarding where they drew the line from none other than King Nebuchadnezzar himself:

> "They trusted in him [their God] and defied the king's command and were willing to give up their lives rather than serve or worship any god except their own God."[483]

Sometime later, when Babylon was overthrown by the Medes and Persians, King Darius the Mede was persuaded to issue and enforce an edict "that anyone who prays to any god or human being during the next thirty days, except to you, Your Majesty, shall be thrown into the lions' den."[484]

And what did Daniel do, even though he held a high position in Darius' administration and was well aware of the decree? "He went home to his upstairs room where the windows opened toward Jerusalem. Three times a day he got down on his knees and prayed, giving thanks to his God, just as he had done before."[485]

Daniel was subsequently thrown into the den of lions, but his life was miraculously preserved. And his drawing the line with respect to worship and his ultimate allegiance prompted another decree from Darius, "that in every part of my kingdom people must fear and reverence the God of Daniel."[486]

2. Faith in the sovereignty of God

Whatever else the exiles had to surrender, they never surrendered their faith in the sovereignty of God—their belief that in the final analysis God was sovereign over their lives, their circumstances, and the kingdoms and political systems in which they were embedded.

[482] Daniel 3:16–18.

[483] Daniel 3:28.

[484] Daniel 6:7.

[485] Daniel 6:10.

[486] Daniel 6:26.

Joseph, for example, clung to this belief throughout his trials as a slave and a prisoner when it would have been easy for him to succumb to the idea that God, like his own faith-based family, had abandoned him. He affirmed this belief in the sovereignty of God, even when he was a public official ostensibly under the sovereignty of Pharaoh, telling his brothers, "It was not you who sent me here, but God. He made me father to Pharaoh, lord of his entire household and ruler of all Egypt."[487] Note that he attributed his political ascendancy to God and not to Pharaoh.

Likewise Daniel, while serving as an advisor to and servant of one of the most violent, unpredictable, and self-centred rulers of the ancient world—Nebuchadnezzar of Babylon—does not hesitate to declare his belief in the sovereignty of God over human affairs. He declares to the king himself, "the Most High is sovereign over all kingdoms on earth and gives them to anyone he wishes."[488]

3. Personal moral standards

In the case of Joseph, he refused to compromise his personal integrity and moral standards by succumbing to the sexual temptations of Potiphar's wife. Notwithstanding the sexual mores of Egypt and his master's wife, this is where he chose to draw the line—a refusal to compromise, which cost him dearly, as her false accusations then resulted in the loss of his position and imprisonment.[489]

In the case of Daniel, as a teenager forcibly inducted into the Nebuchadnezzar School for Public Servants, he sought to be allowed to follow the dietary edicts of the Mosaic law to which he was personally committed, rather than to adopt a Babylonian diet. This might strike us as a rather strange place to draw the line in that there were undoubtedly many other aspects of the school curriculum (such as its teachings about the multiplicity and superiority of the Babylonian gods) that would be even more foreign and unacceptable to a believer in the God of Israel.

Nevertheless, diet was the issue on which Daniel chose to make a stand personally, and note the way and the wisdom with which he went about it. He didn't propose a compromise between the Hebrew and

---

[487] Genesis 45:8.

[488] Daniel 4:25.

[489] Genesis 39:1–20.

Babylonian diets, nor did he go on a hunger strike. Instead he proposed a contest—let me and my three fellow exiles eat and drink what the Mosaic law prescribes, let the other students eat and drink what the Babylonian Food Guide prescribes, and then let's see who is healthier at the end of the day. Most importantly, the point at which he chose to draw the line coincided, not coincidentally, with the movement of God's grace on the heart of his Babylonian custodian, who was led to accept rather than reject Daniel's proposal.[490]

With respect to drawing the line on issues of personal morality, it is important to allow that not all believers will choose to or be led to draw the line at the same place, and we should be careful about judging another man's servant. Where, for example, if anywhere, does Esther draw the line? It can hardly be in accordance with the Jewish laws governing sexual morality—she is an involuntary member of King Xerxes' harem. Nor is it in the area of diet, the point where Daniel and his companions first drew the line. She eats what they tell her to eat, dresses as they tell her to dress, and conforms in every respect to the rules of the harem and the palace. In the end, however, she draws the line at the one point in common with all the other exiles we have studied—her willingness ultimately to identify with God's people, even if it costs her life.

4. Identification with the household of faith

Although they were members of a tiny faith-based and ethnically distinctive minority in a hostile environment, the exiles faithfully identified with the household of faith when it was dangerous—even life threatening—to do so. In Joseph's case, he was willing to identify generously and openly with the household of faith to which he truly belonged, even when it was that household that had betrayed him. And he was willing to be publicly identified with the household of faith (his family) despite his awareness that the Egyptians generally loathed nomads, in particular shepherds.[491]

Likewise Daniel, throughout his life, continued to identify with the people of God and the household of faith and to be so identified in the eyes of the Babylonians. With each of the rulers whom he served, he was always introduced or referred to as one of the exiles from Judah.[492] Daniel

[490] Daniel 1:9.

[491] Genesis 46:31–34.

[492] Daniel 2:25; 5:13; 6:13.

was in Babylon, immersed in the Babylonian culture and administration, but he did not disguise the fact that he was an exile and was willing to be known as such.

5. Speaking unpalatable truths to power

On many occasions these Jewish exiles must have been sorely tempted to compromise the truth in providing advice and counsel to the foreign rulers whom they served—to tell those rulers what they wanted to hear, to flatter them or to sugar-coat the unpalatable, rather than to tell them what they needed to hear. But to their immense credit the exiles drew the line at compromising the truth. This is highly relevant since one of the most dangerous things for any leader in any era or system is to be surrounded by people who tell you only what you want to hear.

Joseph told Pharaoh that mighty Egypt was to be brought to her knees by a terrible famine, something Pharaoh undoubtedly didn't want to hear but needed to hear so that grain could be saved and stored away in the bountiful years that were to precede the famine.[493]

Esther had to tell King Xerxes that the man whom he had most trusted and exalted to the highest position in the kingdom, Haman, was an arrogant, vindictive planner of genocide, undeserving of his position or the king's confidence.[494]

Daniel faithfully interpreted Nebuchadnezzar's nightmare—the dream that foretold that Nebuchadnezzar's pride was going to bring him down from his exalted position as the supreme ruler of Babylon to that of an animal grazing on grass and wet by the dew of heaven.[495] And Daniel fearlessly interpreted the handwriting on the wall amid the drunken revelry at Belshazzar's feast—the prediction that the kingdom would be overthrown because of Belshazzar's arrogance and sacrilegious behaviour.[496]

WHAT ABOUT US?

When tempted and challenged to give our supreme allegiance to the systems in which we are embedded—the academy, the school, the

[493] Genesis 41.

[494] Esther 7.

[495] Daniel 4.

[496] Daniel 5.

company, the market, the charity, the NGO, the church, the team, the party, the department, the government—rather than to God, do we succumb or draw the line?

When adverse circumstances and misfortune overwhelm us—the crop fails, our project flops, we fail the test, we lose our job, we lose a loved one, the business goes belly-up, the stock market crashes, we lose the election, we lose the war—do we believe that God has abandoned us? Or do we cling to the belief that he is still sovereign over the affairs of humanity and disposes of them as he sees fit?

When tempted and challenged to compromise our personal morals in order to "fit in," do we succumb or draw the line?

When we are tempted and challenged to hide or blur our identity as followers of Jesus and children of the Father, do we succumb or draw the line?

When we are tempted to keep silent in the presence of evil or to substitute half-truth, near-truth, and compromised truth for the whole and unvarnished truth, do we succumb or draw the line?

In all these circumstances let us draw insight and inspiration from the lives of the exiles—believers embedded in cultures and systems indifferent or hostile to their faith—who served effectively while remaining faithful to the God who placed and sustained them there.

4.9 RE-ESTABLISHING THE FAITH COMMUNITY UNDER HOSTILE CONDITIONS

SPIRITUAL RENEWAL

AFTER THE DAYS OF KING DAVID, THE SPIRITUAL LIFE OF Israel and Judah experienced a long decline, a decline attributed by the prophets to the departure of the people and their rulers from adherence to the law, will, and worship of God. This decline culminated in the Assyrian and Babylonian conquests of the Promised Land and the carrying off of the people of God into slavery and exile in foreign lands. In those foreign lands, under hostile rulers and conditions, the embers of a vital relationship with the living God were kept alive by a faithful few. But would those embers also be extinguished, suffocated by the hostility and unbelief of their environment? Or would they, could they, in the purposes of God be fanned to life again? Was it possible that the spiritual life of the faith community could be revitalized and restored under such conditions?

The same questions are relevant to the Christian community in the 21st century. We too, at least in Western Europe and North America, have been in spiritual decline, attributable to the same causes that led to the spiritual decline of Israel and Judah centuries ago. Believers are now a minority in cultures and political systems indifferent or hostile to our faith. And while the embers of a vital relationship with God through Jesus Christ are kept alive by a faithful few, the questions remain: Will they, too, be slowly suffocated by the indifference and hostility of a secular and materialistic environment? Is a genuine renewal of faith in God through Jesus Christ possible under such conditions?

In the case of Judah, a revitalization and restoration of the faith community actually did take place under precisely such conditions. The story of how it came about is told, at least in part, by Ezra and Nehemiah. Both Ezra and Nehemiah were exiles in Babylon and Medo-Persia. Both were used by God to lead the return of a significant portion of the faith community to Jerusalem to rebuild its temple and walls and restore the worship of God. The study of their experience and the lessons derived from it is highly relevant to Christians today who desire a genuine spiritual renewal of the Christian community in our times.

WHERE DOES IT START?

The spiritual renewal described by Ezra and Nehemiah had its beginning in a sovereign and simultaneous movement of God's spirit on two very different kinds of hearts: the hearts of the exiles themselves and, strangely enough, the hearts of their captors—in particular, Cyrus, Darius, and Xerxes, rulers of the Medes and Persians. As we have seen from previous examinations of the lives of exiles such as Joseph, Daniel, and Esther, significant events occur when the sovereign movements of God intersect with human hearts—hearts that either respond to or resist his leading.

In the case of the exiles themselves, Ezra described those who were led to go and rebuild the house of God in Jerusalem as "everyone whose heart God had moved"—in particular the family heads of Judah and Benjamin, the priests, and the Levites.[497]

This movement of God on the hearts of the faithful few appeared to manifest itself in two ways, as reflected in the prayers of exiles like Daniel and, later, Nehemiah.[498] It moved them to

- Acknowledge and repent of the acts and attitudes that had led to their people's alienation from the person, will, and work of God in the first place.
- Reaffirm and reassert their faith in the promises of God, in particular the promise communicated by Jeremiah that in due time God would restore his relationship with the faithful and restore them to their place of worship in Jerusalem.

In the case of the rulers of the Medes and the Persians during whose reign this restoration took place, Ezra asserted, "the LORD moved the heart of Cyrus king of Persia" to make the proclamation that authorized

[497] Ezra 1:5.

[498] See Daniel 9:1–19 and Nehemiah 1:4–11.

it.[499] When the enemies of the Jews who had inhabited Judah during the exile endeavoured to stop the work by advising the king that Jerusalem had a history of rebellion, letters were sent from Ezra to the Persian rulers defending their right to proceed.[500] In the end, both Darius the Mede and Xerxes re-authorized the rebuilding of the temple and the city, starting with its walls, leading Ezra to exclaim, "Praise be to the LORD, the God of our ancestors, who has put it into the king's heart to bring honor to the house of the LORD in Jerusalem in this way and who has extended his good favor to me before the king and his advisers and all the king's powerful officials."[501]

It is significant that both Ezra and Nehemiah give as much attention to recording the movement of God on the hearts of the Median and Persian rulers as they do to the movement of God on the hearts of his own people.

THE RESPONSE OF THE FAITHFUL TO THE MOVEMENT OF GOD IN THEIR HEARTS

The great prayer of the exile Daniel provides a classic and instructive model of the prayer for spiritual renewal:

> In the first year of Darius son of Xerxes (a Mede by descent), who was made ruler over the Babylonian kingdom—in the first year of his reign, I, Daniel, understood from the Scriptures, according to the word of the LORD given to Jeremiah the prophet, that the desolation of Jerusalem would last seventy years. So I turned to the Lord God and pleaded with him in prayer and petition, in fasting, and in sackcloth and ashes.
>
> I prayed to the LORD my God and confessed:
>
> "Lord, the great and awesome God, who keeps his covenant of love with those who love him and keep his commandments, we have sinned and done wrong. We have been wicked and have rebelled; we have turned away from your commands and laws. We have not listened to your servants the prophets, who spoke in your name to our kings, our princes and our ancestors, and to all the people of the land.
>
> "Lord, you are righteous, but this day we are covered with shame—the people of Judah and the inhabitants of Jerusalem and all Israel, both near and far, in all the countries where you have scattered us because of our unfaithfulness to you. We and our kings, our princes and our ancestors are covered with shame, LORD, because we have sinned against you. The Lord our God is merciful and forgiving,

---

499 Ezra 1:1.

500 Ezra 4:6–6:12.

501 Ezra 7:27–28.

> even though we have rebelled against him; we have not obeyed the Lord our God or kept the laws he gave us through his servants the prophets. All Israel has transgressed your law and turned away, refusing to obey you …
>
> "Now, Lord our God, who brought your people out of Egypt with a mighty hand and who made for yourself a name that endures to this day, we have sinned, we have done wrong. Lord, in keeping with all your righteous acts, turn away your anger and your wrath from Jerusalem, your city, your holy hill. Our sins and the iniquities of our ancestors have made Jerusalem and your people an object of scorn to all those around us.
>
> "Now, our God, hear the prayers and petitions of your servant. For your sake, Lord, look with favor on your desolate sanctuary. Give ear, our God, and hear; open your eyes and see the desolation of the city that bears your Name. We do not make requests of you because we are righteous, but because of your great mercy. Lord, listen! Lord, forgive! Lord, hear and act! For your sake, my God, do not delay, because your city and your people bear your Name."[502]

There is of course much to be learned concerning the conditions and factors that have led to the periodic renewal of the Christian faith down through the centuries from the vast library of scholarly work that exists on this subject. I refer particularly to works on the history and nature of such movements of God as the Reformation, the Counter-Reformation, the First and Second Great Awakenings, and national and local revivals. The latter would include those that have occurred in Wales, Scotland, and New England and more recently in Africa, Latin America, and Asia.

This is not the place to more thoroughly analyze and discuss those factors and conditions and their relevance to our day and age, nor am I suitably qualified to do so. However, I encourage each of us to begin to identify from our own perspective what a genuine, divinely inspired renewal of the Christian faith in our time might look like, particularly within Canada.

From my own perspective as a Christian in politics, by referring to the need for a renewal of the Christian faith in our time I am not referring to some restoration of the past political influence of Christianity. I am not referring to the gaining of control by professing Christians over the institutions and services of the state, nor am I referring to some dramatic increase in the size and impressiveness of church attendance, church buildings, or church budgets.

---

502 Daniel 9:1–19.

Rather I believe that such a spiritual renewal should manifest itself in the following ways:

- In a renewal of our awareness of evil and its roots in our own lives and in the world in which we live, including the diabolical nature of the violence, crime, addictions, injustices, and self-destroying obsessions that afflict so many human lives today.[503]
- In a renewed passion for healthy relationships with ourselves, our families, our neighbours, our environment, and our Creator.
- In a renewed recognition of the necessity of a right relationship to God through a personal relationship to Jesus Christ, and acting upon that realization.
- In a renewed concern leading to action on behalf of the poor, the sick, and the victims of injustice and oppression.
- In a renewed commitment to creation care—environmental conservation, protection, and restoration—as an integral part of our Christian commitment.
- In a renewed recognition of the reality that God is at work "to reconcile to himself all things" and that we are to join him in that work as reconcilers of conflicting interests in whatever situations we find ourselves placed.
- In a renewed faith in the reality of God and the love of God for humanity, and his willingness and ability to communicate with us and transform us from within.
- In a renewed belief in the efficacy of spiritual practices such as prayer and Scripture study that draw us closer to him and the necessity and benefits of spiritual fellowship.
- And most importantly, in a renewed vision of who Jesus Christ is and what he has to offer in terms of deliverance from evil, the healing of broken relationships, and enabling self-sacrificial service on behalf of others.

---

[503] Since we invariably reap what we sow, is not any society that increasingly entertains itself by viewing, hearing, and reading about evil increasingly likely to be afflicted in real life by those very same evils? Do we not need a heightened awareness of the possibility that for every murder, assault, and deception whereby we entertain ourselves via our literature, movies, plays, and video screens, we may well be destined to experience real-life murders, assaults, and deceptions on our streets and in our communities? Although the context is different, the principle is the same as that referred to by Abraham Lincoln in his second inaugural address when he declared, "Fondly do we hope, fervently do we pray, that this mighty scourge of war may speedily pass away. Yet, if God wills that it continue until all the wealth piled by the bondsman's two hundred and fifty years of unrequited toil shall be sunk, and until every drop of blood drawn with the lash shall be paid by another drawn with the sword, as was said three thousand years ago, so still it must be said 'the judgments of the Lord are true and righteous altogether'" (*Second Inaugural Address* [March 4, 1865]).

THE RESPONSE OF POLITICAL LEADERS TO THE MOVEMENT OF GOD ON THEIR HEARTS

For a person with political interests and involvements, the most striking aspect of the restoration of the exiled faith community as described in the books of Ezra and Nehemiah is the role of rulers who did not share that faith in facilitating its restoration.

The prayer of Daniel previously cited indicates what the movement of God on the hearts of the exiles moved *them* to do—to pray, to repent, and to claim his promises for renewal. Likewise Ezra's citing of the proclamation of King Cyrus of Persia in the first year of his reign indicates what the movement of God on the heart of this political ruler moved *him* to proclaim throughout his realm:

> "This is what Cyrus king of Persia says: 'The LORD, the God of heaven, has given me all the kingdoms of the earth and he has appointed me to build a temple for him at Jerusalem in Judah. Any of his people among you may go up to Jerusalem in Judah and build the temple of the LORD, the God of Israel, the God who is in Jerusalem, and may their God be with them. And in any locality where survivors may now be living, the people are to provide them with silver and gold, with goods and livestock, and with freewill offerings for the temple of God in Jerusalem.'"[504]

Here then is a pertinent question for those longing and praying for a renewal of the Christian faith in our time: Should we also be looking for some movement of God on the heart of some secular political leader who does not share that faith but that would nevertheless facilitate genuine spiritual renewal and complement the movement of God on the hearts of his own people?

In a secular pluralist state such as Canada, this facilitating and complementary action by a political leader or government could not take the form of an explicit endorsement or provision of support for the Christian faith and its institutional forms. But it could conceivably take the form of a genuine and renewed championing of freedom of conscience and belief from which not only Christians but also others with faith-based convictions would benefit.

The historians tell us that Cyrus the Great of Persia was a remarkable ruler for that age and time in that he did not try to impose the religion

[504] Ezra 1:2–4.

of Persia on the nations and peoples he conquered. Rather, he was magnanimous in allowing captive peoples to retain and even restore their traditional religious practices.[505]

In a similar vein, one of the first major acts of the Roman emperor Constantine (emperor from AD 306 to 337 and the first emperor to claim conversion to Christianity) involved proclamation of the Edict of Milan in AD 313. Contrary to popular opinion, the edict did not make Christianity the official religion of the empire (this came much later in AD 380). Instead, it expressly granted religious liberty not only to Christians who had been the targets of ruthless persecution but also to the practitioners of all religions throughout the empire.[506]

It was the granting of such freedom of conscience and practice, as much as the favour of the emperor himself, that then permitted the Christian faith to flourish and expand its influence throughout the empire.

If there is one thing a secular political leader, for example, in Canada could do to facilitate a renewal of the Christian faith in our time without explicitly endorsing or supporting it, it is simply to ensure that the guarantees of freedom of conscience and belief contained in our *Charter* are actually honoured and accorded in practice to those whose consciences and beliefs are rooted in a faith perspective, just as those guarantees are presently applied aggressively to expressions of conscience and belief rooted in secular and non-religious (even anti-

---

[505] A famous document inscribed in clay and dated to the days just after Cyrus' conquest of Babylon describes how Cyrus had improved the lives of the citizens of Babylonia, repatriated displaced peoples, and restored temples and cult sanctuaries. This Cyrus Cylinder is preserved at the British Museum in London; while some scholars dispute its interpretation, it is generally accepted that Cyrus permitted considerable religious liberty among those peoples and nations he conquered.

[506] The Edict of Milan states, "When you see that this has been granted to them [Christians] by us, your Worship will know that we have also conceded to other religions the right of open and free observance of their worship for the sake of the peace of our times, that each one may have the free opportunity to worship as he pleases; this regulation is made that we may not seem to detract from any dignity of any religion" (Lactantius, *De Mortibus Persecutorum*, ed. O. F. Fritzsche, II, 288 sq. [Bibl Patr. Ecc. Lat. XI], in *Translations and Reprints from the Original Sources of European History* 4, no. 1 [Philadelphia: University of Pennsylvania Press (1897?-1907?)], 28–30).

religious) perspectives.[507] Such a new birth of freedom of conscience and belief in Canada, in particular freedom from the dictates of political correctness and the imposition of secular values by our media, academic, judicial, and political elites on those who do not share those perspectives, would be highly conducive to a renewal of genuine Christian faith in our time.

THE NEED FOR CAUTION

In scanning the political horizon for proclamations or actions by secular leaders and governments that might, even inadvertently or indirectly, facilitate a renewal and reinvigoration of faith in Christ, it is especially important to guard against the dangers of such leaders using a revival of religion for strictly political reasons.

In Russia, for example, while it is dangerous to impute motives to leaders most of us only know about through the media, Vladimir Putin's efforts to revitalize the role and influence of the Eastern Orthodox Church would appear to be more related to his interest in stimulating a revival of Russian nationalism than it is to restoring the influence of the Christian faith in Russian society.

In the same vein, I recall a conversation I had a number of years ago with a Chinese Communist official concerning the professed efforts of his party to stamp out corruption. He acknowledged that "religion" in many societies had played a role in establishing and enforcing moral standards such as "thou shalt not steal." While it would be inconceivable for the Communist Party of China, being atheistic in principle, to consider facilitating a renewal of theistic religions for the purposes of combatting corruption, it was not inconceivable that it could facilitate renewed interest in a non-theistic religion such as Confucianism and harness it to that task.[508]

---

[507] Part I of the Canadian *Charter of Rights and Freedoms* reads, "Everyone has the following fundamental Freedoms: (*a*) freedom of conscience and religion; (*b*) freedom of thought, belief, opinion and expression, including freedom of the press and other media communication; (*c*) freedom of peaceful assembly; and (*d*) freedom of association" (*Constitution Act, 1982*, c. 11, p. 1, s. 2).

[508] The Chinese government has been encouraging the revival of Confucianism, including the teaching of Confucian classics in secondary schools and promoting Confucianism abroad through Confucius Institutes. See Daniel Bell, "China's Leaders Rediscover Confucianism," *Herald Tribune* (September 14, 2006), available at https://nyti.ms/2q0kvRK.

CAN CHRISTIAN BELIEVERS LEARN FROM SECULAR EFFORTS TO RESTORE THE MORALE OF DEMORALIZED ORGANIZATIONS?

One of the strangest and most arresting stories told by Jesus was about an unjust steward. The man was about to be sacked from his position by his master so he used his last days on the job to ensure a favourable position for himself with his master's debtors by writing down their debt notes. While Jesus was obviously not condoning the dishonesty of the unjust steward, he did draw attention to his shrewdness and what might be learned from it, remarking that "the people of this world are more shrewd in dealing with their own kind than are the people of the light."[509]

Without carrying this line of reasoning too far, it might nevertheless be helpful to those longing for a renewal of the faith community—weakened and demoralized by past defeats and years in exile in hostile environments—also to study some of the examples of successful attempts to restore the vigour and morale of non-religious communities and organizations that have been down and out.

This is a subject that leaders must frequently consider, especially political leaders after one personally loses an election or one's political party has suffered a devastating and demoralizing electoral defeat. In my case, a story of rebuilding that I have found most instructive is that involving the revitalization of the British army in Burma during the Second World War as told by its leader, Field-Marshall Viscount William Slim.[510]

In 1942, the British army was systematically driven back across Burma by the Japanese all the way to India, suffering defeat after defeat and horrendous casualties along the way. After retreating to India, its shaken leader, William Slim, was instructed to rebuild its ranks, rebuild its morale, and rebuild its fighting capacity—all of which he did. This reinvigorated army then successfully fought all the way back across Burma and by 1945 secured complete victory over the retreating Japanese forces.

Field Marshall Slim's memoir, *Defeat into Victory*, is regarded as a military classic and is still studied at military academies around the world. In it he urges the leaders of defeated and demoralized troops to

[509] Luke 16:8.

[510] Field-Marshal Viscount William Slim, *Defeat into Victory: Battling Japan in Burma and India, 1942–1945* (Lanham: Cooper Square Press, 2000).

"remember only the lessons to be learned from defeat—they are more than from victory."

He then specifically addresses the question of how to restore the morale of a defeated army: "Morale is a state of mind ... which will move a whole group of men to give their last ounce to achieve something, without counting the cost to themselves."[511] He then argues that if that morale is to endure, it must "have certain foundations ... spiritual, intellectual, and material, and that is the order of their importance."

Slim uses the word *spiritual* not in its strictly religious meaning but as "belief in a cause," in particular, a just cause, a "great and noble object" larger than one's self and self-preservation. Slim would likely argue that an army whose members' sole interest is in saving themselves will never experience victory in the broader sense, something that we evangelicals with our heavy emphasis on personal salvation need to reflect upon. His observations and perspectives are well worth study by anyone involved in efforts to renew the morale and effectiveness of a defeated and demoralized community, including a faith community.

---

[511] Slim, *Defeat into Victory*, 182.

4.10 GUIDELINES FOR BELIEVERS LIVING IN EXILE

WE TOO ARE BELIEVERS LIVING FOR THE MOST PART IN cultures and political systems indifferent or hostile to our faith. So as we close these lessons in leadership from the lives of Joseph, Daniel, Esther, Ezra, and Nehemiah—also believers living in exile—it is appropriate for each of us to ask what aspects of their experience are most meaningful and applicable to us personally.

Is it their faith in the sovereignty of God—the belief encouraged by the inspired words of Jeremiah instructing them to settle down, to build, to pray, to disregard false spiritual advice, and to trust in the providence and promises of God—even in dire circumstances and while living in societies and organizations hostile to their faith?

Is it the realization that God can and does use major disasters and calamities in the lives of individuals and nations to lead and place believers in positions of influence and authority that they might not otherwise come to occupy—economic crises, environmental crises, health crises—at the international, national, local, and personal levels? Could it be that he is even now using some such crisis in your life or community to position you for service in advancing his kingdom and the well-being of others?

Have we perhaps gained from these studies a deeper understanding of the perverse spiritual dialectic whereby the author of evil endeavours to twist things that are in themselves good or potentially good—faith, science, freedom, public and private service bureaucracies—toward evil and destructive ends? Has that understanding strengthened our resolve to guard against and resist such abuses? And have we gained insights into opportunities and means for doing so—such as protesting and addressing the abuse of freedom by extremists, including religious extremists, or recognizing and addressing the dark side of science, technology, and bureaucratic organizations?

Have we also gained from these studies a deeper appreciation of the grace and work of God in preventing such transformations of good into evil and in effecting counter-transformations of evil or potential evil into good? Have we resolved to enter into God's work of counter-transformation in some way?

With respect to safeguarding and delivering from evil the bureaucratic organizations in which so many of us as believers find ourselves embedded today, do we sense ourselves being led

- To insist that other caregiving alternatives be considered before automatically consigning persons in need to such systems?
- To frequently visit the front lines of such organizations and expose ourselves to the conditions and experience of those who work there and those whom they serve?
- To be, within such organizations, that ethical salt and light of which Jesus spoke—to listen to that still, small voice of our spiritually sensitized consciences and to follow its dictates?
- To accept responsibility for some of the negative outcomes of bureaucratic organizations and behaviours, even at personal cost?

Have we, through examining the lives of the exiles, gained a deeper appreciation of where and how to draw the line between co-operation with those systems and cultures in which we are embedded and actions that compromise our faith? Have we ourselves drawn the line at some point in our own circumstances—for example, at the point of

- Granting our ultimate allegiance to God and not to someone or something else?
- Upholding rather than compromising some personal moral standard?
- Identifying with rather than disassociating ourselves from the faith community?
- Being willing rather than reluctant to speak uncompromised truth to power?

Finally, have we been challenged to pray for and participate in some way in the restoration of faith in Christ in our times and circumstances through the movement of God on our own hearts and on the hearts of those responsible for our public affairs?

All of the preceding are valuable leadership lessons from the lives of the exiles—believers in another time and space embedded in cultures and organizations indifferent or hostile to their faith. May those of us who find ourselves providentially embedded in similar situations today derive inspiration and guidance from their experience.

As believers living in cultures and political systems indifferent or hostile to our faith we of course have one huge advantage over these ancient exiles. We have the example of Jesus living and working under even more trying and hostile circumstances, since in his case his oppressors and persecutors sought and achieved his death. What was his great guideline for those called to work out their faith in the public arena? Be wise as serpents and gracious as doves. It is the great guideline for believers in any and every circumstance. It is the great guideline for believers in exile. It is the Jesus way.

ACKNOWLEDGEMENTS

MERE WORDS ON PAPER ARE NOT ADEQUATE TO THANK those who have truly helped me and my associates along the spiritual and political journey that has made this book possible. But the following words represent my sincerest effort.

First of all, thanks to my family—in particular my wife, Sandra, whose spiritual insights and qualities are different than but wonderfully complementary to mine and who has soldiered on beside me through all my political adventures and misadventures. Thanks also to our children—Andrea, Avryll, Mary Joy, Nathan, and David—for their understanding and support, notwithstanding my absence from their lives at critical times due to my political involvements.

I also wish to recognize with thanks the role model provided for me by my late father, Ernest C. Manning—a committed Christian who spent 46 years in public life as a member of the Alberta legislature and the Canadian Senate—and express appreciation for all the encouragement and prayerful support provided to both of us by my late mother, Muriel Manning. And special thanks as well to my long-time researcher and executive assistant, Jean Marie Clemenger, who is virtually part of our family and who faithfully researched, typed, retyped, and reviewed every paragraph and word of this manuscript.

Second, heartfelt thanks to my closest political colleagues—Cliff Fryers, Rick Anderson, Andre Turcotte, Ian Todd, and the Reform Party executives and members of Parliament with whom I served. Thanks also to the board and staff of the Manning Centre for Building Democracy. Much of the material in this book, especially on the public life of Jesus, was first developed for courses on navigating the faith-political interface offered by the Manning Centre. Note that the views and positions expressed herein are entirely my own and do not necessarily represent those of the centre or its board and staff.

Special appreciation is due to the first and long-time chair of the board of the Manning Centre, Cliff Fryers, and Rick Anderson, who succeeds me as managing director of the centre. While Cliff and Rick may have legitimate reservations about some of my religious views and activities, they have been loyal and competent executives, managers, advisors, confidants, and friends for many, many years, and their support has been absolutely essential to whatever I may have been able to accomplish in the political arena.

Third, I wish to specifically thank the Marketplace Institute of Regent College at the University of British Columbia for making me a fellow of the Institute and encouraging me to write many of the preceding chapters as lecture materials or articles for the institute's website. I wish to express my deepest gratitude to Professor Paul Williams, director of the institute during my fellowship there, and staff members Mark Mayhew, Ceri Rees, and Rebecca Pousette for their friendship, encouragement, and practical help. Russell Pinson of the institute has been particularly helpful in editing my articles and the original text of this book—his dedication, skill, and diligence deserving special recognition. Once again, the views and opinions expressed in this book are mine alone and are not to be attributed to the Marketplace Institute or Regent College.

I wish also to convey my appreciation to Richard Thompson of Regent's development department and to the generous donors whose support of my fellowship and the institute made the initial work on this book possible. Thank you therefore to Rodger and Carol Woods, Roger and Carol Laing, Bruce and Carol Woods, Warren and Debbie Blair, David and Gisela MacPhail, Rod and Nancy Blair, Herb and Myrna Styles, Roy Ferguson, Sam and Diane Aylesworth, Drew and Geri Fitch, Howard and Janet McLean, Cecil and Inge Hards, Terry and Marina Mochar, Rick and Julie Marzolf, Alan and Carolyn Winter, Bob and Mary Catherine Acheson, John and Kim Hamilton, Robert and Anne Smart, and Roger and Hilary Selby.

With respect to publication of the material contained in this book, thanks are due to Bill Reimer of Regent Press for arranging for the publication of my original lectures in booklet form. Finally, I am greatly indebted to, and highly appreciative of, all the encouragement, help, and support provided by Larry Willard, publisher of Castle Quay Books, and editor Marina Hofman in bringing this work to completion in its current form.

There is one further acknowledgement which needs to be made in any commentary on navigating the interface of faith and public life by a Christian layman such as myself who is also a practitioner in the rough-and-tumble world of partisan politics. And that is to frankly acknowledge the likelihood of errors in both my lay interpretation of the Judeo-Christian Scriptures and in my understanding and interpretation of political events.

If my observations and interpretations on either front are found to be inadequate or faulty by those of you more learned or experienced in these matters than myself, my hope is that you will expend your knowledge and energies on developing more insightful observations and superior interpretations rather than belabouring the inadequacies of mine.

As John Wesley once wrote in the preface to a volume of his sermons defining the principles of life as he understood them, "Are you persuaded that you see more clearly than me? It is not unlikely that you may. Then treat me as you would desire to be treated yourself upon a change of circumstance. Point me out a better way than I have yet known."

Preston Manning
Calgary, Alberta, Canada
September 2017

CASTLEQUAYBOOKS.COM

CASTLE QUAY BOOKS

OTHER BOOKS ON LEADERSHIP

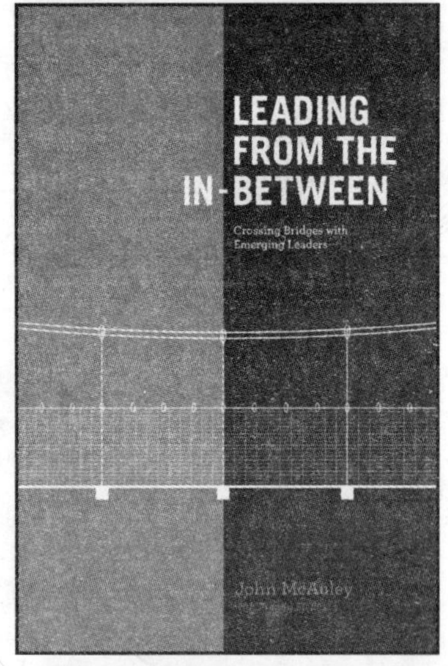

CASTLEQUAYBOOKS.COM